# SOUTH AFRICA

*Adventure, laughter and tears*

PETER S FARLEY

## COPYRIGHT

Copyright © 2025 by Peter S. Farley

All Rights Reserved.

It is illegal to reproduce, duplicate, or transmit any part of this book in either electronic means or printed format without the full written permission of the author.

ISBN No: 978-0-9932824-9-2 Paperback

First printing: 2025*

## About the Author

The author was born in Darwen, Lancashire, U.K. His hobbies include electronics, the paranormal, travel and writing. He holds a degree in Theology awarded by Liverpool University.

Other titles written by the author are:

'Mysterious Tales from Turton Tower'
'The Red Tabs'
'Laugh n' Scratch'
'A Pensioner Visits Peru'

To
Sandra, Elanor, Nicola and Andrew
With my warmest thanks for our shared memories

# GLOSSARY

BLACK: The common name to describe a person of the Nguni groups of South African peoples.

BANTU: The plural form of the word muntu.

BAKKIE: A light delivery vehicle. Usually, having an open back with the driver's cab sealed off from it.

BILTONG: Sun-dried salted edible beef. Cut into strips or small pieces. It is able to be stored for long periods of time.

COLOURED: The South African name given to describe a person of mixed race.

KAFFIR: An old name given to describe a Bantu person originating from the south-eastern regions of southern Africa. Today, it is considered to be a derogatory term.

KHAKI-BOS: A wild-growing weed of large proportions

KNOBKERRIE: A single piece of hardwood of 2-3 feet in length. At one end is a carved ball ('knob'). The item is used as a weapon.

MAGEU: A traditional non-alcoholic drink. It is served cold and made from maize-meal porridge with added yeast.

MUNTU: The singular form of the word Bantu. One who is a member of the Nguni race of people, born in South Africa. Examples are Zulu, Xhosa and Sotho.

ROBOTS: A set of lights used for controlling the flow of vehicular traffic. In the United Kingdom, they are known as *traffic lights*.

RONDAVEL: A cylindrical shaped dwelling made from dried mud or bricks. Covered with a thatched roof and fitted with a singular door and window(s).

STOEP: An area of floor space usually found outside the entrance to a house. In the United Kingdom, it is known as a veranda.

VELD: An open tract of land covered with little or no wild grass.

# Contents

About the Author ................................................................. i
GLOSSARY ........................................................................ iii
INTRODUCTION ................................................................ 1
PROLOGUE ....................................................................... 7
1 PREPARING TO EMIGRATE ........................................... 9
2 THE ADVENTURE BEGINS ........................................... 24
3 WELCOME TO JOHANNESBURG ................................. 33
4 A JOB INTERVIEW ........................................................ 44
5 WALKING IN JOUBERT PARK ...................................... 48
6 21 CHESTERFIELD HOUSE .......................................... 58
7 MY FIRST DAY AT WORK ............................................. 69
8 THE DRIVE-IN CINEMA ................................................ 75
9 SUNDAY MORNING AMBULANCE ............................. 88
10 OUR FIRST SOUTH AFRICAN HOME ........................ 95
11 A NOCTURNAL ENCOUNTER ................................... 101
12 A VLEISBRAAI WITH FRIENDS ................................. 107
13 GOLD MINE TRIBAL DANCING ................................ 113
14 VENTERSPOST GOLD MINE TOUR .......................... 127
15 ISANDHLWANA AND RORKE'S DRIFT .................... 141
16 KYALAMI RANCH HOTEL ......................................... 160
17 PRIMROSE GOLD MINE ........................................... 168
18 HILLBROW'S REVOLVING RESTAURANT ................ 181

19 THE STERKFONTEIN CAVES ..................................................188
20 OUR CAMPERVAN EXPEDITION............................................194
21 A MOVE TO THE WEST RAND................................................217
22 SPION KOP AND BOSJESPRUIT COLLIERY .....................225
23 WIND-PUMP AND WATER......................................................236
24 CHILDREN SEE GHOSTLY FIGURES.................................243
25 JIMMY THE DOG......................................................................249
26 THE 'BULL NASTY' ..................................................................268
27 TOPSY AND TIM ......................................................................277
28 A TALE OF TWO HERBALISTS .............................................282
29 SPIDER AND SERPENT.........................................................300
30 'BIG BALLS' GETS A SHOCK ................................................310
31 MEETING WITH SPIKE MILLIGAN ......................................315
32 SEARCHING FOR A ZULU KING'S GRAVE ........................322
33 KARMA COURT .......................................................................338

*REFERENCES*.................................................................................349

# INTRODUCTION

South Africa's institutionalised system of Apartheid was based on racial segregation. It dictated the social structure in both South Africa and South West Africa (now Namibia) from 1948 until the early 1990s.

Apartheid was characterised by an authoritarian political culture rooted in White Supremacy, or 'Baasskap' as it was known. It enshrined South Africa's minority white population as the dominating group in politics, society and its economy. Within the Apartheid system, white citizens had the highest social status, followed by Asians and Coloureds and then black Africans.

In 1949, the Prohibition of Mixed Marriages Act was the first Apartheid law to be passed. It was followed closely by the Immorality Amendment Act of 1950. These laws made it illegal for most South Africans to have sexual relationships across the racial divides, defined by the classifications that would later follow.

The Population Registration Act No. 30 of 1950 classified all South Africans into one of four racial groups. These were 'Whites', 'Blacks', 'Indians' and 'Coloureds' (people of mixed race). They were based on appearance, known ancestry, socioeconomic status, and cultural lifestyle.

In June of 1977, the South African Prime Minister, Mr John Vorster, told a reporter, "As far as the blacks are concerned, it is a question of one man, one vote - but in their own countries, among their own peoples."

The South African Foreign Minister, Roelof F. Botha, made the comment that his Government was committed to moving away from discrimination based solely on the colour of a man's skin. He added, "But we cannot abandon our right to self-determination. All other African black nations govern themselves. We have been in Africa for three hundred years and have the same right to govern ourselves as they do. This right we cannot and will not forfeit."

In his view, he stated that the search for human rights and values, dignities and freedoms by South Africa's tribal blacks would end successfully but in their own homeland nations, not as citizens of South Africa. He also voiced the opinion that "the alternative of forcing disparate peoples into one system will cause untold misery to both black and white." [1]

The system of Apartheid was humorously put into context by the British ventriloquist Mr. Arthur Worsley. During a television broadcast, his assistant 'dummy' was heard to say:

"Ah, South Africa, that's the place where even Black and White mints are placed into separate packets!"

Furthermore, what may surprise the reader to learn, is that in South Africa, the famous Enid Blyton's Noddy books were banned for a time.

The reason given was that the character called *Gollywog* (who had black-coloured skin) lived in the same village as Big Ears and Mr Plod. They were two of the book's characters who happened to have white-coloured skin!

Not surprisingly, the system of racial oppression did not go unnoticed outside of South Africa. It was frequently condemned by the United Nations, which called for an extensive trade embargo. Some very influential social movements were formed as a result of the oppression.

During the 1970s and 1980s, resistance to the system became increasingly militant. The country's ruling National Party reacted by introducing crackdowns. These served to promote protracted sectarian violence, after which a state of emergency was declared in 1985.

Some reforms followed and, when implemented, allowed Indian and Coloured political representation in parliament. However, this did little to appease the majority of those who wanted to see Apartheid abolished.

Eventually, in 1987, the ruling National Party entered into negotiations with the African National Congress – which was the leading anti-Apartheid movement. Their discussions centred on ending segregation and introducing a majority rule. The year 1990 saw South West Africa become independent under the name of *Namibia*.

Later that year, the South African government began talks with the African National Congress. The state of emergency was lifted, and the A.N.C. agreed to a ceasefire.

Nelson Rolihlahla Mandela - the most prominent figure of the anti-Apartheid movement - was released from prison after serving a total of twenty-seven years. In 1991, Apartheid legislation was repealed, and the acts limiting land ownership, separate living areas and classification of people by their race were abolished.

Finally, in the year of 1994 the first fully representative democratic election was held. Thousands of people from all race groups flocked to the polling booths. The majority found themselves voting for the first time in their lives. The result was an African National Congress Government. Its leader was Nelson Rolihlahla Mandela, who became the first black president of the Republic of South Africa. He served in the post from 1994 to 1999.

Against this political backdrop, my two friends left England during the mid-1970s to live in South Africa. Previously, they had worked in a brewery at Ndola, Zambia. From their Zambian habitat, they wrote me glowing letters about their African life. However, one letter was somewhat critical in its condemnation of their employment's African management. They wrote:

"The management here is so dumb they couldn't organise a 'piss-up' regardless of the fact that we *are* in a brewery!"

By contrast, their views of South Africa were far more complimentary. Their regular letters painted a rosy picture of South African life, describing the glorious weather and good job prospects to boot.

By 1974 I was married and later that year was blessed with a first daughter. Apart from the usual struggles of establishing a home and starting a family, life in England was fraught with political problems. Two years earlier, coal miners took strike action for the first time in almost half a century. During the months that followed, inflation dramatically increased.

In 1973, there was an oil embargo that doubled prices within weeks. To meet the demand for heat in the winter months, the Conservative Government returned to utilising the country's coal deposits. In November of that year, the Government declared a state of emergency. At the beginning of 1974, in order to conserve power, all non-essential businesses were limited to three days of electricity each week. Three years later, the country's fire-fighters took strike action. Once again, the Government responded by declaring a state of emergency. But this time it brought in the troops to act as replacements. With these unsettling events taking place, the thought of life in a sunny clime seemed increasingly attractive.

The following pages contain a collection of memories from the years our family spent in South Africa. It is my hope they may contribute - albeit in a small way - to the recorded history of life for an immigrant family, to South Africa at that time.

The events described took place decades ago. Some words frowned upon by today's society were acceptable back then. This narrative is merely "telling it as it was".

In 1978 when my family and I arrived in South Africa, we were young and adventurous. It was a time when the metaphorical dog, named 'Apartheid', was giving its last dying kicks. But even so, indications of its existence were still visible. Painted signs on park benches or railway carriages and buses, stated which race group were allowed to use them.

We soon discovered that Johannesburg was the commercial and industrial hub of South Africa. Different cultures had met and mingled there, and although the style was often American and the manners frequently British, the atmosphere remained uniquely South African.

At the time of leaving England, I was paying 33% income tax. But, after arrival in the Republic of South Africa, I was pleasantly surprised to see that only 12% was deducted from my employment's first monthly salary.

Furthermore, the Government announced that in the following year, it was to reduce taxation to 8%, which was due to a positive balance of payments. The future seemed bright!

# PROLOGUE

It was another hot and sticky day in the South African city of Johannesburg. Like the tentacle of a giant octopus, the Main Reef Road stretched west from the city centre and towards the gold-mining town of Randfontein. For the most part, it was easy going, but numerous random pot-holes seemed to act as a form of speed control! Arriving at Randfontein, I steered my car towards the town of Carletonville. Passing through the hamlets of Finsbury and Kochsvlei, I finally reached Hillside - a place I knew well. At a sign labelled - *Road No 1* - I turned the car's steering-wheel hard-right. Stretched out before me was a familiar view. A sudden feeling of nausea filled my stomach. This was my first return visit in all of forty years. Halting the car at a tee-junction is where I joined another road named *Pemberthy*. To my left and right were plots of land, while straight ahead lay distant hills; each peppered with various small dwellings.

My particular interest lay in the plot of land at the end of *Road No. 1*. It had belonged to a Portuguese family who lived and worked there. They had sold their home-grown produce in the town of Randfontein. But now, the many rows of vegetables that had grown in profusion on their land, was gone. So, too, was their house. In fact, few clues remained to indicate that any activity had ever taken place there. Poking upward from the ground was the ruin of a brick-built water storage-tank.

A stunted tree grew from within its confines. At the upper end of the plot was a tubular steel-gate, which marked the entrance to the former property. It was open, and leaned forlornly against a perimeter of barbed-wire fencing. Following the faint outline of a pathway, I expected to see an adjacent property. It was where my family and I had lived.

There should have been a wind-powered water-pump that served a four-bedroom house. In attendance should have been a double-garage and a circular water-dam; together with a large rondavel. But now, all was gone.

For a few minutes, I gazed at the empty plots and visualised what once stood there. Like a river in a spate, memories of past events flooded my mind. Ironically, those memories had their beginning six thousand miles away, at my home in the north-west of England.

# 1

## PREPARING TO EMIGRATE

In a north of England cotton town, the weather was mild for the time of year. High above a church pulpit, sunlight scintillated on stained-glass windows. A pair of houseflies gambolled in a rising torrent of warm air. The parish priest's white robe rippled as he gave a blessing to the congregation. His spoken words - "Go in peace and love one another"- reverberated from the walls of the sanctuary. An outstretched hand moved to and fro, as he made the sign of a cross. Carefully, the priest descended the pulpit's wooden steps. Practically gliding along the floor, he reached the exit-door of the church - and waited. Worshippers genuflected as they vacated their pews and followed in the priest's footsteps. Smiling at the departing parishioners, the priest shook hands with some and exchanged words with others.

"Sandra! Come with me," I whispered to my young wife.

We had almost slipped away when the priest caught sight of us. Practically singing the words, he called out, "Good to see you both!"

Since our marriage we regularly attended church services. And in recent years our two daughters were baptised there. Without stopping we returned the priest's greeting. Protruding from a nearby wall was a stone water-trough.

Resembling the bottom lip of a gawping mouth, it was partly filled with Holy-water. Dipping a finger into the cold liquid, we quickly crossed ourselves. Nearby was an open doorway. It seemed to beckon us towards the outside world - and its sinful ways! Seconds later, we followed the flock of God's sheep. As we hurried along a narrow pavement, above the buildings the sun shone brightly. In the distance was a young couple. They headed towards us at a steady pace. Drawing closer, I recognised the man.

"Hello George!" I called out. "Long time no see. How are you doin'?"

"Well I never! I'm fine, thanks," answered George, his face expressing a look of pleasant surprise.

"And what have *you* been up to? Are you still workin' at the cinema?"

"Oh no - I gave that up some years ago. It was shortly before Sandra and I got married. And now we have two young daughters!"

My head turned towards my wife and lured George into following suit.

"You remember Sandra, don't you?"

"Oh yeah, of course I remember Sandra. But two kids? Wow! That's good going!"

At that moment, George thought of his partner, and sounding slightly apologetic, introduced her to us.

"Oh, erm, sorry, this is Janet, my bride-to-be. I don't think you've met before?"

Everyone smiled and exchanged pleasantries.

"What are the names of your children?" Janet asked.

"Well" said Sandra, "Elanor is three and a half years, and her sister, Nicola, is eighteen months."

"Wow, that's nice. I'd like to have two children one day," Janet admitted. "And I must say I love the richness of Nicola's curly red-hair."

"Thank you," said Sandra, "I think it must be a family trait."

"Sandra is probably correct," I chirped, "After all, both her mother and my mother's sister are red-heads."

Smiling broadly, I quickly added, "They have no hair - just red-heads!"

Everyone chuckled.

During a brief pause in the conversation, I casually dropped the proverbial cat among the pigeons.

"Incidentally, we won't be around much longer".

A shocked look formed on our friends' faces.

"That's 'cause we're emigrating to South Africa," I quickly revealed.

"What!" exclaimed George, "Why the heck are you going there? You'll get an assegai in your back!"

Everyone laughed.

"It's possible," I said, forcing a smile, "But I don't think so. Besides, I've got a friend who lives there, with his wife and their children. He often writes to me and says they're doing great".

"He describes the sunshine, good food, lots of jobs, and especially the low taxation."

A wry smile appeared on George's face as he worded a response. "Sounds like a good place to be," he acknowledged. "But aren't the black people who live there treated harshly?"

Before hearing my answer, his partial smile slowly gave way to a frown, and he quickly posed another question.

"And what about the system they call 'A-PART-HIDE'?"

George's mispronunciation of the Afrikaans word caused me to smile.

"I'm sorry, George," I said, "but the Afrikaans word *Apartheid* is not three separate words. It's all one".

"The letter 'd' is pronounced as a 't' and when spoken, the word sounds like *Apartheight*."

George gave a quick nod, affirming he understood. At that moment, I grasped the initiative and continued with my explanation.

"The word actually means the development of separated groups of people. That is to say, people who live in different areas of land. For example, it's like the people living in Scotland and others in England."

As George contemplated my explanation, I suddenly remembered something else.

"Oh yes, and my friend, the one who lives in South Africa - remember? He tells me that things aren't as bad as our newspapers make them out to be."

George seemed perplexed as he raised a further question.

"But wasn't it two years ago when they shot some people at that place called, erm, - oh, what's its name?"

As he struggled to remember, Janet sprang to his rescue.

"Do you mean 'Soweto'?" she asked.

"Yeah, that's it, Sow-et-toe. It's just outside Johannesburg, ain't it? And the police shot some children there too - didn't they?"

Calmly, I answered.

"Yes - that did happen - it was in 1976 - but things are generally much quieter now."

Janet stole a moment and whispered discretely into George's ear. She shared with him an idea. Nodding approvingly, his lips adopted a knowing smile. Turning slowly to face me, George proffered Janet's question.

"So, tell me, Peter, does that mean you will be selling your house? Or are you going to rent it out?"

I glanced briefly at Sandra, giving her the opportunity to say something but she chose to let me do the talking.

"Well," said I, deliberating for a second or two, "I expect we shall put the house up for sale. It's been a long process, you know. We are going to South Africa on the Government scheme of assisted immigration. It simply means we won't have to pay anything. We've already had our medical examinations, which included some X-rays. I expect they wanted to see if we had tuberculosis. Oh, and we had some lovely injections, too. "

"They were meant to ward off smallpox and yellow fever!"

Pausing for a moment, I looked again at Sandra to see her reaction. Again, she chose to remain silent.

"Next week", I added, "we have a meeting in Manchester, with an official of the South African Government, who wishes to assess our college certificates."

"Why yes!" George exclaimed, "You're an electrician, aren't you?"

"Yes, that's right, and Sandra is a biology teacher. We both have skills the South African government is looking for.

George spoke again and slowly pronounced the strange-sounding Afrikaans word.

"I suppose that's got something to do with A-PART HEIGHT?" he asked with a pinch of cynicism.

"Well, it is a young country, and things will take time to get right. The official figures say the population consists of around twenty-six million natives and about six million Europeans. I expect because of the huge untrained population, it's taking time to put things together. Anyway, we're going out there to try to make a difference."

Turning towards my wife, I asked, "Isn't that right, Sandra?"

Silently, she smiled and nodded.

"And to make some big money too, I've no doubt?" blurted George.

"Aye, hopefully, that as well," I admitted.

Janet surreptitiously squeezed George's hand. It was a gesture that caused him to realise he needed to say more.

He responded to the hint.

"So, Peter, tell me. Whereabouts is the house you are likely to sell?"

"Do you know Limes Avenue, at the top of Belgrave Road?"

"Why yes, I do. Isn't that where they built some new houses a few years ago?"

"That's correct, George, spot on! Sandra and I bought one of the first to be built. It's a lovely quiet part of town and yet near to all the amenities."

Janet immediately quipped,

"Oh, Peter, you sound like an estate agent!"

Everyone chuckled.

As the jollity subsided, Janet asked a question.

"Have you any idea when you may be ready to sell your house?"

Sandra looked in my direction. We both expected each other to answer. But this time, Sandra took the lead.

"Well, Janet, we are very near to completing our emigration plans. I think within two months at the most, and we would want to be on our way."

Janet seized the opportunity she was hoping for.

"Amazing!" she exclaimed, "That's more or less the time we are planning for our marriage."

During the following brief lull in conversation, Janet fell deep in thought. Suddenly, her eyes widened as she spoke.

"Of course, we shall need somewhere to live. And where you are, it sounds like a nice place to be. Do you think it might be possible for us to have a look at your house? Sort of, give us a head start?"

Sandra looked at me in a 'give me some help' kind of way. Responding to her silent invitation, I answered.

"Yes, Janet, I'm sure you could. We are home most evenings from five o'clock onwards. When would you like to call?"

Janet declined to answer and motioned George to respond.

"Let's see," he mused, "it's Sunday today, isn't it?"

"Yes, George, all day!" I quipped with a smile.

George was ardently thinking of a suitable visiting date and failed to see any humour in my little jibe.

"I know!" he said with a start, "What about Wednesday evening? Let's say at about half past five?"

Sandra and I nodded in agreement.

"So, what is the house number?"

I spoke slowly and deliberately.

"It is number FIFTY-THREE Limes Avenue."

Before departing, George had the final word. He smiled as he said,

"Okay, we'll see you both on Wednesday evening - Bye!"

At our home later that day, I watched the setting sun; before drawing together our lounge curtains. Relaxing in our Swedish-designed chairs, Sandra and I were kept hypnotised by the television. Meanwhile, our children were in their beds and fast asleep. Limes Avenue was a quiet strip of road at the busiest of times. But on this particular evening, you could hear the cough of a stray dog - that is, of course, if one happened to be nearby! Under such conditions I had no difficulty hearing a car halt outside our house. Its engine continued to idle for more than a minute. Gradually the sound became too much for my curiosity. Reaching the lounge window, I peeked out from behind the edge of a curtain. Two figures were seated in a shiny, red car. Surprise, surprise, they happened to be George and Janet. They were obviously having a sneak preview of what might be their future abode!

Wednesday evening eventually arrived, and once again, the familiar shiny, red car stopped outside our house. George and Janet were made welcome and given a guided tour of the palatial dwelling. As mentioned earlier, we bought it new and had lived there for just under four years. During that time, it suffered a few alterations. They included an extension to the garage and a service pit for our car.

Sandra's taste in decor was modern, which was reflected in our choice of furniture. Although somewhat scant, it was expensive and not least stylish. In the lounge were our Swedish chairs and, for effect, an antique wooden rocking-chair. Each faced a hand-built simulated, stone-fireplace, which stretched across the full length of a wall. At its central point was a gas fire encased in teakwood.

The kitchen's main feature was a round wooden table with four matching chairs, all in white. Suspended from the ceiling above them was a Swedish light-fitting. Yellow in colour, its spherical ceramic construct allowed it to be raised or lowered as required. Aside from the aforementioned, the house was fitted with good-quality carpets. Whilst outside, the gardens to the front and rear of the house were neatly cultivated.

George and Janet were delighted with everything they saw and excitedly announced their desire to buy. And then came another and yet unexpected question.

"We like your furniture", admitted George. "Are you taking it with you?"

Some days earlier Sandra and I had discussed this very question. As a result, I replied with a ready answer.

"No, we plan to sell it".

It was the answer the couple wanted to hear. They asked me to give them a price, and within a few seconds, a deal was made. They agreed to buy, not only the house, but its furniture as well! Eventually, when arrangements were finalised, my family and I had only to pack our bags and go! Well-almost. There was still a formal meeting to be had in central Manchester, with the South African Immigration Authority.

Manchester's Victoria railway station was bristling with people, as Sandra and I stepped down from the train. We were due to keep an appointment with an official at the Department of South African Immigration.

Hot footing our way along the streets, we reached Piccadilly Gardens. Fringed with trees, the oblong-shaped tract of land was considered to be the hub of the city. Wooden benches stood alongside garden beds, and each was filled with gaily coloured flowers. The gardens were a popular destination for people of all ages. Especially those who desired to escape the hustle and bustle of city life. But Sandra and I hadn't time to stand and stare.

Beyond the gardens and the traffic-filled roads were numerous multi-storey buildings. Many had stood since the Victorian era. One of them had a small room, which served as an office for the South African representative. Holding hands, my wife and I hurried towards the tall, designated building. Loitering near its entrance was a skinny-looking individual. His gabardine raincoat was old, crumpled, and stained. Come to think of it, his face had a similar appearance! Anticipating our arrival, he stepped forward as we were about to enter the doorway. Holding a pile of printed leaflets, he gave a sardonic smile as he spoke.

"Would you take a leaflet, sir? Help to dismantle Apartheid in South Africa."

Without looking, I took the leaflet and followed Sandra through the entrance door. We climbed the stairs to the second floor. At the end of a short corridor, artificial light cascaded from an open doorway. It acted as a beacon which guided us to our destination. A small sign attached to the door was painted with the words: 'South African Immigration.' They confirmed we had reached our goal.

Sandra knocked on the open door and walked into the room. A tall, slimly built, blond-haired man stood behind a wide, oak-wood desk. He spoke to us politely.

"Ah, Mister and Missus Farley, I presume? I've been expecting you. Please come in and take a seat."

When the man spoke he gently rolled the letter 'r' in a way similar to that of a Scotsman. And when he spoke the word 'black', it sounded like 'bleck'. Also, when saying the words 'South Africa,' they sounded like 'Seff Effrica.' His accent sounded strange to my ears but after all, it *was* the first time I had heard a South African speak.

Four upright wooden chairs stood in a line. They faced the man's leather-topped desk. Sandra sat nearest the entrance door, and I sat next to her left. The blond-haired man sank into his leather-covered chair. He introduced himself as Meneer Van Tonder. He asked to see our documents. These included our qualifications and medical reports. Smiling encouragingly as he spoke, he proceeded to tell us about life in 'Seff Effrica'.

At this moment, the skinny-looking individual - whom we had side-stepped outside the building - hurriedly entered the room. He breezed past Sandra and me and sat on a vacant chair to my left. The South African official looked vaguely surprised at the unannounced intrusion. Nevertheless, he continued to speak and voiced what seemed like a well-practised piece of descriptive prose.

"I would like to explain the Government of Seff Effrica's concept of Apartheid," he said. He quickly shuffled his posterior on the leather seat, seemingly seeking a little extra comfort. "It wishes for the Republic," he continued, "to reach a point where there are no bleck citizens. By that, I mean the millions of blecks, who are now considered only 'subjects' of Seff Effrica, would be assigned citizenship according to their tribal identification."

Meneer Van Tonder stole a glance in our direction. I imagined he had hoped to sense a level of our understanding. Whether he did or not, I don't know, but at any rate, he continued to speak.

"That would mean," he added, "the creation of ten areas of land called *homelands*. Each homeland would be cared for by the individual tribal groups. The people would, therefore, be citizens of their particular homeland. And each homeland is to become an independent nation."

Meneer Van Tonder smiled. Having made his little speech, he appeared to express a sense of relief. But for Sandra and me, it was all too much for our minds to absorb. Acting like puppets, we simply smiled and nodded in acknowledgement.

Meanwhile, during the short pause in the dialogue, the skinny-looking individual stole an opportunity to speak out.

"Is it not true that the homelands are to be nothing more than labour pools for the white minority?" he asked.

This was clearly an embarrassing question for our host. He apparently chose to side-step the challenge by offering a little more information.

"Ah - well, the first homeland to achieve independence was the Transkei. And that was in 1976..."

Our host was on the brink of presenting more facts when the skinny individual challenged him again.

"That may be so, but is it not true to say that no other country in the world recognises the Transkei as an independent country?"

The South African was clearly ruffled.

But snatching at a moment of time, he attempted to adjust his tie. Perhaps he wished to make his breathing a little easier, or maybe it was to give him a chance to prepare an answer. However, it was just about then I noticed Sandra was showing signs of feeling disturbed.

Our host made another attempt to broaden our minds.

"If the homelands policy progresses as planned, there will be eleven nations: ten black and one white. And all would be within the present boundaries of the Republic," he said.

The skinny individual straightened his back. He appeared to revel in his perceived status of importance. And like the proverbial boxer, he came out of his corner again. He mouthed off another volley of incriminating words.

Meanwhile, Sandra surreptitiously shuffled to the edge of her seat and was now slightly forward of me. Her fresh position gave her a clear sideways view of the intruder. I gave her a momentary glance and noted her body language. She put me in mind of a venomous snake, which had slowly uncoiled its body in readiness to strike. The skinny man was in mid-sentence when Sandra suddenly erupted. Turning her head in his direction, she leaned forward and blatantly called out.

"Listen!" she exclaimed loudly, "If YOU don't want to listen to what this man has to say - WE DO - so please be quiet!"

Feeling a tinge of embarrassment, I practically shrank in my chair. At that moment the room fell silent. The South African looked aghast. He waited for a reprisal, but none came. Without uttering a word, and like a soldier on parade, the skinny individual stood to attention.

He quietly and hastily fastened the top button of his raincoat. And like a dog with its tail between its legs, he swiftly left the room. His footsteps could be heard growing fainter as he hurried down the corridor. A noticeable glimmer of relief appeared on the South African's face. It was followed by a twinkle, which seemed to appear in his eyes. Seconds later, Meneer Van Tonder had regained his composure. With renewed vigour, he continued to verbalise an eloquent picture of his prized country!

Weeks later, our five suitcases were packed and ready for departure. With them was a blue-painted steel box, which contained my engineering tools. It might also be said that it contained our livelihood. Next came the difficult part. Resigning from our jobs and saying goodbye to all our friends was not easy. But saying goodbye to our parents was particularly painful. We could not be sure if we would ever see them again. But we garnered some consolation when various people shared the words: "You can always come back!"

At the time of departure, I didn't realise what a momentous undertaking it was. We were effectively depriving our parents of the pleasure of seeing their grandchildren growing up. But by the same token, they were also *our* children. And we believed that we were giving them a chance of a better future. To our youthful outlook, the whole episode seemed like a great adventure. But we couldn't know that it was to be a life-changing experience - and it was about to begin!

# 2
# THE ADVENTURE BEGINS

The South African government offered us two cost-free modes of travel. We could either sail aboard a passenger mail-ship or fly in a jet-airliner. Steam ships had dominated long-distance travel for decades. They carried cargo and postal items to different parts of the world. Fare-paying passengers were something of an afterthought. But a revolution took place with the advent of the jet-airliner. Long-distance travel and postal communication became quicker and more convenient.

The England to South Africa route had mail-ships, owned by the Union-Castle Line. The sea voyage took days to reach Cape Town, and with meals and entertainment provided, it could make for a wonderful holiday. Amongst the things to enjoy were a swimming pool and various deck games. But what intrigued me most was the mention of a special sea-going ceremony. During the 1970s, my knowledge of the world was limited. I believed the equator to be a mystical place. And rumour had it there was a King, named Neptune, who lived beneath the sea and ruled the oceans. He was said to visit the ship and 'initiate' each sea-faring passenger, who crossed the equator for the first time. The thought of meeting with King Neptune appealed to my sense of adventure. Unfortunately, Sandra had a different idea! She thought we should reach our destination as soon as possible.

Perhaps, and rightly so, she was thinking of the long sea voyage and our two small children to look after. And so, the choice was made to travel by air.

The Boeing 747SP, quad-jet airliner - or *Queen of the skies*, as it was affectionately known - awaited us at London's Heathrow airport. What a magnificent sight she was! The airliner's wings, with a span of 195 feet, each supported two Pratt and Whitney turbofan engines. They were capable of taking the aircraft to a cruising height of 35 000 feet and attaining a speed of over 600 m.p.h. The 747 was the first twin-aisle airliner to be built and the first to be called a *Jumbo Jet*. It had three seats on the window side of each aisle and four seats in the centre.

Boarding the craft, I briefly thought of my first air flight. It was back in 1966 as part of a package holiday. Taking off from Manston airport, in the county of Kent, I flew in an old Dakota DC3. Crossing the English Channel in little more than one hour, it touched down in Belgium. The final part of the journey was made by omnibus to the coastal village of Pietra Ligure, in Northern Italy. The DC3 was fitted with twin, propeller engines and carried twenty-one passengers. It was a far cry from the Boeing 747SP, capable of carrying 341 passengers. And the flight across the English Channel seemed insignificant when thinking of our 6000-mile flight to Johannesburg - which was expected to take sixteen hours! At that time, certain countries opposed to Apartheid chose not to allow South African 'planes to fly in their air-space. Consequently, our flight would take a longer route across Africa. We would first land at Rhodesia's (Zimbabwe) Salisbury (Harare) airport and, having re-fuelled, continue to Johannesburg.

A kindly member of the cabin crew directed us to a set of four spacious seats, which reclined at the press of a button. A small cloth apron hung over each headrest, adding a touch of hygiene. To our inexperienced eyes, this was the height of luxury. A smiling air-hostess gave each of us a sizeable plastic wallet. Inside was a pair of earphones which resembled a doctor's stethoscope. Two plastic pipes, fitted with earpieces and a moulded plug, could be pushed into a socket on the seat's armrest. Quite literally, 'piped' audio could then be enjoyed! Carefully wrapped in a cloth napkin was a set of metallic cutlery. Keeping it company was a moistened cloth to wipe our hands and small packets of salt, pepper and sugar. And there was even a plastic toothpick! Such items gave me hope of a meal to come. Our seats were grouped in the middle section of the aircraft and faced a toilets compartment. Mounted on its facing wall was the in-flight movie-screen. One might say we had a first-class view of the picture show - the fact is we couldn't get any closer to it!

Nicola was generally a bright and bubbly child, but she was troubled with bouts of crying. It was a problem which manifested long before our intended flight. Our family doctor assured us there was nothing physically wrong. In fact, we were told that, in all likelihood, she would "grow out of it." However, our main concern was that she might be troubled during the flight. Consequently, our fear prompted a final visit to the doctor's office. He prescribed a bottle of *medicine* which was meant to promote sleep. "To be used sparingly", he said, "One tea-spoon measure to be taken every two hours - as necessary."

Preparations for the night-time journey were made. A lightweight carry-cot was placed on the floor next to our seats.

Nicola was bedded down, and our little family prepared for the take-off. All went well until a few minutes after we became airborne. Nicola sat up in her cot and promptly began screaming. Sandra desperately tried to console her. Fortunately, the general noise of the aircraft helped to dull her sounds. But they hadn't gone unnoticed by the nearby passengers. Their distant eyes stared in our direction. A few bore expressions of sympathy, whilst others projected scornful looks!

Sometime into the flight, a meal was served, and our two girls tucked into their food with relish. Sandra and I did likewise and enjoyed the added bonus of a peaceful interlude. When the food trolleys had trundled away for the last time, Nicola was bedded down again. But within minutes, she started to cry. Sandra looked at me in desperation. I responded with a question.

"I think it's time to try the medicine, don't you?"

I guessed it must have had a pleasant taste since the first dose of the liquid went down well. With bated breath, Sandra and I carefully watched our child and wondered if she was she showing any signs of sleep. But during the passing of minutes, Nicola managed nothing more than a singular yawn. Perhaps it was caused more by boredom than anything else. Meanwhile, Elanor had stretched out across two of the seats. And by the time the cabin lights were doused and the in-flight movie began, she was fast asleep.

Charles Bronson starred in the movie titled *Telephon*. Little did I know its name was to be forever imprinted on my memory. Projected images appeared on the screen directly in front of us. Their reflected light illuminated our every move. Thankfully, it also managed to distract Nicola from crying.

But the quiet time was short-lived. Without any prompting, Nicola began another epic performance. Her screams actually surpassed those of a movie actress who appeared on the screen!

It must have been horrendous for the passengers seated behind us. Periodically, they would see my dark silhouette appear above the top of the seats. It would soon be followed by that of Sandra as we took turns to lift Nicola from her carry cot. Shortly after administering a second dose of the medicine, a flight attendant approached us. Standing in the aisle, she leaned across the seats and anxiously asked Sandra if there was anything she could do to help. The two of them hurriedly discussed the offer as Nicola continued to wrestle.

Their brief conversation reminded me of an amusing story I once heard. It was about an airline flight during which the Captain made one of his usual announcements.

"Ladies and gentlemen, welcome aboard the aircraft today."

As he spoke, a passenger's little girl began a loud vocal protest. The lady tried hard to console her distraught child, but all the while, her voice grew louder. The Captain continued to address the passengers but his words were disrupted by the child's ongoing outburst. A flight attendant rushed to the pair and hastily inquired: "Is there anything I can do to help?"

The infant was startled by the attendant's sudden arrival. She ceased making a noise and cast a furtive glance at the intruder. During the brief pause, the Captain's voice was heard again.

"We are travelling at 500mph and an altitude of 33,000 feet."

The fresh announcement jolted the child from her passive state. She recommenced her unruly performance and this time with gusto! Whilst trying hard to keep her composure, the flight attendant leaned closer to the woman. Ever so politely, she asked a pertinent question:

"Would your child like to play outside?"

Managing to stifle a chuckle, I thought that under the present circumstances, it might be prudent not to mention the story. Meanwhile, having done all she could to help, our flight attendant walked away. Directly in front of us, Charles Bronson was still strutting around the movie screen. In desperation, Sandra administered a *third* dose of the doctor's medicine. Nicola didn't object; in fact, she actually appeared to relish the liquid! However, a minute or two later, her mouth opened wide. She appeared to be impersonating a roaring lion – albeit noiselessly. Amazingly, she was actually yawning! Her eyes reacted empathetically and slowly appeared drowsy. I flashed an expression at Sandra, suggesting a question.

"Is she finally going to sleep?"

Moments later my unspoken question was answered. Nicola's tiny face contorted and resembled a miniature gargoyle. She released a long and loud burp. As it slowly subsided, she suddenly unleashed a torrent of dark regurgitated medicine. It gushed from her mouth and sprayed Sandra's face. Remaining speechless, Sandra took a cloth and wiped the dripping liquid from her chin. Meanwhile, Nicola looked puzzled. She appeared to wonder where all the liquid had come from. But soon after creating, what resembled a scene of destruction, she finally chose to sleep. And Sandra, who was exhausted from her ordeal, quickly joined her.

Meanwhile the movie continued unabated. The projected images created patterns of bright, fluctuating light, on the reflective screen. Annoyingly it had the undesired affect of keeping me awake for the duration of the show. And unable to follow the movie's storyline, I wistfully gazed at the faces of my family, who were now blissfully sleeping. In retrospect, *Telephon*, the movie, will always serve to remind me of that night - it was amongst the worst of my life!

With bleary eyes I witnessed the dawn of a new day. Shortly before ten o'clock that morning, the aircraft touched down at Salisbury (Harare) airport. Ground crew wheeled gantries up to the forward, port exit-doors. Each gantry was fitted with a canvas-covered framework. They were designed to protect the disembarking passengers from the searing sunshine.

Following hours of incarceration, the people enjoyed the opportunity to stretch their legs. Meanwhile the Boeing's long-range masterpiece stood motionless. The backdrop of a deep-blue sky served to accentuate her majestic stature. Airport personnel peppered the scene in an animated but relaxed way. Wearing a white topee, a uniformed African stood next to a port-side engine. Its metallic-silver-casing was shimmering in the morning sunlight.

Standing next to the adjacent engine was a bereted guard. Smiling broadly, he chatted to a European staff member, who wore an aviation-styled peaked-hat. Over his white shirt and blue tie, he wore a white-cotton, short-sleeved boiler suit. A fuel tanker drove under the aircraft's wing and stopped. Personnel scurried about as they proceeded with their task of refuelling.

Bringing my 8mm cine camera into action, I filmed the passengers' exodus from the aircraft. There was a mix of people, both young and old who casually strolled across the asphalt. Many wore jerseys or jackets from the night before. A senior lady with a mop of white hair ambled along towards the airport's main building. Wearing a thick overcoat, with buttons unfastened, she seemed hampered carrying a large, leather shopping bag. Its long handles strained from the weight within.

A woman half her age breezed past. By contrast, she flaunted jet-black hair - which hung loose around her shoulders. Wearing a thigh-length, waist-hugging, tweed jacket, it was complimented by a pair of dark, tight-fitting trousers. With little effort, she carried a canvas shopping bag. As my cine camera panned a view of the aircraft, I was abruptly confronted by a tall African soldier. The brown-skinned figure held an AK47 rifle. His dark-brown eyes glared at me with a firm countenance. Pointing the gun in the direction of the airport buildings, he silently motioned me to move on. One look at the gun's barrel convinced me not to argue!

Enormous metallic letters attached to the main building spelt the word SALISBURY. Beneath them was a round analogue clock. It displayed the local time of a few minutes after ten a.m. From the aircraft to the airport buildings was a short walk. Every step of the way was observed by the eagle-eyed armed soldier. My daughters, along with their mother, gleefully picked up their pace. We all wanted some refreshment, and the children were especially anxious to receive their promised "sweeties!"

Standing behind the refreshment counter was an African employee. Displaying a broad smile, he greeted us.

"What would you like, sir?" he asked.

Looking over his shoulder, I noticed a shelf stocked with sealed plastic packets. They appeared to contain loose chocolates.

"Hello to you", I answered and pointed towards the shelf. "Could I have two packets of chocolates, please?"

The man turned his head to look where I was pointing. Apart from the plastic packets, there was little else to see. Sounding surprised, he proffered a question.

"You want biltong, sir?"

His previously smiling face had changed to a look of mild confusion.

"Er, yes, okay - biltong chocolate", I replied, whilst not wishing to argue with him. All the while, I was thinking that *biltong* must be the trade name for the packets of local chocolates. Still pondering my request for *biltong chocolate*, the confused man completed the sale. In the meantime, our two girls looked on with eager anticipation. Opening the first packet, I examined the contents. With eyes wide open and like two voracious dogs on the point of salivating, the girls watched my every movement. To my utmost surprise, the pieces - which I expected to be chocolate - were actually small chunks of dried, preserved meat, called 'biltong'!

Biltong - as I later discovered - is a traditional African food. Produced mainly from sun-dried, salted beef, it remains edible for many days.

At that moment, the girls weren't the only ones to feel disappointed!

# 3

# WELCOME TO JOHANNESBURG

It was the afternoon of June 16th 1978, when our flight ended at Johannesburg's Jan Smuts, International Airport. At passport control our family was singled out from a long queue. Nervousness gripped me as an Immigration Officer spoke. His voice had a distinct Transvaal (Gauteng) accent. Robotically, he uttered the words,

"Velkom toe Johannesburg en Suid Africa."

Inspecting our passports, he asked if we carried any drugs or firearms.

"No sir!" was my quick and sharp reply.

With suspicious eyes, he looked us up and down. Gradually, his stern facial expression changed to one tinged with pity. Finally, he waved us on. I wondered if, following the eventful flight, our dishevelled appearance had influenced his response!

Our family hurried towards the airport's main entrance. Basking in the morning sun-shine was a single-deck bus. As we hurried to find some vacant seats, friendly, dark-skinned hands loaded our luggage. Within minutes the bus would take us to a hotel, located in central Johannesburg. It was ear-marked to accommodate newly arrived immigrants. Awaiting its departure, I looked from the crowded bus and took-in the scene.

With flights much fewer in those days, everything appeared relaxed outside the airport building. An airport employee stood at the entrance. Lazily, he played water from a hosepipe onto a wide concrete pavement. Simultaneously, a colleague pushed a stiff broom to sweep the ensuing water into the gutter.

As I envisaged our family's future, a feeling of excitement grew inside me. The heat from the risen-sun enveloped my body, which felt sticky with increasing perspiration. My dreamlike state had caused me not to notice the last of the passengers, who boarded the waiting bus. Suddenly, its engine roared into action. The exhaust-pipe coughed and belched a ball of black smoke. With a crunch of gears and a further roar from the engine, the bus lurched forward. Our journey to Johannesburg - aka the 'Golden city' - had begun. The title alluded to the copious amounts of gold which had been mined there down the years.

Travelling along the highway revealed what seemed like a new world. To our left and right stood newly built office blocks and some factories, which gradually gave way to private homes. Each house stood on its own piece of walled-ground. Many had swimming pools, with sunlight reflecting from the water's surface. It was a far cry from the north of England, with its rows of tightly packed terraced houses.

Like an old style mail-coach, the bus struggled onward. Shortly after reaching the brow of an incline, the view resembled a newly-turned page of a picture book. In the far distance, tall oblong-shaped buildings, of concrete and stone, pointed skywards. Rising from low-lying haze, they appeared like stalagmites in a mystical fairyland; this was the city of Johannesburg.

As the highway stretched before us my heart skipped a beat. Whilst disappearing amidst the surreal scene, it reminded me of the literary yellow-brick road, which led to the 'Wonderful Land of Oz'!

Sitting diagonally opposite to me was Sandra, who had noted the spectacle at much the same time. Turning her head in my direction, she gave me an encouraging smile. It seemed that telepathically we had shared the same excited thoughts.

Within a few minutes our transport arrived at number 35 Quartz Street. Here stood a Government sponsored building. It was named *The Constantia Hotel*, and it boasted a one-star rating. Our suitcases were carried by the bus driver and placed in the foyer. He set them down in front of three African staff members. Standing to attention in military style, their dark-brown skins contrasted sharply with their starched, white cotton-jackets. Black trousers and white shirts, along with black bow-ties, complimented their apparel. And in addition, white pillbox hats, perched jauntily on the side of their head, added a touch of professionalism.

Poised behind a polished-oak reception desk was a dumpy, low-set European lady. Her bouffant-styled, grey-hair and mode of dress, betrayed her age. Raising a hand, she adjusted a pearl-beaded necklace, festooned around her neck.

"Velkom to Sout Africa ant de Constantia 'otel" she said. "My name is Mrs Isaacs, ant my husband ant I are de joint managers."

Opening a large-sized ledger, which lay on the desk top, her bird-like eyes flashed me a look, as she politely asked a question.

"Vould you please sign de visitors' book?"

*Constantia Hotel - Johannesburg (1978)*

*Mr. & Mrs. Isaacs at Constantia Hotel (1978)*

Taking hold of a pen, I suddenly decided the lady's accent sounded distinctly Jewish. Seconds later, her husband appeared from an adjoining room. Reacting swiftly, Mrs. Isaacs swivelled her head in his direction. Although relieved to see him, she expressed her pent-up annoyance by barking a few words.

"Ah, zere you are! It's two zirthy! You should 'ave been 'ere at two o'clock!"

Mister Isaacs' face erupted into a look of surprise. With eyebrows raised and eyes opened wide, he presented a bewildered expression. Almost immediately, he spoke.

"Vhy?" he asked "Vot 'appened at two o' clock?"

Exhaling a long sigh, his wife turned her head away. She rolled her eyes and gently shook her head from side to side. Glancing over her shoulder, I noted Mister Isaacs. Acting like a mischievous schoolboy he flashed me a smile. It was quickly followed by the wink of an eye! His actions suggested he had the makings of a comedian.

Following a few pleasantries, Mrs. Isaacs reached for a small hand-bell. It stood expectantly next to the visitors' book. Giving it a quick shake, she barked some instructive words at the hotel employees.

"Take de luggage to apartment fourteen!"

With their brown faces emitting beaming smiles they happily jumped to the task.

At first glance, our apartment appeared to be a relative of austerity. It might also be said it was in keeping with the remainder of the hotel! But at least all was spacious and clean.

It had two bedrooms, each with twin single-beds and a singular bathroom. A wall of one bedroom was adorned with two, framed photographic prints. One of which portrayed a South African Airways 747SP jet airliner in flight. I guessed its intention was to remind us of our horrendous journey. And after remembering the event, we might appreciate our meagre surroundings! By way of contrast, the other framed print was an ocean liner. In a similar way, I guessed it too, was meant to impact on any observer, who may have immigrated by ship!

After unpacking our suitcases, a quick inspection of the bathroom convinced me the hotel had seen better days. At that moment, I reminded Sandra of the hotel's one-star rating. From within the bathroom I called out.

"I now know why the hotel is rated as ONE star!"

"Why is that love?" she asked.

"Because I can see ONE star in the night sky - and that's through a hole in the bathroom ceiling!"

We both laughed.

But after taking everything into account, we agreed that its condition wasn't so bad. A little dated perhaps, but none-the-less adequate. We eventually settled in for a good night's rest.

Breakfast time arrived the next day, and none too soon. Our family was more than ready to eat. The hotel's dining room was fairly plain, with a few iron-framed tables occupying the floor space. Perhaps in an attempt to disguise their age, white, starched table-cloths were draped over them. And each of the tables hosted straight-backed, tubular-framed chairs.

Offering basic comfort, they were fitted with thin cushions. We sat at a centrally placed table and patiently waited for some service. A quick look around the room confirmed we were the first diners of the day. Double, swing-doors separated the dining-room from the kitchen. They reminded me of Hollywood's Wild West movies, when gun-toting cowboys were often portrayed, pushing them open upon entering a saloon.

As I contemplated the surroundings, our two daughters amused themselves by pretending the cruet-set were people. The unfortunate salt and pepper pots were made to tirelessly walk around the table top! Meanwhile, Sandra was engrossed in reading a single-sheet breakfast menu. Our peaceful state ended unexpectedly when we heard the loud slamming of a distant door. Seconds later, the double swing-doors flew open! A tall, and skinny, uniformed waiter, entered the room. His face displaying a vacant expression, he sauntered towards our table with all the makings of a Stan Laurel. Slowly, he inquired what we chose to eat. We took pains to explain, and in exact detail, our requirements. The fully informed waiter returned to the kitchen.

Minutes later, another loud bang heralded the arrival of a second waiter. His grand entrance was made backwards, having used his posterior to push open the swing-doors. His white-cotton, gloved-hands, carried food-laden dishes. Assuming a half-crouched position - in the style of Groucho Marx - he approached our table. Leaning his upper-body slightly backwards, he lifted his right-leg off the floor. Then keeping his left foot grounded, so as to maintain his balance, he performed a unique dance. In a harlequinade fashion, he turned full circle, and all the while, tightly held our breakfast plates!

Having twice performed this curious stunt, the food was finally placed on our table. Throughout the performance Nicola and Elanor giggled with amusement. As for me, I wondered how the food had ever reached us, without first touching the floor!

When all four plates had been delivered, Sandra and I looked them over. Much to our chagrin, we soon discovered the first waiter had got the orders totally wrong! It was then we realised the two men were a double act. And it was one which was to be repeated many times during the days which lay ahead!

After breakfast, we left the hotel to explore our new found world. Carrying a camera and a few South African Rand, our feet took us along the spacious Johannesburg streets. Unlike our English home town, they appeared cared for. There was an absence of familiar dog droppings and discarded fish and chip papers! Wherever we walked, multi-storey apartment blocks towered above us. We felt like a family of ants, walking through a field, filled with corn stalks. Seemingly everywhere we looked was black African people. Curiously, they appeared to attain their individual identity by donning a particular headdress. It was amusing to see the various styles. Flat cloth-caps were commonplace, and reminded me of the ones frequently worn in Lancashire. Knitted bob-caps, trilbys, and safari-hats were all evident in varying numbers. Occasionally, a straw boater put in an appearance and there was even a bowler hat to be seen!

Walking towards the central post office, I noticed a group of Africans. Standing in a space between parked cars, the scene looked as though there may have been an accident. Two or three of the men gesticulated as they uttered loud, verbal sounds.

As a precaution, I ushered our daughters to the opposite side of the street. From the relative safety of distance, I observed the action. To my surprise the group was busily engaged in a game of dice-throwing! Some stood on the pavement watching, whilst others used the gutter and the edge of the kerb to act as a buffer for the thrown dice!

Continuing on our way, we came upon an entrance to Johannesburg's central railway station. Scores of Africans sold foodstuffs and trinkets from little tables they had set-up along the pavement. The diversity of saleable goods was fascinating to see. But slowly an awareness came upon us that we were the only white people in that area! A mild sensation of panic began to take hold and we felt it best to move on. For days afterwards, whenever walking in the city's central area, the thought of being attacked was always present. But eventually, I realised the African people were much like any other, and in the main were quite friendly.

For the average South African, the day begins early and most people are on their way to work by 0600hrs. School children normally follow an hour later. But by the same token, the day ends early. There is no twilight, and during the winter months of June and July, the sky is usually dark by 1800 hrs.

My first evening stroll along the streets of central Johannesburg was interesting to say the least. Hundreds of lights shone from different directions and from sources of all kinds. Some examples were hotel display signs, shop windows, street lamps and even burning braziers. At this time of the year it was common to see a burning brazier placed outside many of the large apartment blocks.

*Street vendor near Johannesburg railway station (1978)*

*View from Johannesburg's central library steps (1978)*

Standing around them would be one, or more, uniformed Africans. Employed from six o' clock in the evening, until six o' clock the following morning, they represented a visual form of security. A uniform usually consisted of an old army great-coat and a khaki-coloured peaked cap. Sometimes, the cap might be seen to be perched on top of a knitted balaclava helmet!

For personal protection, a security guard normally carried a *knobkerrie*. Essentially, it was a long wooden stick, with a carved ball-shaped *knob* at one end. Prior to serving as a weapon, it had originally been the short branch of a tree. The security guard could swing the knobkerrie, like an international golfer might swing a number seven iron. But the African could achieve a far more devastating result!

My continuing investigative wander took me to Eloff Street. Rounding the street's corner, I was surprised to see distant flames shooting merrily skywards. Initially, I thought some rubbish had been deliberately lit and possibly with evil intent. But after hurrying closer, I saw the flames rising from the confines of an upturned oil drum. Sitting next to it, on an improvised seat, was a black African. Wearing a shabby-looking overcoat, together with a knitted hat, his appearance defied the concept of fashion. For him, however, during the present season of the year, warmth was more important than style. Next to him was an orange coloured steel cabinet, which stood around five feet tall. At the start of the day, it could be opened into a miniature book stall. And from there newspapers, magazines or paperbacks, could be sold to a passing pedestrian-trade. The man explained to me that he awaited delivery of a newly printed batch of Johannesburg's *Star* newspapers. He then hoped to sell them at twelve cents each!

# 4
## A JOB INTERVIEW

On arrival to South Africa, I was required to report to the Government's Immigration Department, in central Johannesburg. There, I was to be assessed for future employment. Before my due appointment I was required to do two things. The first was to complete several official forms and the second was to wait a long time!

Eventually, I spoke with an employment officer named Meneer Raas. He was Afrikaans speaking and a no-nonsense type of person. Whilst examining my trade papers, he asked many probing questions. Finally, I was given an address, where I was to attend a job interview. Surprisingly, my mode of transport was a trolley-bus! I had never seen one before. The ungainly-looking vehicle was a cross between a tram-car and a double-deck bus. Painted two-tone burgundy and cream, its wheels were two at the front and four at the rear. Two long poles attached to its roof had their 'free' ends resting against catenary cables. Suspended high above the road, the cables carried electricity, from which the electro-motorized vehicle derived its power.

Climbing aboard, I noticed a wooden sign placed prominently near the entrance door.

Painted on it, in bold white letters, were the Afrikaans words, 'SLEGS BLANKES.' Translated to English, they read, 'WHITES ONLY'. In essence, the sign meant that only European passengers were allowed to travel on the bus. This was my earliest introduction to Apartheid.

At that time, Afrikaans was the first of the country's two official languages. In the main it had evolved from the language of the early Dutch settlers. In addition to that, eleven different Bantu languages were spoken in the country but the State declined to give them equal status!

Like a large and laggardly mechanical-beast, the trolley-bus rumbled along the streets. It took me away from the centre of Johannesburg to the distant Empire Road. Notch by notch, the driver ratcheted a control lever, which allowed the bus to reach its top speed. I felt sure it couldn't have been more than twenty miles per hour! With every move of the lever, I heard what seemed like the grinding of gears. Furthermore, the whole bodywork rattled at every turn in the road. It seemed as though it might fall apart at any minute. But before I could find the courage to jump off, the tortuous conveyance arrived at my destination!

My interview was conducted in an old, single-storey house, which was presently used as the head office for a construction company. It specialised in refrigeration and ventilation work. On my arrival, the interviewer was entertaining a travelling salesman, who had called from a Siemens' factory, based at Isando. The word *Isando* is of Zulu origin, meaning - *to work*. But in this case, it was the name given to a suburb of Johannesburg, which was near the present-day Oliver Tambo International Airport.

Part way through the interview it unexpectedly became a three-way conversation - which included the travelling salesman! Taking me by surprise, the interviewer suddenly interrupted his string of questions and began to tell a joke.

"Did you hear about the Afrikaans policeman?" he began. "He was sent to the scene of an accident, where a motorist had driven his motorcar into a horse! The policeman arrived at the junction of two streets where the animal lay dead. The motorist explained to the police officer how he was driving from one street and entering the other. He described how he had been unable to avoid the collision. The officer carefully studied the position of the dead horse. With a pencil poised over his notebook, the officer asked a relevant question.

"Nou meneer, wat is die naam af die straat?"

(Now, Mister, what is the name of the street?)

The English-speaking motorist was quick to reply.

"It's called BEZUIDENHOUT STREET."

Writing in his notebook, the policeman spoke each word loudly. "Horse found dead at the junction of..."

But in mid-sentence he stopped speaking. After pausing to contemplate the spelling of the street name, he continued to write. "B...err...um..., E...err...um...Z..."

The spelling of the word BEZUIDENHOUT became too much for him. Suddenly, he exclaimed,

"Oh, damn it, man! Couldn't we just drag the horse around the corner into SMIT STREET?"

The joke eased the tension of that initial meeting, and the interview continued. Without me realising, the salesman pondered my answers to the various raised questions. Perhaps it was something I said which caused him to share some information.

"There's a vacancy for a job at the Isando Siemens' factory" he said. "They are looking for someone with experience of electric-drives".

Admitting the name *Siemens* was new to my ears, he hastened to enlighten me.

"Siemens is a large company with branches throughout Africa," he said.

Seeing my expression change to one of growing interest, he added,

"If you like, I can arrange for you to have an interview."

Some days later, following a couple of interviews at the Isando factory, I was offered the position of *Motor Production Planner*. My new appointment was expected to start in two weeks' time.

# 5

# WALKING IN JOUBERT PARK

In the sun-soaked city of Johannesburg, nestling between the streets of Twist and Wolmarans, lies a stretch of land named *Joubert Park*. It was a veritable oasis in the heart of the bustling city. As it was close to the Constantia Hotel, it soon became my family's regular haunt. At its centre was a circular stone-enclosure. It contained a water fountain, which gushed like a newly 'blown' oil-well. Surrounding it were smaller and less powerful spouts of water, which might be compared to the petals of a large flower.

An asphalted track formed a perimeter around the outer limits of the park. And like the spokes of a wheel, four walkways reached out from the circular stone-enclosure. Each of them connected to the asphalted track. The overall layout resembled a giant wheel of an ox-wagon. And occupying the spaces in-between the 'spokes' was turf-covered land. It provided for a mix of flower-beds and rose-gardens. The flowers displayed a kaleidoscope of colour and saturated the surrounding air with their perfume. While here and there, palm trees towered above them, resembling giant umbrellas.

A Victorian conservatory - or 'Hothouse' as it was known - was situated at the north-west corner of the park. Inside was a large water enclosure, which contained gold-fish and floating water-lilies.

Surrounding that was a collection of green-ferns and exotic flowers. At another section of the park was a stone-built art gallery. It contained many interesting pieces of art. Two of them were oil paintings, created by Picasso and Monet.

The main entrance to the park was located on Twist Street. Standing next to it was a redundant German field gun - a relic from the First World War. It occurred to me that it looked out of place in that peaceful setting. But then I noticed the gun stood diagonally opposite the old military *Drill Hall*. And as the name suggests, during past decades, cadet soldiers had used the building's spacious hall for training purposes. Perhaps the gun was a left over from those earlier times.

Another point of access to the park was from Wolmarans Street. Near its entrance was an area set aside for an open-air chess game. Coloured concrete paving-slabs formed a chess-board, on which players could stand. Chess pieces about two feet tall were made of fibre-glass. On one occasion, I saw an African player who stood on the 'board', whilst concentrating hard on the game. Sporting a brown, two-piece suit and a brightly coloured shirt, he looked resplendent. But sadly, his affluent image was somewhat tarnished by wearing a pair of scruffy, open-toed plimsolls! Meanwhile, his opponent was a well-fed European. With hands pushed deep in the pockets of his designer wind-jammer, he studied an impending move.

On another occasion, three European ladies watched a game in progress, whilst seated on a park bench. It was intentionally placed next to the chess-board to offer a good view. Meanwhile a short distance from them stood two contesting muntus.

Both appearing well-dressed, they carefully perused the chess-board. One wore a neat, two-piece suit and a brown trilby-hat. But it was his highly polished, black-leather shoes, which particularly captured my attention. By way of contrast, his less affluent opponent wore a denim jacket and a light-coloured flat-cap. After considering both occasions, what impressed me most was the mix of Bantu and European people, who appeared relaxed and happy, as they spent time together.

Park lands usually have some form of entertainment for young children, and Joubert Park was no exception. Set aside was an area which provided some traditional recreational equipment. A steel-horse, pivoted on a steel-post, stood silently awaiting action. Its head, with a fixed grinning-mouth, was separated from its tail by an oblong body. A row of seats, each with a short grab-rail, was fixed along its back. The infant riders, who sat astride the horse, were expected to hold the grab-rails tightly.

To motivate the beast, someone was obliged to push its tail-end. It was designed to perform a rocking motion and without leaving its support. But what a motion! The head would dip and rise like the bow of a ship on turbulent waters. And if the 'pusher' was sufficiently vigilant, the mechanical equine could emulate the action of a bucking-bronco! Before long, it would require the rider's entire strength to remain seated. Come to think of it, the children who chose to ride the horse would need to be very brave!

Nearby were a row of swings, a roundabout and a *jungle-gym*. The latter was a cubic-shaped, tubular-steel climbing-frame.

It had a singular slide, allowing children to glide gleefully from its top level to the ground. Aside from their obvious function the play items had another thing in common. They were uniformly painted in green and red colours. But due to the regular clamour of numerous tiny shoes, most of the paint was long gone!

At Christmas time, the park was transformed into a magical world for children and also for adults, who were children at heart! Trees festooned with coloured lights, helped to create a mysterious setting. Amongst the various flower beds, statuettes made from plaster of Paris were arranged in fairy tale themes. Snow white and the seven dwarves was a popular choice to view. Whilst for the Afrikaans speaking populace, the character named Jan Pineritz, was another firm favourite. Secreted in the trees were loud speakers, which emitted recorded music and singing-voices. In particular, they produced all the familiar Christmas carols. Families from far and wide would travel to enjoy the free and spectacular display.

In 1974, the Johannesburg City Council relaxed the application of the Reservation of Separate Amenities Act (1953). Thereafter, black Africans were allowed access to Joubert Park. However, at the time of our arrival in Johannesburg my family didn't know that! When making our first visit to the park it was one which we treated with caution. Before leaving England, the media, friends and some work colleagues, had contributed to conditioning our way of thinking. We had come to believe that South Africa was a most fractious country. But our friends, who actually lived in Johannesburg, had assured us that all was well.

Elanor, our eldest daughter, caught sight of the swings. Suddenly, with gay abandon she ran towards them.

With trepidation, I watched as she crossed the grassy area. But then I became aware of something else. To my horror, two young black boys arrived at the swings before her. Competing against each other, they strained to keep the swings air borne. My immediate reaction was to stop our daughter. But before I could holler a word, she reached the boys and took command of a vacant swing!

I couldn't help thinking black and white race groups were not allowed to mix. I was on tenterhooks in case an official came along to reprimand us. But, before the word, 'Apartheid' could be uttered, Nicola, our other daughter, was making a bee-line for the roundabout. Within seconds, she joined Bantu and European children of a similar age. Meanwhile, two black nannies were standing a short distance away and keeping a watchful eye over them all. Everyone was happy, and no one complained.

At the end of an hour of trouble-free fun, our family set off back to the hotel. Along the way I remembered the verbal warnings I had heard before leaving England. But considering what I had just witnessed, the contrasting impressions left me mentally challenged!

During one of my numerous visits to Joubert Park, I chanced to meet an old school chum. It had been more than a decade since we last met. As he ambled towards me he exclaimed,

"What the hell are you doing here?"

"Well, John" I replied, "I might ask you the same question!"

I learned he had been living and working in Johannesburg for eighteen months but was shortly due to return to England.

Naturally, I asked about his experiences during his time in Africa. He explained how the Africans were collectively known as 'Bantu'. Or singularly, they were known as a 'black' or a 'muntu'. He also added how the majority generally lived in salutary surroundings.

As we discussed the Bantu's lifestyle, John shared with me an interesting observation. One day he and his pal had driven some miles from the city to see a rural area. John described how they had found a house abandoned by the Bantu. Made from compacted-mud, it was standing in the open veld.

"Do you mean a genuine 'mud-hut'?" I asked excitedly.

"Yes, of course" he answered nonchalantly.

John proceeded to tell me how the hut was built.

"Of course, before you can build a mud-hut, you need mud bricks." he said. "The Bantu first knock together some pieces of wood to assume an oblong box. Dry soil is mixed with water to form a thick sludge. The sludge is poured into the wooden box and left to dry in the midday sun."

My friend paused to ask if I 'followed' his explanation.

"Yes, yes," I hurriedly replied, please continue.

"Okay," he said. "In a short time, the sludge becomes a hardened block. The blocks are then used to build free-standing walls. Finally, another mix of soil and water forms slurry, which is plastered over the walls to create a bond. The end result is an extremely sturdy piece of architecture."

At this point, I responded to John's mini-lecture.

"That's very interesting," I remarked. "But what happens to the walls when it rains? And what is done to make a roof?"

Smiling broadly, John continued to enlighten me.

"Rainfall in this part of Africa is tempered with prolonged bouts of sunshine, so the walls resist downpours reasonably well. As for the roof, old corrugated, tin-sheets are laid flat across the wall tops. They are held down with makeshift rope of plaited straw, or often just randomly placed stones."

John added that he and his pal had tried hard to kick down one of the abandoned walls. But to their surprise, it failed to budge - thus testifying to the inherent strength of the dwelling.

The mention of a 'dwelling' caused me to ask where he was presently living. John revealed he rented an apartment in a high-rise block and not far from Joubert Park. I quizzed him about the Apartheid situation. He acknowledged that things were generally improving. But he added that certain members of the police force frowned upon the mixing of the race groups. John unexpectedly chuckled as he remembered a personal experience.

"Why are you laughing?" I asked.

"There was a time", he laughingly recalled, "When a dark-skinned maiden spent a few days living with me."

"Oh, really?" I exclaimed, "Pray tell me more!"

Restraining a laugh and with a twinkle in his eye she explained.

"Well, let's just say she was seeing to my needs. If you know what I mean?"

John suspected a bigoted neighbour had informed the police of his contravention of the Race Relations Act.

One morning, about breakfast time, he was rudely awoken from slumber. A loud banging was heard on the front door of his apartment. Still half asleep, John stumbled from his bedroom. Wearing nothing more than a pair of shorts and a tired look on his face, he opened the front door. Instantly, he was confronted by the blare of the morning sun. It caused him to raise a hand to shield his eyes. A second or two passed before he was able to see reasonably well. It was then he suffered a severe shock.

Standing in the doorway, whilst silhouetted against the blinding sunlight, were the uniformed figures of two policemen! Along with their blue-coloured tunics, they wore regulation Sam Browne belts. The taller of the two had the peak of his regulation cap pulled down over his eyes. Without invite, he stamped a booted foot against the inside of the open door.

"Doen 'n swart frau bly hierso, meneer?" he growled.

(Is a black girl living here, mister?)

At that moment, John's eyes focused. A startled look formed upon his face. As he stared dumbly at the policeman's tunic, adrenalin coursed through his veins. His startled expression quickly morphed into one of puzzlement. Reacting to the silent response, the policeman repeated the question. But this time - realising he was speaking to an immigrant - halfway through the sentence he switched from his mother tongue and spoke English.

"Ek sy Meneer err, um Mister - Is a black woman living here?"

"No sir!" was John's instant and submissive reply.

But unfortunately for him, at that precise moment the dark maiden chose to leave the bedroom. She lazily shuffled her feet on her way to the bathroom. The distant movement of her body was enough to attract the attention of the vindictive policeman. Seeing her semi-naked form caused him to wonder why she was there. But instinctively, he reacted. Like a compressed spring having been released, he raised an arm into the air. Stabbing a forefinger accusingly towards the girl, he loudly and caustically called out.

"Den vot is dat, meneer?" (Then what is that Mister?)

John's head turned to follow the direction of the pointing finger. He was instantly shocked to see the incriminating evidence. Blissfully unaware of the unfolding drama the girl continued her journey. It was then John made a mistake. He simply shouldn't have looked back - but seconds later, he did!

In one swift motion, the policeman lowered his arm, and with the back of his hand, swiped the face of the accused. Responding to the blow, John staggered backwards. The policeman snarled some final words.

"Get dat fokken kaffir uit van daar before we come back!"

Having uttered the threat, the two policemen left the building.

My friend's experience reminds me of a joke which was popular around this time. It has a certain bearing on the previous story. The joke involves an American tourist, the Carlton International Hotel, and a muntu lady-escort. But before writing the joke, allow me to describe the actual hotel.

Located in central Johannesburg, the Carlton International Hotel was built as a five-star venue and was the finest in South Africa. The multi-storey structure has something of a unique shape. From the lower third of the building, its front and rear faces extend outwards at a sloping angle. They give it the appearance of a stationary space-rocket - albeit oblong in shape and having a flat roof-top. Its roof area features a large open-air swimming pool, with a retractable glass-panelled ceiling.

At ground level, above the hotel's main-entrance, and perched on a concrete ledge, was a row of flag-poles. Flags of various nations flew there - silently testifying that the Carlton was truly an international hotel. Today, they fly no more, since the hotel closed its doors for the last time in 1997. Anyway, returning to the joke:

An American tourist arrived in Johannesburg and spent a few days at the Carlton Hotel. During a lonely period, he contacted a local escort agency. Somehow, he managed to have a muntu lady-escort visit his hotel suite. That night, they whiled away the hours enjoying copious amounts of champagne. The next morning, they awoke in the blissful comfort of a double-bed. Gradually recognising his surroundings, the American turned his head and was shocked by what he saw. Lying next to him and smiling sweetly, was the naked form of the muntu lady-escort. With his southern-American drawl he exclaimed,

"Who the hell are you?!"

The lady-escort gazed at him lovingly and replied.

"Baas - I don't know who I is dis mornin' - but last night I was de Yellow Rose of Texas!"

# 6
## 21 CHESTERFIELD HOUSE

With my employment at the Siemens' factory confirmed, Sandra and I decided to find an apartment. They were plentiful in and around Johannesburg and rental costs were moderate. But since my job was at Isando, it seemed logical to find a place near there. However, transport was a problem.

At that time public transport was limited. PUTCO was an acronym for Public Urban Transport Corporation. It provided single-deck buses but they catered almost exclusively for the indigenous populace. Designed to travel within the townships, with their many unfinished roads, the buses were robustly built and certainly lacking in comfort.

Eventually, we decided to hire an automobile. Squeezing into a *Datsun 120*, we fastened its seat-belts. In South Africa at that time, unlike in England, the wearing of safety-belts was compulsory. Edenvale, a town on the East-Rand, was our chosen destination. Leaving Johannesburg's Eloff Street, our car joined the M2-East motorway. In this part of the city, the motorway is built on concrete stilts and passes above the roof tops of certain buildings. From the elevated road system, it was possible to see the spread of the city and beyond. And rising from the ground at numerous places were tall, man-made mounds of sand.

Commonly known as 'mine-dumps', they were the product of processed ore. Countless tons of rock had been extracted from gold-mines during past mining operations. In 1978, the mine-dumps were exposed to the elements. On windswept days, their loose sand was whipped-up into the air and deposited over the city. This resulted in many shops in central Johannesburg displaying signs on their entrance door. Printed words read: 'CLOSED ON ACCOUNT OF THE WEATHER'. In this case, the word 'weather' was related to the air-borne sand.

During the winter period of June and July, the wind was particularly active. Intermittently, it drove cloud-like formations of sand across the M2-East highway. And for a brief time, it was under these conditions I drove the car. Keeping to the maximum speed limit of 60kph, we travelled in the central lane of three. What followed next was an experience best forgotten.

Totally unexpected, a car from the inside lane, and another from the outside lane, shot past me. Like two guided missiles running amok, they instantly crossed the middle lane in front of me and both at the same time! One of them headed into the nearside lane and quickly joined an off-ramp. While the other, entered the offside lane and accelerated away. It was a nerve racking experience which momentarily took my breath away!

The day spent in Edenvale, looking for an apartment to rent, produced no positive result. But I did learn something about traffic procedures. For instance, a set of traffic lights in this part of the world are known as *robots*. Their sequence of change is like the British system with a difference.

In both countries, the solitary green changes to green and amber, followed by red on its own. All well and good, you may think. But in the R.S.A. and unlike the British system, the solitary red-light changes directly to green - without showing amber!

On many occasions I witnessed cars halted at red stop-lights, whilst waiting for the light to change to green. The motorists would display their impatience by revving their car engines. The resultant sound was similar to that of an orchestra preparing for a concert - although far less melodic! When the red light finally changed to green, it was instantaneous. And as if taking part in a Grand Prix, the waiting cars raced away! In those days, noisy exhaust systems were commonplace, and many drove around making as much noise as they liked!

Another example of South African traffic procedures was the mandatory 'Stop' sign. At road junctions without robots, there was a metal road-sign displaying the word 'STOP'. Painted on the road surface adjacent to the sign, was a broad white line. It indicated where the front wheels of any vehicle must stop. And that was *behind* the white line. If, for any reason the vehicle's wheels rolled over the line, without first coming to a halt, a penalty fine of fifty Rand would be issued. In light of this, it was not unusual for an overzealous traffic officer to be seen waiting at a road junction. His sole purpose was to issue a ticket to any unfortunate motorist who happened to flaunt the rule!

What surprised me most about South African vehicles was the number of very early models in daily use. The majority were rust-free and generally appeared in good mechanical condition.

The lack of rust was undoubtedly due to the abundance of sunshine and the low humidity of the Highveld. The region surrounding Johannesburg, known as the 'Highveld', sits at an altitude of around 6000 feet above sea-level and enjoys a low annual rain fall.

Continuing with the subject of automobiles, in the Republic of South Africa a Road Worthy Certificate is the equivalent of the English M.O.T. (Ministry of Transport) test certificate. Both are issued when a road vehicle meets the required safety standards. However, unlike the English M.O.T. test the R.S.A. variety need only be performed each time the vehicle changes ownership. It is therefore possible to buy a vehicle and keep it for years, or even for its lifetime, without it being officially tested again!

Returning the rental car was fraught with difficulty. The Eloff Street area of Johannesburg had numerous one-way streets. I found myself needlessly driving around in circles and clocking up some extra kilometres. In desperation, I eventually abandoned the car in a parking lot! The next morning, I was successful and after the car was inspected, I was presented with the bill.

The fee, which included a mileage charge, insurance, and a Government stamp duty, amounted to a grand total of sixteen Rand! With an exchange rate of R1-88 = £1, it seemed like a reasonable amount to pay. Feeling generally happy with the rental service, I was bowled over by an added bonus. When I happened to mention I was about to visit the *1820 Settlers'* office, which was situated in central Johannesburg, I was given a free chauffeur-driven ride!

Opposite Johannesburg's Carlton Hotel were the headquarters of an organisation known as the *1820 Settlers*.

A feature of its service was to assist newly arrived immigrants to resolve any problems they may encounter. Of course, our family's immediate hurdle was one of finding suitable accommodation. And with no joy in Edenvale, Sandra and I agreed to find an apartment in Johannesburg. As for transport to my new job, the Siemens' Isando factory kindly provided a private bus. It ferried its employees, who lived in Jo'burg, to and from the factory gates. Fortunately for me, the pickup point happened to be close to our hotel.

At the 1820 Settlers' office a kindly lady issued us with a printed list of available rental apartments. And before leaving the office she advised us to buy a copy of the *Witwatersrand Map Book* - which was a comprehensive street plan of Johannesburg. She said it would help us locate the various street addresses on our list. With her words freshly in mind we called at the nearest C.N.A. shop. The letters C.N.A. represent Central News Agency, and a shop is usually found in every town. On sale at the shops are books, newspapers, magazines, stationery, and even children's games and toys.

Entering the shop, I spoke to a male European assistant.

"Do you have a copy of the Wit-Waters-Rand Map Book?"

My north of England accent placed particular emphasis on the letter 'W'. The shop-assistant calmly picked up a copy. Handing it to me, his face took on a questioning look, and his voice spoke with a hint of sarcasm.

"I take it you haven't lived very long in Johannesburg, have you, sir?"

Shaking my head in agreement he began to explain.

The word *Witwatersrand* stems from the Afrikaans language and means 'Ridge of white waters'. Allegedly, when the early Dutch-speaking settlers entered the region, they saw a distant rocky ridge. Streams of water flowing over it reflected the sun's rays. This caused them to appear white in colour and hence the given name.

The shop assistant proceeded to explain the correct pronunciation of Witwatersrand. I discovered the letter *W* is pronounced as a *V*. Therefore, Witwatersrand becomes Vit-vaters-rand. And if one wishes to be absolutely correct, the letter *d* is pronounced as a *t*. So, finally, we have, 'Vitvatersrant'. Newly armed with a map book, and a decidedly small understanding of the Afrikaans language, our family set off on another day of exploration.

How does the song go? The one sung by *The Lovin' Spoonful*?

"Hot town somewhere in the city back of my neck getting dirty and gritty..."

Well, that's how it was for us. And following hours of foot slogging around the city streets, amazingly we found an apartment to suit our needs. And guess where? It was literally around the corner from the Constantia Hotel!

The ten-storey *Chesterfield House*, stood on the corner of Koch and Twist Streets. As our family approached the main entrance the superintendent greeted us. We headed towards an elevator, where he opened its metallic door. Immediately, I noticed the words *SLEGS BLANKES* (Only whites) stencilled in white paint at the top of the door frame. This was another tangible example of Apartheid.

The superintendent said the Bantu seldom showered, and to travel in an elevator, close to an un-showered person, was something to be avoided; especially on a hot Johannesburg day!

Located on the second floor was apartment number twenty-one. At that moment we weren't to know it but was soon to be our future home. Stepping inside, the superintendent was quick to tell us there was an attached balcony.

"It offers an uninterrupted view of the nearby Joubert Park," he proudly announced.

Sandra and I gave it a cursory look, but my attempt to view the park was interrupted by a commotion in the street below. It happened to be the collection day for refuse. A wagon of giant proportions slowly roared along the street. The driver's cab reminded me of an American long-distance truck, with its wide frontage and enormous wheels. Next to the driver's door was the combined exhaust pipe and silencer, which pointed skywards. The rear of the cab was attached to a large steel container, which carried the collected refuse. Wearing their everyday clothing, six or seven muntus ran alongside the moving truck. They laughed and shouted like playful schoolboys, as they managed to empty the bins into the moving wagon.

As Sandra and I edged towards another room, she discretely whispered in my ear.

"Did you see Joubert Park?"

"No - did you?"

"Sure - It's a great view from the balcony", she declared. "And you *can* see Joubert Park; if you happen to be a contortionist!"

The apartment had a large living room, two double-bedrooms, a bathroom, a separate toilet and a fitted-kitchen. When I say 'fitted-kitchen', I mean there were cupboards and a sink. But there was no electric oven or 'stove,' as they are called in South Africa, and there was no refrigerator. However, with a rental cost of R154 per month and the assurance that a stove would be installed on the date of occupancy, it seemed like a good deal.

Whilst the paperwork was being arranged, I managed to steal a quiet moment to ask Sandra a question.

"Do you have a good memory for faces?"

"Why is that?" she asked.

"Because", I replied, "the bathroom has no mirror!"

A contract was duly signed, which meant that number 21 Chesterfield House was to be our home for the next six months. However, for the time being we remained residents of the Constantia Hotel.

Before our eventual re-location, my persistence in asking the superintendent to install an electric stove finally produced a result. Two muntus brought one from a storage room, located in the dark basement of the building. They placed it in the kitchen of our new apartment. But rather than spend more time waiting, I volunteered to connect it to the electricity supply.

One evening, later that week, I arrived at the empty apartment with my tool-box. Entering the darkened kitchen and switching on the light, my eyes beheld a frightful sight. The floor area appeared to be moving! On closer inspection, I saw a veritable sea of cockroaches.

Their writhing bodies gave me the impression an insect convention was in progress. As I looked on in amazement, more of them gradually joined the merry throng. Acting like commandoes on a training exercise, they cascaded from the oven compartment. Seconds after my initial shock, I began stamping on the intruders. However, most of them evaded my shoes and darted back inside the stove! But the job needed to be done. Proceeding with caution, I connected the electricity supply to the oven and switched on the power. My hope was that the oven's heat would drive out the unwanted occupants. In due course it seemed the idea had worked and feeling satisfied the battle had been won, I triumphantly returned to the Constantia Hotel.

The lease for our apartment commenced on the first day of July. Some furniture, purchased from a local supplier, was due for delivery on the third day. But although Sandra and our children waited for some hours, the furniture failed to arrive. Finally, on the seventh day, our beds and lounge suite were delivered. Along with them was a *Blaupunkt* music-centre. The German-made state-of-the-art appliance featured a three-speed turntable, a double cassette-deck and a multi-channel radio-tuner. Its amplifier claimed to deliver twenty-eight watts to each of its twin speakers - this was technology at its best!

Having arranged the new arrivals, our first evening away from the hotel, was spent in the luxurious comfort of our own little 'palace'. But sad to say, our enjoyment was short-lived. Another batch of the troublesome cockroaches appeared in our kitchen. Previously, someone had suggested using a chemical spray which was aptly named *Doom*. Because it was a spray, it could penetrate narrow crevices and secluded corners.

Applied liberally, in and around the stove, the *Doom* fulfilled all expectations. More insects appeared; having been forcibly evicted from their hiding places. However, the chemical had also produced an unpleasant odour.

Sandra suggested the best course of action was to switch on the power to the oven. The idea being to burn off any deposit left over from the spray. Her idea was put into practice and the kitchen window was opened to allow the fumes to disperse. With the kitchen door closed, all seemed to go well - at least for a time.

An unexpected clattering sound brought our peaceful evening to an abrupt halt. There was no doubt it originated in the kitchen. Imagine the thoughts that seethed through my troubled mind.

"Had the god of the dead cockroaches affected their resurrection? Had they mustered together and were about to launch a retaliatory attack? Were they perhaps armed with items of kitchen cutlery? And above all, were they now waiting for me to re-enter *their* domain?"

What followed was a brief high-level discussion between me and the Advisory Committee of the War Department - aka the Farley family. It resulted in me being elected to investigate the cause of the noise. Surreptitiously, I approached the kitchen. With my ear pressed against the closed door, I listened intently. All was quiet on the inside. By opening the door slowly, and peering through the enlarging gap, I could see the inside floor area.

Expecting to find a legion of knife-wielding cockroaches, I was surprised to see the floor was empty. Gingerly, I entered the room. The stove continued to emit low heat and the odour from the sprayed *Doom* had all but gone.

Nearby, lay a few cockroach cadavers. Across the room the kitchen curtains gently flapped. They indicating a slight breeze was blowing through the open window.

But suddenly, like a scene from a horror movie, a large winged object appeared. Its fat, bungling, feathered-body arose from behind the stove. It was a pigeon!

Attempting to perform a lap around the room, its outspread wings flapped past my face. And before anyone could say the words, *Nelson Mandela*, I back-stepped out of the kitchen and pulled the door closed! The Advisory Committee had been nervously waiting. Their shock at seeing my reaction immediately prompted another meeting. Shortly, everyone agreed to wait a few minutes before having a second look. It was thought that following a lull in activity, perhaps the pigeon might be induced to leave the premises.

Opening the kitchen door for a second time, I anticipated another airborne attack. Fortunately, I was pleased to find all was quiet. A quick look behind the stove and then around the room, proved beyond doubt that the bird had gone! Flown away - I presumed - and through the open window. "Clever bird," I thought. All that remained was the few deceased cockroaches, which lay strewn around the stove.

But wait! - There *was* more! A close inspection of the floor beneath the open window, revealed a generous dollop of pigeon droppings. It was a parting gift from the winged intruder!

# 7

## MY FIRST DAY AT WORK

The first day of my Siemens' job eventually dawned. I awoke from sleep feeling apprehensive. For a time, I lay in bed, basking in the darkness of the bedroom; while enveloped in the peaceful silence. A distant noise - sounding like a buzzing bee - broke the pleasant spell. Starting around Anderson Street, in the south of the city, a motor-bike engine was in motion. The sound increased as it gradually drew nearer.

On its journey along Twist Street, the 'buzzing bee' morphed into a roaring lion! And as it passed our apartment, its noise filled the bedroom's air-space. Moments later, the motor-bike accelerated towards Hillbrow, and its sound gradually faded away. An abrupt jingle of the alarm-clock signalled an end to my days of unemployment. Six o'clock seemed like an unearthly hour to awake. But I was reassured by the thought that the sun would soon be rising. It was a far cry from my working days in England, where the comparatively miserable weather had been left behind. Nevertheless, I struggled to do three things. The first was to get out of bed - the second was to get dressed - and the third was to keep my eyes open!

A cabin-trunk, containing bespoke items of kitchenware, dispatched earlier from our English home, remained in transit.

Consequently, some improvisation was deemed necessary. A hot-ring of the electric-stove brought a pan of water to the boil. It provided for a refreshing morning cuppa, with enough left over to shave my face. Later, a walk of about a mile, would take me to De Korte Street. It was there the Siemens' bus offered free transport to the Isando factory.

Leaving the apartment, I found the outside air chilly but dry. At the end of the street some Bantu sat next to their newspaper stand. Warming themselves around a burning brazier, they waited for customers to buy morning newspapers. At regular intervals along my journey, the scene appeared to repeat itself.

Gradually, pavements filled with people, as they walked to their places of work. An assortment of vehicular traffic darted along the streets. Catching my attention as it rumbled passed me, was a British-built Leyland-wagon. With its open flat-back, of about thirty feet in length, it carried rows of coal-filled hessian sacks. Precariously placed at the tail-end of the wagon, was a small steel drum. Containing chunks of burning wood, flames and sparks flew skywards. A few Bantu workers huddled around it, intent on keeping warm. Whilst on their way to deliver the sacks, they appeared unconcerned by the wagon's erratic motion. And as I watched the entertaining spectacle, it seemed as if I was the only one who took notice.

At the end of De Korte Street, a single-deck bus was waiting. Climbing aboard, I sat next to a bright-looking Indian youth. Following an initial introduction, we chatted about his life in South Africa. He told me he was originally from Durban and was training at the Siemens' factory to become an Electrical Engineer.

As the bus motored along the highway, towards the Siemens' Isando factory, the Indian youth related to me a recent experience.

One afternoon at around five-thirty, he was on his way home from work. And as he was about to enter Johannesburg's Central railway station, he was surrounded by some muntus. Four of them pushed his body against a wall and held him there, whilst another frisked him. Rummaging through his pockets, the thief brought to light, a handkerchief, a fifty-cent coin, a fish-cake, and a *prune!*

Personally speaking, I could understand him carrying a handkerchief and the fifty-cent coin, and perhaps even the fish cake but the *prune* had me puzzled. Thankfully, my new friend confessed to having bought the fish-cake on his way home. He said he had intended to cook it for his evening meal. The explanation was acceptable but I felt compelled to ask another question.

"Why did you carry a *prune* in your trouser pocket?"

My friend explained he was a Muslim by faith, and on that particular day he was called upon to fast. As for the prune, it was meant to see him through his religious obligation. He openly admitted that since he had little money with him, he feared the men would do him harm. Fortunately, however, they allowed him to go on his way. But that was not before relieving him of two items. And they were; the handkerchief and the *prune!*

Within the hour, the bus arrived at the factory gates, where its passengers disembarked. They were obliged to walk past the security check-point, with its two muntu security guards and their European overseer.

*Siemens' security guard* (1979)

*Bare-footed boy Joubert Park* (1979)

It was their responsibility to inspect the identity-cards of the arriving personnel. But since it was my first day of employment I had no card. However, I expected to receive one in due course. Now, I'm not saying the security was lax, but for *five* weeks, I walked past the guards without carrying an identity card and without being stopped!

The walls of the entrance to the two-storey factory displayed large colour-photographs, which depicted Siemens' products. A flight of stairs led to an office area, where I would spend some working months. For a few days, my daily climb up the factory stairs left me feeling breathless. The temporary condition, I was told, was due to Johannesburg's rarefied atmosphere. The city is situated at a height of 6,000 feet above sea level, and its ambient air has reduced oxygen content. I later learned this condition causes a fifteen percent drop in an automobile's engine-performance.

The office area in which I worked had a mix of nationalities. Comprised of two German ladies, two South African European males, one Bantu male and two English males; it was a rare combination. Fortunately for me our shared common language was English. But there was one exception. The German ladies addressed male persons using the word *Herr*, (Mister) as a prefix to their surname. And in like manner, the males reciprocated by addressing the ladies as *Frau*, (Missus). Initially it sounded very formal but I soon learned it was part of the German culture.

Celebratory gatherings regularly featured at the office. The Germans called them *ankunfte* and *abschiede*, which meant *arrivals* and *farewells*. Tea and freshly baked cakes were normally provided.

Almost any event was acknowledged from, say, the receiving of a letter from Berlin, to the farewell of a visiting mother-in-law!

The factory produced a range of electric-drives, mainly for the South African Government's projects. My job title was *Motor Production Planner*, and it entailed close liaison with the design office and various suppliers and customers. In addition to this my duties pertained to the manufacture of electric machines for the Sasol Two and Iscor projects.

Throughout the various departments there was a diversity of nationalities. Surprisingly perhaps, a contingent of English ex-pats was employed. Needless to say, they tended to gravitate towards each other. On such occasions, stories were shared about their earlier South African experiences.

One lad recounted his long-gone arrival to the region. Living near the city of Pretoria, he had an apartment in a building, surrounded by tall trees. During the first two nights he felt distinctly ill at ease. When asked, "Why?" he explained that during the night, he could hear the not too-distant sound of wild animals. And in particular, there was the intermittent roar of lions!

Naturally his imagination worked overtime, causing him some concern. He earnestly inquired if he was at risk of being devoured by the wild beasts. Responding to his question someone asked him to explain the precise location of his apartment. Having done so, the frightful spell under which the poor man was held, was mercifully broken. Hearing the description of the apartment's locality, a knowledgeable listener suddenly exclaimed:

"Hey mate; you're living next to Pretoria's Zoo!"

# 8

## THE DRIVE-IN CINEMA

Before leaving England and bound for South Africa, the sale money from our house was entrusted to a local bank. Subject to currency control procedures, our money finally arrived from England. Naturally, its arrival prompted a desire to spend some. During a little chat, Sandra and I decided that two main items were missing from our daily lives; they were a refrigerator and an automobile. When discussing cars, my earlier days of motoring sprang to mind. For the most part, I had driven 'old bangers', and when Sandra and I married, the situation hardly changed. In time, we became the owners of a well-used Morris Minor saloon. One night, in an attempt to make it more presentable, I spray-painted the body-work dark-green. With limited facilities at my disposal, I used a reversible, tubular-type vacuum cleaner to do the job! I have to say the resultant finish wasn't too bad. But afterwards, my workmates nicknamed my car -*The Flying Apple!*

The thought of buying a car and straight from the showroom had been a long-time unfulfilled dream. But now we had the money to buy one! For three weeks, the trawling of ad-columns in Johannesburg's *Star* newspaper became a daily ritual. The search eventually culminated in 'phoning various car dealers.

A question put forward to the different sales people was always the same.

"What car do you have within our price range?"

Predictably, each dealer offered a model newly arrived to the South African market. It was the 'German-designed', Chevrolet Opel Ascona. Powered by a 1300cc engine, it also had a Stromberg carburettor. The car was fitted with inertia seatbelts and four doors. The two at the rear had child-proof locks, which was a new innovation at the time. A national newspaper glowingly advertised the car as *'German engineering at its best!'*

With its tanned-leather seats and its ruby-red paintwork, the Opel Ascona had us nibbling at the bait. But there was one dealer who offered us an alternative. It was a larger vehicle and known as the *Chevrolet Chevair*. After we expressed some interest, a salesman actually drove it to our apartment. It looked resplendent with its metallic-blue paintwork and a beige-coloured, vinyl-covered roof.

Complimenting this combination was a set of chrome-alloy wheels. But it was its 2.3-litre engine that completely captured my attention. Apart from looking magnificent, a test drive proved the car to be the personification of comfort. Sadly, its price was higher than we had planned for. However, after due consideration, and even though our budget would be stretched, Sandra and I decided to buy it! The necessary paperwork was signed, and the following day, we were due to become the proud new owners. Unfortunately, the next day was heralded with a bombshell. The salesman 'phoned with some disappointing news.

"I'm very sorry to tell you," he announced.

"I made a mistake with my calculations. The car will now cost you an additional two hundred Rand above the agreed price!"

The news was shocking to hear and pushed us well over our budget. Sandra and I had an urgent discussion to decide our next move. In the end, we agreed to buy the cheaper Opel Ascona. A quick return 'phone-call confirmed the salesman's selling price; which was actually cheaper than his competitors. But before we committed to buying the car, I received an unexpected call from another dealer. We had previously spoken to each other, but unlike the others, this particular salesman had taken my 'phone number!

He offered the Ascona at a price lower than the present dealer. This latest development was unusual, to say the least, but it started a chain reaction. For the remainder of the day, I played a ping-pong telephone game with the two punters. I baited the first salesman against the newcomer. And each time I spoke to the first dealer, I intimated that his competitor had offered me a further discount of ten Rand. Eventually, the first salesman capitulated.

"All right!" he exclaimed. "This is my final price for the car and I'm not going any lower!"

In terms of numbers, from a starting price of R4245 - which included number plates, plus R170 sales tax and R25 for the cost of registration - it was reduced to R3861 and six cents! Armed with this vital information, I made one more strategic 'phone call. It was to ask the second dealer to better his price. Adamantly he announced a final figure of R3866 and refused to budge. Politely, I informed him that we had received a better offer from the other man and had accepted it.

With that said, he conceded defeat and gracefully bowed out. It was time to play my trump card in this metaphorical game of poker. Once more, I 'phoned the first dealer.

"I have to tell you," I said, "The other dealer has matched your price." There was a brief silence. "But", I added, "If you round-up your price to R3860 you have got yourself a deal!"

The man was flummoxed.

"How are one Rand and *six cents* going to make a difference?"

"Well," I replied, "I think they're better in my pocket than yours!"

Nonplussed, the man exclaimed,

"Oh, all right-I'll give you the difference myself!"

That was the end of the matter. Sandra and I were now the proud owners of a showroom, Opel-Ascona. We had saved ourselves the princely sum of R385 – and not forgetting the six cents!

With our new car safely garaged, I turned my attention to finding a fridge. Unfortunately, I was to discover that buying a fridge was a totally different ball-game. Another trawl through the newspaper adverts revealed a suitable sale item.

*'Second-hand-fridge - Good condition - Large capacity - Price R40.'*

The sale price seemed acceptable, and by a stroke of good fortune, the seller lived in Hillbrow, which was within walking distance from our apartment. Next day I made a 'phone call and arranged to pay the seller a visit.

A little old Jewish man opened the front door of his seemingly little old apartment. Smiling broadly, I announced my presence.

"I 'phoned you earlier today and I've come to see the fridge".

"Ah, Ja. Do come in."

As the front door closed behind us, the man pointed a grimy, gnarled finger towards another door.

"Zey are in zat room at zee end of zee passage - please take your pick."

Measuring about four metres square, it surprised me to see the room packed with fridges, and all were more or less the same physical size.

"Which is the one for forty Rand?" I asked.

"Zey are all forty Rand - take any vone you vont."

Casting a glance over them I spotted one to suit our needs. Its bulbous shape brought to mind the picture of a 1950s Juke box. On closer inspection, I realised it was probably as old as a 1950s Juke box! Nevertheless, it was clean inside and out. And it even had a large freezer box fitted into a top corner. Furthermore, I noticed that a newly fitted electrical-plug was attached to its power cable. The sight of the 'new plug' filled me with hope.

"Does it work? - Can I try it?" I inquired.

"Ja, of course, zey all verk but vee cannot try it because zere is no power point in zis room. But you can allvays bring it back if you are not 'eppy."

Naturally, it would have been better to see the fridge working.

But when the man agreed to deliver it for free and said it was returnable, I accepted his offer. A small deposit was exchanged for a pledge to deliver the fridge two days later - namely on a Saturday afternoon.

Saturday was a day of excitement for our family. That evening, we intended to visit a 'Drive-in' cinema for the first time in our lives. Our children were thrilled at the prospect. The 'Drive-in' was something of an institution for South Africans. It offered a cheap form of entertainment for the whole family and a means by which they could share 'bonding-time'. In this part of the world, television was in its infancy, having been introduced as recently as 1976.

A browse of *The Star* newspaper revealed a list of the available Drive-ins. Some were advertised as *Inry-Bioscopes* - which was the Afrikaans language alternative. We chose one located at the West-Rand, which stood on the outskirts of Krugersdorp. It was sited next to a waste-dump of a disused gold mine. Of course, it was a fair drive from Joubert Park to Krugersdorp. However, that didn't matter much to us; after all, we would travel in our newly purchased car! The movie to be shown was titled *Live and let die* and starred Roger Moore. It was the first movie in which he acted in the role of James Bond.

The arrival of the fridge was long overdue. Eventually, we gave up hope of its delivery and prepared to leave the apartment. That evening, the air temperature was expected to drop. Preparing for the worst Sandra and I gathered together various items. Blankets were placed in a pile, along with some pillows for extra comfort. A large carry-bag was packed with fruit-juice and bottled-beer, and packets of crisps and sweets.

Elanor and Nicola donned their pyjamas and carried their favourite dolls. And just as we were about to step out of the apartment; fate stepped in! There was a loud knocking on the entrance door. Two healthy-looking muntus wheeled a white, bulbous-fridge into our kitchen. With little time for formalities, I quickly plugged the power cord into the wall-socket. The fridge motor whirled into action. And when I opened the fridge door, the interior light shone. Everything was looking good. The balance of the sale money was paid, and we climbed into our car. Along the way, knowing that we now had a fridge, Sandra and I shared a *warm* feeling. Please excuse the oxymoron!

We arrived at the Drive-in just under the hour and with some time to spare. Essentially all Drive-in cinemas were built to a similar pattern. But Krugersdorp's example was surrounded by trees. It consisted of a large car-parking area, with a singular driveway, providing for both entrance and exit. An entrance fee of two Rand and twenty cents was charged per vehicle and not per person. Due to this concession, it was not unusual for a camper-van to arrive with up to six people on board! And it was quite acceptable for them to bring small folding chairs, on which to sit. Of course, because of its size, the vehicle would be required to park at the far edge of the parking area. I expect the Drive-in was compensated for a reduction in entrance fees, by the sale of the additional passengers' refreshments. As a matter of interest and by way of contrast, at that time, the cost of a traditional indoor cinema-seat was two Rand per person. Clearly, the Drive-in represented good value for money.

Positioned midway, at one of the parking area's longer sides, was the movie screen.

It was a sturdy structure built to withstand the elements. The actual screen, on which the movie-image was projected, consisted of corrugated iron-sheets. Painted matt-white, they were bolted to a tubular-steel framework, which stood upwards of fifty feet tall. The metallic screen spanned the framework's width and occupied two-thirds of its height. As night-time arrived, the darkened sky - together with the addition of a few twinkling stars - created a satisfactory back-drop. Large electrical flood-lights were attached to the steelwork. Before and after the movie was shown, they illuminated the screen and the ground below it. Under the watchful eye of parents, the illuminated ground provided a safe place for children to play. And for that purpose, a few items of playground equipment, namely swings and a jungle-gym, were permanent features.

The asphalt parking area had parallel undulating lanes - which ran transversely at the front of the movie-screen. Arriving cars would turn to face the screen and park with their front wheels at the top of a chosen undulation. The procedure had the effect of raising the car's nose. And while seated in a semi-reclined position, passengers found it easier to view the movie. Parking places were demarcated by the use of short, vertically-placed, steel poles. Standing at the height of a car's wing-mirror, the poles were spaced at regular intervals along the length of the parallel lanes. They served as anchor points for loud-speakers, which provided the audio from the movie's soundtrack. When not in use, the heavy alloy, speaker-enclosure was designed to hook on top of the pole. A tough, electrical-cord connected the two. But when the movie began, the loud-speaker was usually hooked onto the inside of the car-door's open window.

The arrangement usually worked well. But at the end of the show, if the driver forgot to replace the speaker, it could result in the car driving away and ripping the electrical cord from the pole! Sometimes, it did happen!

A singular movie-projector was housed in a room, which stood at one side of the parking area and opposite to the movie screen. Its projected images shone over the tops of parked cars. Near to it was a toilet block. There was also a shop, which sold refreshments. And in addition to the usual pop-corn and soft drinks, which could be had, there was beef burgers with fried chips, or hot-dogs with onions. For the more adventurous, there was a choice of chicken or steak dishes.

Five minutes before the starting time, a male voice interrupted the piped music. His words bellowed from a loud-speaker.

"Dames en here, die show is op die punt om te begin."

[Ladies and gentlemen, the show is about to begin]

Children leapt from the swings and the jungle-gym and raced to their parents' cars. Meanwhile, our daughters - wrapped snugly in their blankets - held their favourite dolls, as they occupied the back seats of our car. Sandra and I had prime places in the front. Packets of sweets were passed around, and the loud-speaker's volume was adjusted. Minutes later, the movie-screen's powerful flood lights were abruptly switched off. A singular beam of light shot through the air, as the drive-in's cine-projector began to roll. The metallic-screen became 'alive' with images of *Bugs Bunny* and other cartoon characters. And the musical sound issuing from the loud-speakers, suddenly changed to the *Looney Tunes* theme.

Our daughters giggled at the antics of their favourite characters, while Sandra and I enjoyed our favourite wine gums.

A varied programme of movies was shown that night. Aside from the animated cartoons, there was a one-reeler titled *'Spiel International'* (Mirror International). It portrayed items of international news events. For the many people without television, it provided a means of keeping up-to-date with world affairs. Next was a short educational movie about South Africa's many species of snakes. Not recommended to watch when obliged to sit in the confines of a car! When the short movies came to an end, there was an intermission lasting a few minutes. This was followed by the first of two feature movies, which was a comedy titled *'Witblits and peach brandy'*. The dialogue was spoken entirely in the Afrikaans language, and although Sandra and I struggled to understand the words, the actions spoke for themselves.

At the end of this movie there was a second intermission and the flood-lights attached to the screen were switched on again. Almost immediately, people of all shapes and sizes emerged from their cars. They seemed like insects appearing from an upturned stone. Some visited the toilet block whilst others made their way to the refreshment building. Minutes later, by ones and twos, they returned to their cars. Some carried boxes of popcorn, while others had burgers and chips. Many carried soft drinks, and some wrestled with a mixture of everything!

A prolonged delay was suffered before the second movie began. Eventually, when everyone was seated inside their cars, impatient spectators began flashing their headlights.

The many circles of bright automotive-light created patterns on the blank movie screen. And as if that wasn't enough, at random places within the drive-in, car-horns began sounding intermittently. The combination of flashing lights and hooting of horns was tantamount to a performance given by an unseen orchestra. Unfortunately, the resultant sound was not quite so pleasing! Finally, as if by an act of submission, the flood lights switched off, and the second feature movie began.

Largely unknown to the many patrons, a rain-cloud had gathered high above the drive-in. It seemed to hang around for a few minutes before it chose to unleash its contents. Our car's windscreen wipers were set to intermittent and did their best to combat the intrusion. But we soon found the swishing of the wiper blades to be distracting. Happily, though, as they reached the point of irritation, the rain obligingly stopped. Meanwhile, our two girls, snugly seated in the back seat, were sleeping soundly. At the end of the show, the familiar movie-screen's flood-lights switched on again. Dozens of car headlights quickly sprang to life. Their pencil beams of light shone everywhere. Cars weaved in and out of the speaker poles and formed orderly lines as they moved slowly towards the exit point.

We arrived home long after midnight. The girls hardly flinched as Sandra and I carried them to their beds. When all was done, Sandra casually reminded me of our newly acquired possession.

"I wonder how our new fridge is getting along," she said.

"Oh yes! I'd forgotten all about it. Let's go and have a look."

We hurried to the kitchen. Thankfully, no cockroaches were to be seen, and I was very pleased to hear the fridge motor running.

"Hey, that's a good sound!" I exclaimed.

After fumbling with the door latch for a few moments, the fridge door flew open and the interior light lit-up. But it soon became obvious that the air temperature *inside* the fridge was somehow hotter than that on the *outside!*

I didn't sleep too well that night. Sunday morning arrived and I 'phoned the Jewish salesman.

"Don't vorry", he said, "I'll get my technician to call you in the morning. He doesn't verk on Sunday."

Monday morning arrived - and went - without any word from the technician. On Tuesday, I made another 'phone call to my Jewish friend. This time, he assured me that his technician would call to see me on Wednesday morning. Another day was wasted!

On Thursday morning, the salesman answered his 'phone.

"Your technician has not yet arrived", said I. "When is he going to repair my fridge?"

"My technician is very busy," he said, "You vill 'ave to fix it yourself!"

"But I paid you for a working fridge, and *you* must repair it", I replied.

"No - You bought zie fridge voetstoots, and zat means you must fix it yourself!"

With those parting words, the salesman put his 'phone down. I quickly learned the word 'voetstoots' is an Afrikaans expression. It simply means 'as is'.

In other words, I had knowingly bought a faulty fridge, and now I must have it repaired!

When a work colleague heard of my dilemma, he sarcastically remarked, "Welcome to Jew-hannesburg!" Meanwhile, another colleague suggested avoiding any conflict and advised me to send the salesman a lawyer's letter. I took his advice. A letter was sent requesting the repair of the fridge. But needless to say, there was no repair and not even a reply to the letter.

"You know," my lawyer began, "If you want to take this matter further, it is going to mean court action. And I'm afraid that is going to be costly."

With the thought of litigation and the mention of more money, the matter was dropped. We were now lumbered with a defunct refrigerator! But fortunately, another work colleague knew a fridge mechanic. The kindly man spent time fixing our fridge and refused to accept any payment. Surprising as that was, almost forty years later the fridge was still working. It was keeping beers cold for members of a certain tennis club!

# 9

# SUNDAY MORNING AMBULANCE

One Sunday morning, as the sun lazily climbed the sky, I ambled along Koch Street. Heading towards me was a white Mercedes estate-car. With red-flashing lights mounted on its roof, the ambulance slowly passed me. Occupying the front seats were two medical personnel, both wearing white clinical suits. The windows, set in the sides of the low-roofed vehicle, allowed me to see inside the rear section. A man lay on a stretcher, wearing a white surgical-gown and with his arms folded neatly on his chest. A thin, flexible-pipe attached to a glass container, entered the man's nose. It was suspended inside the vehicle as part of a drip-feed arrangement.

At the entrance to Chesterfield House, I found the African caretaker sitting on a low wall. As we chatted I was unaware the ambulance had reached the far end of Koch Street. Surreptitiously, it had made a three-point turn and was slowly making its way towards us. Engrossed in conversation, I gradually became aware of a red, pulsating light. With each flash of light, the darkened entrance to the apartment block lit-up. Slowly, it dawned on me the light originated from over my shoulder. Turning sharply around, I was surprised to see the Mercedes ambulance again. It was stationary alongside the nearby kerb.

One of the two medical men stuck his head out of the vehicle's window. He looked furtively up and down the street. And after making sure no one was about, he quietly hailed me. I hurried to his side. Nervously, he glanced up and down the street again. With his gaze now focused on me, the man cautiously spoke from a corner of his mouth.

"Is there a hospital anywhere around here?"

My sense of humour was instantly motivated. The sequence of events seemed like a classic sketch from a television comedy show. Of course, this was no laughing matter. Knowing there was a hospital two streets away; I stifled my thoughts of levity and directed him there!

On the subject of hospitals, there was an occasion when our family had cause to visit one. In the early hours of a weekend morning, a loud thud, followed by a scream and wailing, aroused everyone from sleep. It transpired that Nicola had fallen out of her bed! She had landed shoulder-first on the bare parquet floor. The poor child was in agony. She had discovered that parquet flooring is constructed from particularly hard wood! Because our stay at the apartment was intended to be short-lived, we had chosen not to buy carpets.

As daylight grumpily climbed through the apartment's windows, our family grumpily walked to the hospital. It was located at Upper-Hillbrow, near Johannesburg's Old Fort. Even at that early hour, the reception area was busy. People were milling around as we gave our details to the receptionist. A doctor approached me wearing a white clinical-coat and with a stethoscope hanging around his neck.

He studied some notes attached to a clip-board. At that moment, a wheeled-stretcher was pushed passed us. It carried a male person who was probably in his fifties and appeared to be unconscious. The doctor attending to him saw me looking. In a casual manner, he showed me an x-ray of the man's head. I could clearly see the image of a skull and something that looked like a bullet. It was lodged in the upper part of the man's cranium. Pointing to the 'bullet', the doctor cynically made an observation.

"That's what happens when you choose a small calibre to end it!"

I was left with no doubt the doctor was suggesting the patient had attempted to commit suicide. It crossed my mind this was surely an example of irony? Paradoxically, the patient's life - which he chose to end - was now dependent upon the skill of a surgeon!

Nicola was examined by a doctor who quickly discovered she had fractured her clavicle. There was not a lot he could do besides using bandaging and some foam-rubber to strap her shoulder. Afterwards, her arm was placed in a sling. What a sad sight she looked. The foam rubber beneath her dress caused it to bulge outwards and gave the appearance of a hump above her shoulder. On the way home, the poor child didn't take kindly to me calling her *Quasimodo!*

When living in central Johannesburg, we had lots of matters to take care of. Visits to our chosen bank or the central post-office, were often necessary. Searching stores for items of need was all part of a day's work. Sometimes, I would venture out alone, whilst other times, Sandra might take our children.

Quite often we would see some entertaining incident and when it came time for the evening meal, our daily observations became topics of conversation.

One time, when Sandra and our girls were walking along a busy street, they saw two lanes of traffic which had come to a standstill. Vehicles jostled to avoid the obstruction. Some turned around, whilst others made an exit into nearby side-streets. Curiosity gripped the ladies and urged them towards the incident. When they saw the cause of the hold-up, they simply had to laugh. Some road-work was in progress in the middle of a traffic lane. A deep trench had been dug to expose some underground pipes. Signage was used to indicate the presence of danger, but presumably, an unsuspecting motorist hadn't seen it. A brightly coloured Volkswagen Beetle was compromised. It had been driven, nose first, into the trench! With its rear wheels suspended above the road surface, it looked every bit like a sinking boat!

On another occasion, I witnessed a large, Bantu lady pedestrian, approach the junction of Jeppe Street and Von Brandis Street. Generally speaking she was an overweight person, and the wearing of various layers of clothing added to her size. What she was thinking, I don't know, but as a motorist's van rounded a corner, the lady decided to step off the kerb. Side-swiped by the van, she was lifted a few inches into the air. The van instantly stopped. Landing on the road-surface, the lady actually bounced like a giant rubber ball! Albeit only once; before finishing in a sitting position!

What happened next must have added insult to the lady's injury. A tall, skinny-looking, Afrikaans-speaking individual jumped from the van.

As the poor woman - who must have been shocked - proceeded to stand up, the skinny man stabbed an accusing finger inches from her face. Almost leaving his shoulders, his head and neck strained forward as he lambasted her with a torrent of verbal abuse!

Standing motionless, the lady said nothing. Her facial expression was like that of a lost sheep. I mused at the irony of the situation. The *guilty* party was making all the noise, whilst the chastised *victim* remained silent!

The thought of the skinny man's performance caused me to remember something similar. At a much later date, I was crossing Twist Street on my way to Joubert Park. A short distance from the park's entrance, I saw a European male arguing with a muntu. Their voices were raised, and a small gathering was noticeably enjoying the spectacle. Comparing the two, the European physically out-matched the muntu, who was much shorter in stature. As the discourse between them had seemingly reached a crescendo, the European unexpectedly reacted. He took a half-step backwards, and, like a performing ballerina, instantly lifted a long, lanky-leg off the ground. He swiftly brought it through the air in a wide, controlled arc.

A second later, the muntu's head jolted from the impact of the aggressor's shoe; although not causing much harm. Fortunately, the aggressive action appeared to bring the argument to a conclusion. Meanwhile, standing next to me were two spectating muntus. As the aggressor's shoe made contact with the victim's head, I couldn't help hearing a comment made by one to the other.

Pointing to the European, the muntu said

"Awu - He's just showing off!"

Yet another incident springs to mind. One day when I was shopping, I heard a loud bang. It originated at a nearby road junction. A tall-sided, enclosed delivery van had taken a turning too fast. The van turned over onto its side and slid forward two or three metres. As the body-work ground to a halt, the van's windscreen literally fell out; and all in one piece! Before the attendant dust had settled there was movement from the driver's compartment. Like a caterpillar emerging from a cocoon, the driver wormed his way out of the windscreen-less frame. Once clear of the van, he stood up and, using both hands, calmly proceeded to brush dust from his clothes. His action put me in mind of a movie stunt-man, having fulfilled the role of James Bond!

In addition to incidents such as these, there were other topics of meal time conversation. Sandra and I often discussed the diversity of stores and shops - which lay within an easy walk from our apartment. We talked about the choice of various items and their prices. During one leisurely evening meal, Sandra announced she had seen a shop selling all kinds of animal hides.

"Earlier today", she began, "the girls and me passed a shop which displayed various animal hides for sale. The children were fascinated as I explained to them their different kinds. We saw a lion, a zebra, and a wildebeest hide."

"And a GIRAFFE hide too, mummy!" shouted Elanor excitedly.

"Oh, yes", Sandra agreed, "and a giraffe, too".

"What!" I exclaimed - "A GIRAFFE?"

"Yep," Sandra acknowledged - "A GIRAFFE!"

"Really?" said I, half doubting her story. But then suddenly, I remembered an appropriate joke.

"Whilst we are on the subject of animals" I began, "tell me this. Why do giraffes have long necks?"

Sandra sensed a corny joke was about to be unleashed. She looked at me with a frozen half-smile.

"Go on...Why *do* giraffes have long necks?"

"Because" said I, "their feet smell awful."

Elanor and Nicola giggled loudly.

"Haw - haw" laughed Sandra - almost sympathetically.

"Honestly though", she affirmed, "The shop had a giraffe's hide for sale. But who would buy such a thing? And most of all, how would you display it?"

Adopting a serious expression, I attempted an answer.

"I guess," said I thoughtfully, "Any serious collector of animal hides might buy one. Some people buy zebra hides and use them as decorative floor-rugs - so why not a giraffe-hide?"

"Although, I have to admit it *is* slightly different. And when it comes to displaying the hide, I expect you could attach its body and legs to a wall. As for its neck and head - well - perhaps you could cut a hole in the ceiling!"

# 10

## OUR FIRST SOUTH AFRICAN HOME

The lease to our apartment was fast drawing to a close, and with it came a need to find a house to our liking. Thankfully, regular sorties in our new car eventually paid off. Not far from the Siemens factory, in the area of Edenvale, we saw a house priced at a reasonable R18 000. It was the usual free-standing type and surrounded by turfed ground. But the home owner was something of an amateur ornithologist. At one end of the rear garden was a cluster of small wooden huts. He used them for housing his numerous birds. Unfortunately for him, we decided the house seemed a little small for our taste.

Conversely, at the top end of the price-scale was a house with two storeys and a swimming pool. It was built at *Bruma*, which was an older area of greater Johannesburg. It was for sale - or *Te Koop* in the Afrikaans language - at a cost of R33 000 but it was out of our price range.

Fortuitously as it seemed, a fresh concept in housing was introduced at that time. Recently built 'A-framed' homes were available at a price of R23 000. They were constructed with a two-storey wooden framework. Vertically placed, their two converging sides formed the letter 'A' and their outer faces were covered with ceramic roof tiles. The upper storey was designed to accommodate two bedrooms.

But due to the apex of the two joining sides the bedrooms' space was99 constricted.

Never-the-less, a two bed-roomed home priced at R23000 was not to be sneezed at. Call us old-fashioned if you like, but we felt the 'A' shape was too adventurous for our taste. Instead, we turned our attention to a house-building company by the name of Schachat Cullum.

At that time, Schachat Cullum represented probably the biggest building contractor in South Africa. A salesman duly called at our apartment to discuss having a house built from scratch. The practice of building 'from plan' was not uncommon. A basic drawing showing the layout of a two bed-room home was presented to us. Sandra and I were at liberty to position the various rooms and re-arrange their internal sizes to suit our particular needs. There was also a choice of coloured wall-tiles for the kitchen and bathroom. The sale price of R26 000 included a long, narrow piece of land, located at the rear of the property.

Regrettably, the thought of living in a newly built house resonated with memories of our recent home in England. Purchased from new, it had taken three years of hard work to get it to our liking. So now, the thought of spending more years working on this latest home presented a mental challenge. However, the thought of bartering with the salesman entered my mind. I reasoned that if successful, the reduced sale price would compensate for enduring any future work effort. At the outset, my haggling had a surprisingly positive effect. It reduced the asking price by three hundred Rand.

Of course, the salesman had his limit, and before long I reached it. Risking a final stab, I insisted he reduce the sale price by an additional one Rand. Sound familiar? My opponent refused to budge. We seemed to morph into two rams, both head-butting over a measly one Rand! Eventually, realising I would not withdraw my ultimatum, he slowly stood up. In a theatrical fashion, he took hold of the drawing, and with arms outstretched, he held it in the air.

"Mr. Farley", he said, "You have wasted a lot of time!"

With one swift motion, he ceremoniously tore the drawing into two halves and dropped them. Like falling leaves, they glided onto the table. He then motioned to leave the room.

Sandra - who had remained quiet throughout the transaction - burst into tears! I felt like a cad but it was too late. Pride had gone before a fall - or should that read - *Price* had gone before a fall!

Fortunately, not many days after this momentous disappointment, we found a house to our satisfaction. It stood at *Alarm Road* in the suburb of Solheim, near Primrose. Conveniently located close to the main airport highway - which ran from Edenvale to Isando - the house was within easy reach of my place of work. Our first South African home was over twenty years old and by British standards, it might be described as a bungalow. Built of clinker brick, its roof was covered with sun-faded terracotta tiles. The house was surrounded by established gardens and the stand had concrete panelled-walls, on three of its four sides. They provided adequate privacy from our neighbours. The house frontage was fenced with waist-high wrought-iron railings.

Meanwhile a single entrance gate opened on to a short slasto path leading to the front door. At the base of the railings was a narrow soil embankment. Peppered with medium-sized rocks, it sported a mixture of large cactus plants and flowering shrubs. Next to the entrance gate was an iron-pole. It supported a tin enclosure shaped like a miniature house, which served as the post-box. At the rear of the house was a sizeable lawn consisting of lush kikuyu grass. And at its far side was one of the three concrete panelled-walls. Over the wall stood a house where an elderly Portuguese couple lived. They seemed to spend most of their time cultivating grape vines. In a corner of our garden was a sizeable peach tree with large, juicy peaches hanging from its branches. By chance, a neighbour's grape-vine found its way over the concrete wall. It had wrapped itself around a branch of the peach tree. Given enough time, I visualised grapes growing next to the peaches, which seemed like a pleasant prospect.

Inside the house were two good-size bedrooms and a lounge, which boasted a stone-built fireplace. The floor was made from varnished slasto, being easier to clean than woven-carpet. A single garage was attached to a side of the house and was connected to the nearby road by a short driveway. Behind the garage was a servant's quarters. It consisted of a small shower-room with a toilet, together with a separate, medium-sized bedroom.

At the time of viewing the house I noticed something unusual about the servant's bedroom. A single, iron-bedstead stood freely on the floor. But each of its four legs had a singular house-brick placed beneath them! Curiosity caused me to ask the estate agent for an explanation. Her face slowly adopted a knowing smile.

"Ah yes," she said thoughtfully, "that has to do with a traditional belief amongst the local Bantu."

"Oh," said I, "and what is that?"

By now, my curiosity was fully aroused.

"Well," she began, her smile having dissolved into a serious pose. "They believe in the existence of an evil, dwarf-like creature known as a *tocholoshe*."

"A what?" I exclaimed.

Laughing briefly at my response, she repeated the word.

"A TOCHOLOSHE," she said. "It is similar to the Irish leprechaun. The Bantu believe that an evil doer could send a tocholoshe to visit a person, usually at night time, with a view to causing harm. It is believed the creature could climb up the leg of the bed and choke the victim as he or she slept!"

Following a quick and perhaps cynical chuckle, she ended the explanation by saying,

"The bricks are intended to prevent the entity from climbing up the legs of the bed!"

It didn't take long for our family to settle into the new home. Everything was satisfactory, except for one strange feature. All the window-frames were made from steel! But I soon learned that steel was used as a protection against termites. The frames had a large central, glass-window, with smaller ones running along the top and vertically up one side. And all of them were held closed by the use of metal latches.

One night, whilst sleeping in the main bedroom, I was abruptly awakened by a sound made by the metal latches. All of them rattled, violently but briefly. Sitting up-right and wide-awake, I listened attentively. After a short pause, the latches rattled again, but this time, the whole bedroom gave a quick shudder. It was a frightening experience.

The next day, I learned the phenomenon happened periodically and was considered to be normal. It was explained that our house was near the Primrose and Balmoral gold mines. And sometimes, due to mining activities, there was a shift of rock underground. It was that which produced the potentially frightening effect!

On a happier note, not far from the house, we found a suitable crèche where we sent our girls. In attendance were a sizeable number of children from the local Portuguese community. And because of the mix, it wasn't long before we found our daughters returning home and speaking words of Portuguese to each other. Naturally, they put Sandra and me in a bit of a quandary. The girls soon realised there was power in words and used them to their advantage. Sandra and I were never entirely sure if they might be planning to play a prank on us!

But aside from all of that, after taking time to reflect on our overall situation, we decided that life at Alarm Road was mainly pleasant and things were going well for us.

# 11

## A NOCTURNAL ENCOUNTER

Our new home at Alarm Road, stood diagonally opposite a long building, known as *Transvaal Motors*. It housed a showroom and workshop for Chevrolet automobiles. It was from there we had purchased our 'out of the box' Opel Ascona. One dark, February evening, I arrived home after visiting a friend. Chilled air hung over the stretch of open veld, which lay between Transvaal Motors and the end of Alarm Road. As I locked our car inside the garage, I was surprised to hear distant shouts from people and their spasmodic screams. Unable to see any activity, I entered our house. Sandra welcomed me home and gave me an envelope containing some franked postage stamps. They were a gift from our neighbours' young son, who shared with me an interest in philately.

Shortly after examining the stamps, our joy was interrupted by a loud knocking on the front door. For a brief moment I thought the neighbours' son was calling in connection with the stamps. But then I remembered it was after ten in the evening. South African children, and most adults, are usually in their beds at that time of night. The knocking persisted and grew louder. At length, I plucked up the courage to answer the door. But before unlocking it, I called out.

"Who's there?"

An anxious sounding female voice replied,

"Asseblief baas! Asseblief" (Please, mister, please).

"What do you want?" I shouted. The voice repeated the plea.

"Asseblief baas; Help! Baas"

This time, the words sounded more urgent. Sandra suggested I open a small lounge window to view the entrance porch. Standing in the semi-darkness was a plump African lady. When she spoke, stray light from the house reflected from her pearly-white teeth and the whites of her bulging eyes appeared to hover in the air. Nervously, the woman explained that down the road, a group of people had been drinking liquor. There had been some fighting, and a woman was hurt.

At that moment, Sandra switched on the porch light, allowing me to see the visitor more clearly. I suddenly noticed some irregular-shaped, dark stains, on the woman's dress. They suggested splashes of blood! She pleaded with me to telephone the police.

When I dialled 10111, the emergency number for the police Flying Squad, there was no answer! I tried another number, which was meant to be used if the emergency services couldn't be reached. There was no reply. But after dialling the Flying Squad's number a second time, I was taken aback when an official-sounding voice suddenly spoke. It posed a series of questions, which I was obliged to answer. Finally, after what seemed like a long time, the voice agreed to send help.

Returning to the entrance porch, I told the African lady the police were on their way. Her facial expression instantly changed to reflect her inwardly felt relief.

"Thank you baas!" she loudly exclaimed.

In one swift movement she turned about and hurried down the road. With my curiosity taking charge, I rushed outside to the road and watched the lady as she hurried towards some on-coming people. Light from a tall streetlamp illuminated two African women and one male muntu. The plump lady approached one of the women, who appeared to be staggering.

When the two women met, an argument quickly ensued. Fortunately, the male muntu managed to calm them down. And taking hold of the plump lady, he escorted her across the open veld. In the meantime, the others continued walking towards me. As they drew closer I saw one woman was wearing only a white brassiere and a waist-length under-skirt. She appeared to stagger, as the other woman helped her along. Reaching me without uttering a word, they sank to the ground and sat on the grass verge near my feet. Their action put me in mind of two pet dogs, having just returned home from a romp; albeit not so frisky!

Limited light from a nearby street lamp allowed me to inspect the injured lady. A thin trickle of blood issued from a small but deep gash in her upper arm. It ran down her dark-brown skin. Short, black, curly hair made it difficult to see a second wound on the crown of her head. Breaking their silence, both ladies began a conversation in their tribal language. At length, one of them produced a cigarette and judging by their actions, I surmised they had no matches. Volunteering to get some, I went to the house, where Sandra quizzed me about the incident. When I mentioned the blood oozing from the woman's arm, Sandra promptly grabbed a clean dishtowel.

Dashing outside she began to carefully bandage the wound. Meanwhile, in a totally detached manner, the lady's friend took my matches, lit a cigarette and calmly inhaled its smoke.

Seconds later, at a short distance down the road, the plump lady emerged from out of the darkness. Keeping her company was another woman. Both made their way towards me. On arrival they immediately exchanged heated words with the injured lady. As odd as it might seem, although they spoke in their mother tongue, I was roughly able to deduce most of their conversation. It transpired that the new arrivals were concerned about the trouble that was sure to arise as a result of the earlier fighting.

At that moment a thought occurred to me. It seemed like ages since I had made my 'phone call, but in truth, it was only a few minutes. Amazingly, not long after the thought of police had entered my head, a flash of headlights appeared at the far end of the road. An S.A.P. (South African Police) vehicle - loosely resembling a Land Rover - screeched to a halt in front of the assembly. What looked like a large, oblong-shaped, steel birdcage was mounted over its rear axle. Attached to the rear corner of the vehicle was a tall radio antenna. Closely resembling an extended fishing rod, it swung from side to side, like a metronome. Mounted on the roof of the driver's cab, was a blue domed light; which flashed intermittently.

The doors on either side of the cab flew open. Wearing pale blue cotton safari suits, as part of their S.A.P. uniform, out jumped two young police officers. One officer wore his regulation peaked hat and carried a black, stick-like truncheon. But his companion appeared in a less formal, if not casual, manner.

He approached our group hatless and with a burning cigarette hanging from a corner of his mouth. Both officers addressed me politely in the Afrikaans language.

"Goeie aand meneer". (Good evening sir).

Without further ado, and in robot-like fashion, they proceeded to assist the ladies to climb into the 'bird-cage'. Months later I was to learn that this type of conveyance, as frequently used by the police, was critically called the *'meat wagon.'* No doubt alluding to the human passengers it frequently conveyed.

The injured lady was reluctant to stand up. Perhaps she preferred the soft grass verge to the prospect of the hard, steel-seating of the Police-van. However, following a sharp prod with the policeman's truncheon, and together with a few encouraging words, she entered the van. Meanwhile, another lady surreptitiously wandered down the road. Apparently, she, too, didn't relish the thought of a ride in the Police-van. But the sharp eye of the second policeman saw her and persuasively changed her direction. With relative ease and superb efficiency, all four ladies were soon seated in the van - although somewhat compactly!

My attention was presently drawn towards the plump lady, who was pressed against a sidewall of the cage. Surprisingly, when considering the circumstances, she appeared relaxed, as she awaited her fate. When our eyes made contact, her face erupted into a beaming smile. And I was taken aback when she promptly called out,

"Thank you baas, for 'phoning!"

A padlock closing on a metal door was the final act in securing the ladies inside the 'meat wagon'. With that done the policemen turned their attention towards me. Amazingly, the only information they required was my name.

Turning instantly on their heels, they climbed into their van. Sounds of its doors slamming, and its engine starting up, disturbed the relative quiet of the evening. With its blue light flashing and tyres skidding on the loose gravel, the van sped off. It disappeared into the distant darkness, leaving behind a cloud of rising dust!

In the gutter beneath my feet, a tiny glow of red light caught my eye. A wisp of smoke rose slowly from the tip of a discarded cigarette butt. It appeared as if a policeman had left his visiting card!

The next morning, I saw the plump lady walking across the veld. Dressed in bright-coloured clothing, she was happily on her way to work. Seeing her in that carefree state, and whilst remembering the events of the night before, I considered that the outcome couldn't have been too bad after all!

# 12

# A VLEISBRAAI WITH FRIENDS

My two English friends, John and Patricia Ainsworth, had largely influenced our decision to move to South Africa. They had given us both their help and encouragement. Now we were settled in our home and owned a car, we set out to visit them. They lived south of Johannesburg, at Brakenhurst, which was a suburb of Alberton. Their house was not far from a Bantu township named *Katelong*. Some might say it was a localised labour pool. Perhaps they were not far from the truth. After all, throughout South Africa at that time, many European homeowners employed a Bantu maid. And, of course, any nearby township would be a convenient source of supply. However, distances between the township and the employer might be problematic. But often, a solution was to have the maid live at the employer's home, within a small furnished annexe.

Normally the maid might do the housework and look after the employer's children. And in many instances employees gradually became a valued member of the family. Sometimes their husband or relatives were also employed, and usually in the gardens. In this way, it was a profitable situation for all concerned. In general, providing employment for the under-educated Bantu was a primary concern for the South African Government.

Government training schools were established, which allowed the Bantu to learn certain skills. One example was based at Olifantsfontein, located between Johannesburg and Pretoria. It was there I saw a training programme in action. Bantu were taught the rudiments of working at a filling station, which included how to operate petrol pumps. As a result of such training, many Bantu throughout the country became gainfully employed.

When entering a garage forecourt, motorists may look to the Bantu to provide any necessary assistance. The driver is under no obligation to climb out of the vehicle and it is normal for an attendant to fill the car's fuel tank. Usually, a second attendant 'pops' the car's bonnet and checks the engine's oil and water levels. The two commodities are replenished as needed. The air pressure of the tyres may also be checked. And as a final service the windscreen is washed and cleaned. When payment is made, usually, a few spare coins are given to the attendant as a tip. In this way, and depending upon the volume of customers, the petrol attendant's weekly tips may accumulate into a useful sum of money. This of course, is over and above the usual employee's pay. The system has merit in that it helps to reduce the Government's unemployment figures and is also good for the motorist, particularly when the driver lacks knowledge of automobile maintenance.

On the subject of automobile maintenance, I once visited a certain filling-station and observed an employee at work. He was attempting to change a tyre on a car's wheel. With the old tyre removed from the steel hub and replaced with a new one it was ready to be inflated.

A few of the employee's colleagues stood around watching. The man attached an air hose to the tyre's valve and proceeded to inflate the tyre. Surprisingly, before reaching the required pressure, it suddenly stopped inflating. Thereafter, the tyre rapidly *deflated*. The man was puzzled by the state of affairs. He tried again, only to experience the same result. An inspection of the air compressor proved that it was still running. And so, with renewed confidence, the poor man tried for a third time to complete the task.

Sadly, each time the tyre was inflated, it would somehow stop, and its pressure would be lost! Eventually, the colleagues burst out laughing. The tyre-man looked perplexed and couldn't understand what was happening. I must confess it took me a few seconds before I realised the cause, and then I too laughed.

One end of the air hose was attached to a compressor, while its other end was held by the man. But what he had failed to see was that the hose was resting in-between the tyre and the steel-rim. When the tyre inflated, it squeezed the hose against the steel-rim and effectively cut off the air supply! The unfortunate man eventually saw the problem and while trying to hide his embarrassment, managed to finish the job!

At that time, a popular 'buzz' was being told, which might complement the previous story. It was about an affluent, blonde lady motorist. One day, she drove her top-of-the-range Mercedes car into a filling station. The Bantu garage attendants performed their duties in their normal manner. From her seated position behind the steering wheel, the lady watched closely as an attendant reached under the car's bonnet. He emerged holding the engine's oil-level dip-stick.

The man carried the dipstick to the blonde lady and showed her the present oil level.

"Eish - excuse me, Madam," he said. "Dis stick tells me dat de oil level is low. So, I need to put one can of oil in de engine."

The lady was amazed.

"Oh my," she said, "How clever is that! But please tell me, where can I buy one of those sticks?"

---

It was yet another sun-filled day as we arrived at John and Patricia's home in Brakenhurst. Their free-standing, single-storey house had been recently built and was surrounded by neatly cut turf. In one corner of a walled area was a water feature. A low-powered pump produced water, which cascaded over a gathering of medium-sized, irregular-shaped rocks. The whole arrangement produced a pleasing effect.

John and Patricia welcomed our arrival and introduced us to some of their friends. It wasn't long before their children and our daughters were playing happily together. Meanwhile, John invited us to experience a traditional South African 'braai'.

As the day progressed we were made aware that a *braai* is to the South Africans, as a *barbecue* is to the Australians. Both of which were strangers to us. It was also explained to our inexperienced ears that the Afrikaans word *braai* is a verb, and its meaning is 'to cook'. Whereas the Afrikaans word *vleis* is a noun and its meaning is 'meat'. Putting the two Afrikaans words together creates the word *vleisbraai*, which means 'meat cooked', or as spoken in English, 'cooked meat'.

However, people usually refer to the act of cooking on a 'device,' as having a 'braai vleis' or simply 'a braai'. The 'device' or form of cooking stove is often described by the same words, thereby creating confusion.

John was a dab hand at engineering, and by using house bricks, he had constructed his own 'vleisbraai'. The bricks formed a hollow, oblong-shaped chimney, about waist height. Across its upper opening, he had placed a sheet of steel-mesh on which to cook any food stuff. Another sheet of steel-mesh was located at a lower level. Placed upon it was burning charcoal, which provided the necessary heat.

Never before had I seen so much meat cooked in one place and at one time. Chicken legs, which, judging by their size, looked as though they had been regularly exercised, lay next to equally large pork sausages. And taking up space next to them was something I had never seen before. They were T-bone steaks. As the name implies, they were tee-shaped bones encompassed with succulent beef, and they tasted delicious.

In the meantime, standing close to the vleisbraai were cans of *Lion* lager. *Lion*, being the name of the locally brewed alcoholic drink, which served to slake the thirst of the hard-working chef!

However, we soon witnessed another use for the lager beer. During the cooking process the meat received an occasional splashing. The lager was said to add some additional flavour to the meat. But one cynic was heard to say:

"It's a waste of good booze if you ask me!"

Regrettably, the enjoyable day passed all too quickly, and after saying farewell, our family climbed into our shiny, new Opel Ascona. But as I was about to drive away, the noise of a distant wailing siren reached my ears. It was similar to that made during the 1940s, to warn against air raids over war-time London.

"John - What's that noise?" I asked.

"That's a siren announcing the start of the curfew", he replied. "All the Bantu must be off the streets by nine o'clock or the *meat wagon* will round them up".

Of course, I knew what John meant when he said 'meat wagon,' but the siren was something new. I have to say that apart from this one occasion, during all my time spent in South Africa I don't recall hearing any other siren. But like most of Apartheid's rules which were pending retirement, perhaps this was another example.

# 13

# GOLD MINE TRIBAL DANCING

In the year 1978 it was estimated around 400,000 muntus were employed in the Witwatersrand gold mines. They represented a cross-section of South Africa's tribal peoples. Most of them had left their homes in neighbouring regions to become contract workers. Benefits for the employees were good. In exchange for labour, men not only received a salary but also food, accommodation, and medical treatment. Many of them owned land in distant parts of the country, and their wives continued to live and work there. Money earned by the men folk helped to sustain their assets. However, underground mining was fraught with danger. The risk of injury or death was great. Added to the list was the long-term death sentence known as *silicosis*. This disease of the lungs was brought about by inhaling mine dust over a number of years.

For a form of entertainment and as a means of maintaining their ethnic identity, the tribal groups competed in weekly *Mine Dances*. Selected members of each tribe created dance routines and a bespoke form of dress. After much practice, they performed their skills at a custom-built arena, for the benefit of friends or relatives. But not surprisingly, the lively displays soon became a tourist attraction.

During the month of August, Sandra and I met with our English friends, John and Patricia. We journeyed to Johannesburg's *Kloof* gold mine and saw for ourselves a display of Bantu mine-dancing. The venue put me in mind of a Roman amphitheatre. A steel-framework supported a thatched roof, which served to keep the sun's burning rays off the mix of spectators. An area of compacted soil formed the dance arena. Tiered concrete-seating was built in an arc around it. Vinyl-covered scatter cushions provided a little comfort for the visitors. Encircling the dance arena were waist-high iron railings, which separated spectators from the performers.

Soon after our arrival, my friend John looked for somewhere to sit. His eyes scanned the hundreds of seated Bantu. From personal experience, he was mindful of their general body odour, and after making a calculated choice, he pointed to a row of vacant seats.

"Let's sit here!" he said, "I don't want to sit *down* wind from that lot!"

Keeping a careful watch over the visitors was a sprinkling of security guards. They looked resplendent wearing dark grey uniforms. Their jackets sported large pockets, with brass buttons to fasten the flaps. A brass badge attached to a military-style peaked hat added to their aura of authority. Following a short delay, a man wearing a trilby hat and a shabby suit entered the dance arena. He placed a metal easel against the safety railings. Attached to it was a piece of wood, shaped and painted to resemble a warrior's shield. Poking outwards from its top, like the hands of a clock, were two wooden assegai-points.

Loosely placed across the face of the pseudo-shield was a printed sign. It silently announced the name of the next tribal group to demonstrate their dance routine. After each performance, the man changed the sign. Amongst the many names displayed that day were 'Swazi', 'Pondo' and 'Baca.' It was a novel way of introducing each new group of dancers.

Three muntus arrived, carrying wood and cow-hide drums, of around two feet in diameter. It surprised me to see the thick hair of the beast was still present on the hide. The men wore wrap-around pieces of cloth printed with a traditional Swazi-style pattern. Holding wooden sticks and standing astride the drums, they began to beat out a rhythm. Various drums were struck with great zest throughout the day. Their repetitive sound was essential for many of the dancers to maintain their performance. Mine-dancing, in general, is a noisy affair and has all to do with rhythm, footwork and timing - and particularly lots of style.

An opening performance from a group of ten young Swazi men presented all the above. Their lively foot stamping and high jumping dance was done with gusto. Minutes later, they left the arena, and were replaced by drummers. They continued the rhythmic pounding on large drums, which heralded the arrival of five Zulu dancers. Throughout their routine, the loud beat of the drums reverberated around the arena. One over-enthusiastic musician placed a foot on his drum to stop it from rolling away. And while holding his sticks tightly, he bashed the drum's cow-hide sides as hard as he possibly could!

Responding to the drumbeat, the Zulu dancers' limbs performed with synchronised movement. Their shiny, ebony-coloured bodies were magnificently toned. Not a trace of spare fat was to be seen. They appeared naked, save for two small animal pelts, which covered their front and rear. Each wore a headpiece, sporting a few large feathers, whilst just below the knee were tied the longhairs of a cow's tail.

For the most part, the Zulus had created the look of authentic traditional dress. But one item of their apparel was undeniably European. Worn on their feet was a pair of plimsolls - or *takkies*, as the South Africans call them!

Every member of the dance group carried a metre-long stick, which I surmised was intended to simulate an assegai. Initially, the men swayed gently from side to side, while alternately raising each foot off the ground. Then, without hesitation, bring it down again with force. The sudden impact produced clouds of rising dust. All the while each movement was done to the constant beat of the three drums. The men repeated their moves several times as their makeshift spears were thrust in unison at the sky. And as the Zulus performed their actions, they progressively moved in a circular route around the arena. The manoeuvre allowed everyone in the stadium to share a full view of their performance.

When the Zulus made their exit, members of another tribe entered. Each wielded a stick above their head and wore a red-coloured shirt with a matching bandana. Strips of blue cloth, looking like the floppy ears of a dog, hung on the sides of their head,

*A wicker-work belt around their chest (1978)*

*Gum boot dancers in action (1978)*

Lengths of animal-hair hung around their lower legs and a broad, wicker-work belt was fastened to their chest. The belt carried two parallel rows of mothball-size metal bells. Uniformly dressed and in consecutive rows of four, the men paraded around the circular arena. At times, their arms stretched sideways and parallel with the ground.

Collectively, they bent the knee of one leg and raised the foot off the ground. And after stepping forward in unison, they stamped the raised foot down again. Doing so caused their chest-belt to shake and make the tiny bells ring - which in turn rendered a pleasant melodic sound. Repeating the motion with alternate legs, they steadily edged forward. Their actions simulated a team of strutting stallions and in this way, they circled the arena before finally leaving.

Yet another group of men took their turn to entertain the crowd. They wore red jockey caps and white, short-sleeved shirts, along with white trousers. Attached above and below the trouser knee were rings of animal fur. They reminded me of doughnuts on a stick. Periodically, one dancer stood on the tips of his toes and wobbled his legs. He had possibly never seen or heard of Elvis Prestley, but he gave a very good rendition of his gyrations!

Next in line to perform their dance was the *Ndau* tribal team. They chose to wear white tee-shirts with matching shorts, together with white jockey caps. Their overall display seemed more like gymnastics than a dance. At frequent intervals two men would bend their bodies forward and hold each other's ankles. In this way, they formed a human 'wheel'. And after tightening their grip, they simply rolled around the arena. In the meantime, other members of the team executed individual forward rolls.

Another group of dancers who entertained the audience wore white trousers and white, long-sleeve shirts. Each donned a red jockey cap and wore a red sash around his waist. Two of the men performed foot movements with amazing dexterity. Standing on tip-toe, with outstretched arms, they looked like performing ballerinas. And when their knee-bent legs moved backwards and then forwards, they appeared to be riding an invisible mono-cycle. Meanwhile, the main group squatted on the ground and clapped their hands at a steady pace.

As it happened, they were not the only ones to clap their hands that day. The mix of visitors applauded loudly after each and every performance. And in one section of the auditorium a large number of muntu children were seated together. Under the ever-watchful eye of a uniformed security guard, they made frequent gleeful sounds towards the various dancers. They were simply extending their appreciation of the spectacular displays.

To round off the day's entertainment, a group of men, known as the *gum-boot* dancers, entered the arena. In England, knee-length rubber boots are known as *Wellington's*, or *welli-bobs* and sometimes even *wellies*. Allegedly, they take their name from the footwear worn by the Duke of Wellington, of Waterloo fame. Of course, the boots worn by him were made from leather. In South Africa, this kind of footwear is known as *gumboots*. Perhaps the name is a more sensible choice since they are made from the 'gum' which oozes from the rubber tree.

Strapped to the ankle of each dancer's gumboot was a large boot-polish tin, which contained a number of small glass beads.

As the dancer's gumboots moved, the glass beads tumbled about inside the tin and made a sound like a baby's rattle. Each man wore a black, slouched hat and a bright red tunic, with its shoulders covered with white material. The men also wore black trousers, with the legs tucked inside their gumboots. Six dancers formed two lines of three; and stood opposite each other while faced inward.

Meanwhile, two men similarly dressed, stood a short distance away and strummed their acoustic guitars. The dancers exercised a well-timed routine to the rhythmical sounds of the guitars. It involved leaning their body slightly forward and lifting their right boot off the ground. Held momentarily in that position, their right-hand slapped the outside face of the boot. Just as quickly, their hand swung away from the boot and clapped together with their left-hand. The sequence was repeated with each boot, and as the slapping was made, a step forward was taken. In this manner, the men progressively travelled in a line across the arena. Surreptitiously, the guitarists strummed increasingly faster and in like manner the dancers increased their pace. Finally, everyone appeared as though exhausted, and all collapsed in a comical way to form a heap on the ground!

When the day's mine-dancing drew to a close, I unexpectedly felt someone's fingers lightly tapping my shoulder. They belonged to a young Afrikaans lady. She and her male companion sat behind us. Maybe, having heard our North of England accents, she was prompted to ask a question.

"Have you ever been down a gold mine?"

Straining my neck as I turned around, I politely said "No."

With an outstretched hand, the lady offered two tickets.

"These tickets allow two people to tour the Venterspost Gold Mine", she said, "They're free of charge. Would you like to take them?"

Without hesitation, I plucked them from her hand and smiling gratefully, promised to put them to good use. From that moment we began a conversation. The lady introduced herself as Miss von Maltitz and mentioned that her father, Meneer Adrian A. von Maltitz, was a past President of Johannesburg's Chamber of Mines. She politely requested that we gave her feedback of our future gold-mine tour and I readily agreed. Before saying our farewells, Sandra and I made arrangements for her to visit our apartment.

It was during Miss von Maltitz's visit when she loaned us a book relating to her family's history. The book revealed a disturbing piece of text. It described the fate of Miss von Maltitz's ancestor, who died during the second Anglo-Boer War. Killed at the battle of Colenso, the man was buried in a trench where the Boere force had been positioned. Reading about the British having shot the lady's ancestor made me feel uncomfortable, but she appeared unfazed. And surprising as that was, I was more surprised when she announced she was about to marry an Englishman! Still reeling from her disclosure, Sandra and I received yet another surprise. It was when Miss von Maltitz asked the question,

"Would you like to come to my wedding?"

It seemed like she had taken a liking to us, and we felt honoured.

The thought of a wedding was exciting. Apart from attending the pleasant ceremony, we now had an excuse to buy some new clothes! Until now we had spent money on accommodation, furniture and transportation – so why not a few new togs?

During a wander around the city, I managed to find a shop selling a light-weight, three-piece suit. I bought it for the princely sum of fifty-one Rand. In terms of English values, with an exchange rate of R1.88 = £1, the suit had cost £27. Wow! Of course, the reader should remember this was the year 1979.

The wedding was to be held in a small Afrikaans church in an up-market area of Johannesburg. Set to begin at 1530 hrs, the ceremony was expected to take about thirty minutes. Unfortunately, due to unforeseen delays - which included finding a parking space - what should have been an early arrival, resulted in us being ten minutes late! As we entered the small church, or *kerk*, as they say in the Afrikaans language, the ceremony was in mid-stream. Sandra glanced at her watch, then she turned to me and wryly whispered:

"There's hardly enough time remaining for us to sit down!"

Compared to the weddings I had previously witnessed, this one was decidedly different. The service was part spoken in English, but was mostly conducted in Afrikaans.

There must have been upwards of thirty people present - of which only the bride was known to us. At the close of the marriage ceremony, the priest raised his arms above his head. And with outstretched hands, he pointed them towards the congregation. Speaking in the English language, he openly declared, "And so be it!"

To our inexperienced eyes the wedding reception appeared to be a lavish affair. It took place at the home of the von Maltitz family. And if I remember correctly, the large imposing house was named *The Armada*. It stood on a large plot of land in Pallinghurst Road - West Cliff - Johannesburg.

The front door opened to reveal a large entrance hall. A polished dark-wood table stood against a wall. Sitting on its top was a small bronze sculpture. It took the form of three bare-chested gold miners. Grouped together, they held a drilling machine and were poised in the act of drilling gold-bearing ore. A life-size version of it stands in Johannesburg's suburb of Braamfontein. It is a monument intended to honour the efforts of past miners, who contributed to the wealth of South Africa.

Standing shoulder to shoulder, the wedding guests filled the entrance hall's copious space. While in the adjacent billiard room, a buffet was provided. There was a two-tier wedding cake, which Sandra noted had the two tiers placed directly on top of each other.

"I'm surprised there are no little supporting pillars", she remarked.

She also noted there was an absence of the traditional tiny models of a bride and groom. In this instance, there were two small black cats; presumably for good luck.

Two Bantu servants, wearing starched white uniforms, circulated amongst the guests. The male servant's white-cotton, gloved-hands, held a silver tray.

Bearing numerous crystal glasses, each was filled with sparkling champagne. Wandering amongst the wedding guests, he gracefully encouraged them to take a glass.

Meanwhile, his female counterpart carried a silver tray covered with a mix of canapés. Supplemented by tiny sausages and cocktail onions - all were skewered with little wooden sticks. Appealing to her sense of fun, our youngest daughter ate the different coloured onions; while her sister focused on the more substantial quality of the sausages!

Inside the entrance hall, a wide staircase faced the front door. Its imposing marble steps appeared shaped like a fish-tail. The bottom step being much wider than the ones thereafter. Its highly polished, mahogany hand-rails were supported by sturdy, wrought-iron-work. The stairway gracefully ascended towards a short horizontal landing. The opposite ends of which connected with the upper storey's passageways. And set in the centre of the wall, behind the landing, was a large, wood-framed window. Its two vertical sides merged to form a point, giving it an ecclesiastical appearance. Sunlight shone through its stained-glass panes and cascaded onto the area below.

At a pre-arranged moment, the murmur of the wedding guests was politely interrupted. The head of the von Maltitz family spoke loudly in making an announcement.

"Ladies and gentlemen, could I have your attention, please?"

Meneer von Maltitz paused briefly, allowing the gathering some time to respond. Shortly, the bride and groom entered on to the landing. Facing the guests, they returned the many admiring smiles.

Sunlight invading the space behind them, created a silhouette effect. Taking advantage of the lull in activity, the spokesperson's eyes scanned the gathering. They quickly found the man-servant, who was standing next to the guests. Looking up at the landing the servant saw his employer mouth the words:

"Has everyone got a glass?"

Nodding his head vigorously, the servant answered, "Yes, sir".

His words were unheard, but the head nodding was enough. It confirmed the bride's father could continue with his announcement. Holding a glass of champagne, Meneer von Maltitz raised his arm and held it towards the guests.

"Would you please join me in toasting the bride and the groom?"

Responding to the request the gathering stood still, and each with an arm outstretched, appeared like a forest of one-branch trees. The spokesperson turned to face the newlyweds. Again, with his arm raised, but this time pointing in their direction, he spoke once more.

"We all wish you both happiness and success for now and in the distant future."

Putting the rim of the champagne glass to his lips, Meneer von Maltitz slowly sipped the chilled liquid. The guests quickly did likewise. Meanwhile the bride and groom smiled broadly and looked lovingly towards each other. More announcements followed, during which champagne flowed and refreshments continued to be consumed.

At length, it was time for the groom to make a speech. However, he was delayed by a surprise interruption. Was it the day's excitement? Or was it from eating too many coloured onions? At that moment the reason was unclear, but it was Nicola who brought a halt to the proceedings.

During the quiet but brief interlude, which preceded the groom's speech, Nicola's voice was heard. Looking up at her mother and speaking in a loud, croaky voice, she called out - "I want a ba-ba!" Instantly, she became the focus of attention. Dozens of accusing eyes looked in her direction. It was an embarrassing moment for the Farley family. Elanor stifled a giggle, while Sandra's face froze with shock. But fortunately, the friendly maid-servant came to the rescue. She guided mother and daughter to the nearest toilet!

After the reception, the guests wandered leisurely about the well-kept gardens, which surrounded the house. A large swimming pool looked inviting, as the surface of its clear water sparkled in the reflected sunlight. The rear of the property offered a magnificent elevated view of greater Johannesburg. And from time to time the guests were offered refreshments by the two industrious servants.

With the passing of years, we sadly lost contact with the bride and groom. But during the 1990s, at a factory in the Wynberg area of Johannesburg, I chanced to meet Miss von Maltitz again. After introducing myself, I related past events. Appearing somewhat reserved and showing no signs of knowing me, the young lady said she couldn't remember any of it!

# 14

# VENTERSPOST GOLD MINE TOUR

Before using our free tickets to tour the Venterspost goldmine, I did a little research. The city of Johannesburg is literally built on gold but the gold exists in a reef of rock; which stretches for miles beyond the city limits. Known as the *Main Reef*, the gold is invisible to the naked eye and must be extracted from the processed rock. The Main Reef was discovered over a hundred years ago by George Harrison and George Walker, who were two travelling tradesmen. In the year 1886, they left Cape Town to make their way overland to Barberton in the Eastern Transvaal. (Present day Gauteng) It was said that work was plentiful, and gold could be found there. On their way through the Transvaal, the tradesmen found temporary work in building a small cottage on land owned by two brothers named Fred and Harry Struben. They had been prospecting at a rocky outcrop - a few miles from a farm named Langlaagte - when they eventually struck gold. However, unfortunately for them it was soon mined out. But before that happened, they directed the two tradesmen to the Langlaagte farm. It was owned by a homely widow named Oosthuizen. She had heard about the cottage and agreed to have one built for her. The work went well and was drawing to a close when George Walker, with some time to spare, wandered away from the farmstead to gather his thoughts.

Plodding over the rough veld he accidentally stumbled over a small outcrop of rock. It glittered as it reflected the sunlight. On closer inspection he realised it might be gold-bearing ore. The knowledge gained by working with various prospectors was about to pay off. Ultimately, a sample of the ore was tested and found to be gold-bearing. Furthermore, the reef from which the rock sample was taken stretched for miles. It became known as the *Main Reef* and the simple 'find' began the great gold mining industry of South Africa.

Within a few years, and not many miles from Langlaagte, the city of Johannesburg was built. The Bantu people refer to Johannesburg as *Egoli* or *Place of Gold*. And within the space of a lifetime it has grown from a mining boom-town to one of the commercial capitals of the world.

The South African gold mining industry is a world leader in gold-mining technology. At the gold mine of Western Deep Levels, mining is taking place at depths of 3,608 metres below the surface. At that depth, constant air conditioning is required to keep temperatures just bearable for men to work. In terms of output, the highest yield of any single gold mine is the Crown Mines Ltd. During its life, it has produced a record 1.4 million kilograms of gold. Of course, with the production of so much gold, an even greater amount of waste material was produced. This was formed into giant man-made mounds, or 'mine dumps', as they are commonly known.

By 1975, South Africa was responsible for having produced 40% of the gold ever mined. Three years later, the country mined enough ore to produce 24,849,734 ounces of gold (704,479 kilograms).

At the average price for the year of R168.90 per ounce, this earned a total of just under R4, 200 million. It contributed more than twelve cents to every Rand of the country's wealth. [2] However, by the year 2010 China became the world's largest gold producer. And by July 2018, the Mineral Council of South Africa announced that 75% of its gold mines were now unprofitable due to a decline in gold reserves. At the time of writing, South Africa produces only 4.2% of the world's gold.

My research revealed that gold can be found in three different formats. There is alluvial gold which is visible in small solid pieces. It may be found lying loose in river beds, or attached to the surface of rocks. Secondly, there is 'fool's gold'. It normally appears on the surface of a rock and shines as a golden-coloured streak. But in reality, the golden-streak is actually iron pyrites. Finally, there is the third kind, which sticks to the surface of pebbles. The pebbles are held together with other pieces of rock and collectively they are called *conglomerate or banket*.

The early Dutch miners ate a grey-coloured toffee, which surrounded large, white almonds. To them, it was known as *banket* and because the gold-bearing rock reminded them of their toffee, the name *banket* was adopted. Having mined a mass of rock, a lengthy process is employed in order to extract the gold.

Mentally fortified with this knowledge, Sandra and I excitedly picked up our complimentary tickets and drove to the Venterspost gold mine. Situated on the West Rand, it was some thirty-six miles from Johannesburg . We arrived at the mine during a sunny and wind-less day. Surrounded by barren and rock-strewn ground, it appeared like an oasis.

At its centre was a cluster of tall buildings, each clad on all sides with corrugated tin sheets. Many of them contained equipment for processing gold-bearing ore.

Not far away stood the tall and proud-looking headgear. It straddled a vertical mineshaft, which descended hundreds of feet below ground level. Constructed from iron pieces bolted together, it supported pulley wheels and steel ropes, all of which were used to lower a large, iron-box down the mineshaft.

The iron-box, or *cage* as it is called, is a composite of three storeys or tiers. Each one placed above the other has its own iron entrance gate. The tiers may be filled with mining equipment or human passengers. The cage is suspended inside the mineshaft by a 'steel rope' attached to its top. The other end of the 'steel rope' is wound onto a large, motorised steel-drum, which is situated in a distant control room. An operator controls the drum, enabling it to wind the 'steel rope', which lowers or raises the cage as desired.

Shortly after our arrival, Sandra and I joined a group of visitors at the mine Manager's office. Gathered in the room was a mix of nationalities. Included in the mix were two young ladies from the United States of America. Fresh-faced and wide-eyed, they looked around the office in anticipation of what the day's visit might bring. Following the direction of their gaze, I noticed a framed photograph attached to a wall

It portrayed an image of Danny Kaye, an American film star of the 1950s. The photograph recorded his visit to the Venterspost gold mine during that time.

"Do you ladies remember Danny Kaye?" I inquired.

Their faces responded with a look of surprise and appeared to say: "Are you talking to us?" Moments later, when my question had registered, they glanced at the photograph. Turning to face each other, one of them asked:

"Do *you* recognise the guy?"

With a joint shrug of their shoulders, they quickly agreed on their answer. One of them turned to me and casually said:

"Naa - he was before our time!"

Following the curt admission, they continued to chew some gum.

The mine Manager was a friendly soul. He introduced himself as Meneer (Mister) Joubert and proudly informed the group he had many years of mining experience. As he spoke, a 'mine boy' entered the office carrying a large metal teapot. With steam rising from its spout, he placed it on a table and next to an array of tin mugs. Taking hold of a nearby mug, Meneer Joubert raised a question.

"Would everyone like some tea before we begin our tour?"

The offer was unanimously accepted and as each visitor grabbed a tin mug, I whispered into Sandra's ear.

"Aside from his many years of mining experience, I expect he's had many years of drinking mugs of tea!"

As the Manager spooned sugar into his tin mug, he explained why he had made a point of offering us all some tea.

"When overseas visitors arrive in Johannesburg, they are living at a height of 6000 feet (1828 metres) above sea level" he said.

"At that altitude the air is rarefied and produces breathlessness and dryness in one's throat. It also causes dehydration, which can bring on headaches."

Pausing briefly before raising the mug to his lips, the manager smiled broadly and offered some consolation.

"Don't worry", he advised, "the effects wear off in a few days. Anyway, until then, a drink of tea is always welcome; don't you agree?"

Everyone smiled approvingly. as they followed his example. Each person took tea and a complimentary biscuit. And the manager continued with his well-practiced talk. He explained how the Venterspost Gold Mining Company started life in 1935 and was considered to be an average-sized gold mine. It extracts gold-bearing ore from both the Main Reef and the Ventersdorp Contact Reef.

The two reefs aggregate a total of 90,000 metric tonnes per month. And by utilizing two vertical shafts, the ore is hoisted to the surface. From the total mined rock, the gold-bearing ore averages about 87,000 metric tonnes per month and from that, the average gold yield is 6.8 grams of gold per tonne.

Meneer Joubert ceased talking and observed the assembly of visitors. He studied their faces, looking for signs of boredom. Presumably he decided the people could absorb a little more information and continued with his speech. He went on to say,

"The two vertical shafts accommodate the passage of approximately 3 365 metric tonnes of gold-bearing ore and waste rock per day. And the rock is hoisted to the surface at the rate of 900 metres a minute, or approximately 50km per hour."

"However, the gold-mining personnel are hoisted at the lesser speed of 750 metres a minute."

Pausing once more, the manager checked the placid faces of his guests. He decided to impart one last piece of information.

"At Venterspost mine," he continued, "the deepest level at which men work is 2,543 metres (8343 feet) below the surface; which is roughly 926 feet below sea level. To provide ventilation, a large volume of air has to be circulated underground every minute. And to ventilate the whole mine, the two vertical shafts are served by seven shafts below the surface. They all help to reduce temperature and dust concentrations". [3]

Smiling broadly, the manager announced he had finally reached the end of his talk. There was an instant buzz amongst the visitors. It seemed as though they celebrated the end of the presentation. After all, there is a limit to the amount of facts and figures a visitor can absorb in any one morning.

Our tour began with a visit to the compound where the Bantu mineworkers stayed. The men hailed from various areas of South Africa and represented the diversity of tribes which lived there. Examples of these were the Swazi, Zulu, Themba and the Pondo. To help prevent possible conflict between the groups, the men were housed in segregated military-styled barracks.

Prior to working underground all were trained in various skills; the most important of which was teamwork. Sandra and I witnessed one of the training sessions. A team of five men were given the task of assembling a number of large wooden pieces. Each individually shaped piece was part of a segmented circle.

It was like watching a giant-sized jigsaw puzzle put together. The session was intended to have the various tribesmen communicate with each other and work as a team. Teamwork was essential for safe working underground.

When considering the many different tribal groups, it naturally followed there was a diversity of spoken languages. In fact, in today's South Africa there are eleven tribal languages, which are known to be in use. Due mainly to the mix of tribes, a 'new' language emerged in the goldmines. Known as *Fanakalo*, it evolved from words taken from the various Bantu languages. The result was that Fanakalo could be understood by all the Bantu people. Furthermore, as a means of communicating with their workers, it proved to be most effective for the European overseers.

Leaving the trainee, mine-workers to get on with their lot, our band of visitors was ushered towards a nearby building. Inside, we were given protective clothing to wear. Each person was issued with a white cotton boiler suit and a pair of boots, along with a hardhat and headlamp. Connected to the lamp was a heavy battery pack, which strapped around our waist. Suitably attired, we resembled a line of white mice, as we made our way towards the goldmine's headgear.

The dark metal structure towered high above the open mineshaft. Two 'steel ropes' hung behind some rusty, iron safety-gates. Distantly below ground, the 'ropes' were attached to an iron cage. Meanwhile, above ground, the 'steel ropes' passed over large, grooved iron-wheels. They were attached to a horizontally placed axel at the top of the head-gear. Making their way through the air, the 'ropes' disappeared into an adjacent building.

It was known as the *winding room* and housed an electrically powered winch. Following a short wait, my watchful gaze detected a movement in the 'ropes'. One of them travelled in a downward direction, whilst the other journeyed upward. As they travelled, each wavered slightly from side to side. What followed next was a sound like rushing wind as air escaped from the mouth of the shaft.

Acting like a piston, the travelling cage forced air upwards. And as the cage neared the surface, the sound of rushing wind grew louder. It could be heard above the general murmur of the waiting people. Suddenly, like a magician's trick unfolding on a theatrical stage, an empty three-storey cage appeared before us.

It stopped abruptly inside the mineshaft and swayed slightly on the end of the 'steel rope'. An instantaneous hustle of some Bantu miners hurriedly pushed forward. They climbed a narrow, short flight of wooden stairs. One by one, they entered into the upper storey. An iron safety-gate was quickly closed behind them. Meanwhile, our group was shepherded into the lower compartment. A thin ceiling of perforated iron separated us from the miners. Worming our way through the narrow entrance, we squeezed inside. Small ventilation holes peppered the cage's iron walls. The first people to enter had their backs pressed against them. Like the miners inside the upper-storey, we stood shoulder to shoulder. And like proverbial sardines, we were literally packed inside a tin can! Traces of dirt fell on our heads from the boots of the miners above us. Last to enter, was our guide for the tour. Shutting the clattering iron-gate, he hooked the safety catch. We were securely fastened inside. But where could we go? There was only one direction and that was down!

Suddenly, someone shouted a warning. It was instantly followed by the coded sound of bells. Beginning with a quick jolt - the cage began to move. At first, it travelled slowly and smoothly. Then picking up speed, it dropped swiftly down the shaft. Daylight was speedily left behind and exchanged for darkness; which intensified as we travelled.

Standing next to me was someone I couldn't see. Not even a dimly discerned outline of a person. I was totally encased in darkness. But within seconds, narrow beams of light pierced the air. The passengers switched on the lamps attached to their safety helmets. My body felt the sensation of being pressed against the iron-wall of the cage. Simultaneously, my feet seemed to lift gradually upwards. The momentum of travel caused the cage to buffet marginally from side to side. Within a few seconds, we had descended nearly a thousand feet. But just as rapidly as it began, the descent of the cage slowed.

With a surprise jolt, it abruptly stopped. We had reached our destination. The rusty, iron safety-gate was unlocked and flung open. Passengers clambered clumsily out of the cage. Hastily I followed and banged my helmet on the iron doorframe. The sudden and unexpected impact reminded me to stay alert!

Herded together like a flock of sheep, the surrounding area was called a *station*. Illuminated by electric light, it was the central point on that level of the mine. As we looked about, our leader slammed the cage door and closed its latch. A number of coded rings were heard from an unseen bell. The cage was quickly in motion. It was whisked upwards, on a journey to the upper world.

To my left and right were tunnels, or *drives*, as they are known. They had been blasted out of barren rock.

Our group was directed along one of them. Underfoot, the ground was cemented, and the rocky sidewalls white-washed. Here and there our guide showed us the gold-bearing Reef. It was visible as a speckled band which wound its way through the rocky walls. Varying in thickness, it sometimes appeared broad and, at other times narrow.

We arrived at a gaping hole in the surface of the tunnel. Known as a *stope* it slanted downwards. In the attendant darkness, men were working. Narrow beams of light shining from their safety helmets could be seen. In following the slant of the Reef, the miners had drilled and blasted their way down to their working area. The blasted and broken rock was loaded into trucks and transported to the main shaft to be hauled to the surface for processing.

Powered by compressed air, the piercing hiss of a jackhammer could be heard. In the confined space the noise was deafening. It was surrounded by clouds of ground and powdered granite. We saw a miner drill a neat round hole, about a metre long, into the rock. All the while, the jackhammer's drilling bit was water-cooled. Clutching the vicious kicking tool, his muscular body was taught and trembling, as it strained to keep control. In that way, a number of holes would be drilled and plugged with dynamite. When detonated, the surrounding rock would come crashing down. It would fill the stopes and drives with flying stone pieces of various sizes.

Afterwards, all would be quiet. The blasted rock would be left in the choking untidiness for the next shift of miners. The newly arrived men would continue the process by carting it away to the surface. Once there it would be crushed to access the gold.

When our group returned to the surface, the strong sunlight caused our eyes to screw-up. But after a minute or two we were able to see our way. Stripped of our headlamps and batteries, we were guided to the stamp mills. The deafening, grinding roar of their machinery could be heard as we approached them. Large steel rods, or *stamps* as they are known, pounded away at the chunks of rock brought from underground. The broken smaller pieces of rock were dumped into a steel cylinder, filled with what looked like steel cannonballs. As it rotated, the steel balls ground the rocks into a powder-like state. The powder was mixed with cyanide and carbon to dissolve the quartzite and leech out the gold. From there it was sent to the reduction works, where tanks of dirty-looking water stood - each with a scummy froth floating on top. The tanks contained the powdered rock which formed slime. This, in turn, was poured over a corduroy-covered shaking table. During the shaking process, a patch of yellow substance appeared at a corner of the table. Our group was advised the yellow substance was gold!

Tonnes of rock were crushed to produce a small quantity. At the reduction works the gold-bearing liquid was poured inside steel crucibles. About the size of domestic buckets, they were placed into a glowing furnace. At the right time, a team of men, using iron holders and tongs, lifted the crucibles out of the fire. Appearing like yellow, steaming milk the burning, liquid-gold, was poured into a hollow iron-mould. Finally, when the mould had sufficiently cooled, it was turned upside down. And from it fell a solid gold ingot - about the size of a house brick!

*Gold miner & 'steel ropes' Venterspost Gold mine (1978)*

*'It was called a stope': Venterspost Gold Mine (1978)*

*Wood props for Venterspost gold mine (1978)*

*Venterspost gold mine (1978)*

# 15

# ISANDHLWANA AND RORKE'S DRIFT

During a casual stroll along Johannesburg's Commissioner Street, I saw an interesting shop. It specialised in buying and selling second-hand Africana books. Their prices were generally too much for my pocket, but nevertheless I enjoyed browsing. By chance I found a low-priced, multi-page booklet. It was an illustrated anthology of the Anglo-Zulu War of 1879. Various battles of that period - many of which I had no knowledge - were described in some detail. One of particular note was fought at Rorke's Drift on January 22$^{nd}$ 1879. The name *Rorke's Drift* was given to a crossing point on the Buffalo River. The river forms a natural boundary between the provinces of Natal and Zululand.

On January 11th 1879, from a military camp at Rorke's Drift, a British column of troops invaded Zululand. Its intention was to destroy the main Zulu opposition at their capital of Ulundi. The British left behind approximately 150 men to defend the camp, consisting of tents and a few stone buildings. Days later, an attack was launched by about 4000 Zulu warriors. The camp was successfully defended, and for their part in the action, eleven of the British combatants were awarded the Victoria Cross. The most to be awarded in any one engagement, either before or since.

The Rorke's Drift conflict was immortalised in a 1964 movie titled *Zulu*. It starred the actors Stanley Baker, Jack Hawkins and Michael Caine. But aside from Rorke's Drift, a battle and with much greater loss of life was fought some hours earlier. It happened a few miles from Rorke's Drift, at the base of a hill known as Isandhlwana. On its battlefield, some 1500 British and Colonial troops faced an estimated 20,000 Zulu warriors. At the end of the day, around 800 Europeans and an estimated 4000 Zulus had been killed.

Coincidentally, January $22^{nd}$ 1979 was fast approaching. As it was the centenary anniversary of the Anglo-Zulu War, it seemed like a good idea to visit the battle sites. My wife and I agreed that to see them, and exactly one hundred years after the event, might prove to be a memorable experience. Arrangements to travel quickly took shape and by the twentieth of January, our family was ready to go.

Leaving our Solheim home in mid-afternoon, we drove virtually nonstop before arriving at Dundee, in the Province of Natal. At around eight o'clock in the evening we entered the municipal camping site. Surrounded by high, wire-mesh fencing, an asphalt road formed a wide loop through turfed ground. Tents or caravans were at liberty to stay anywhere within the loop. At one end of the site was a modern and fully equipped ablution block. And surprisingly it was provided with electricity!

Adjacent to the camping ground were the municipal open-air swimming baths. Built during the nineteen twenties, it was still in daily use. After selecting a suitable spot, we pitched our tent under the spreading light of a nearby street lamp.

Considering we were inexperienced campers, the task of erecting our canvas abode went more smoothly than anticipated. Minutes later, as I was preparing some food, Sandra happened to notice a muntu. He was carrying a ledger and a money bag. Realising he was heading towards us, she hailed me.

"Peter! There's a man heading our way. It looks like he's coming to collect some money!"

Engrossed in cooking our food, I only partially heard the warning. Looking up from the gas cooker, I called out:

"What's that? I didn't hear you properly."

Sandra repeated her announcement. But this time, somewhat impatiently, she spoke slowly and deliberately. And to emphasise each word, she stabbed a forefinger in the direction of the muntu.

"THERE – IS – A – MAN!"

As she finished speaking I noticed the muntu was standing near us. Taking one look at him, I quickly realised his intention.

"Oh! Okay," I said, acknowledging the announcement. But at the same time, I recognised an opportunity for some levity. I decided it was *my* turn to do some finger-pointing. And with a stabbing fore-finger aimed towards Sandra, I slowly and deliberately spoke the words:

"THERE - IS - A - WOMAN!"

Soon after, swinging my arm around, I pointed to our daughters. And with the same stabbing motion, I called out:

"THERE – ARE -CHILDREN!"

The muntu witnessed my little performance and approached me laughing. His beaming smile revealed large, pearly-white teeth. In the limited light from the street lamp they seemed to glow. He requested fees for the campsite and asked me to complete some details in his ledger. As we spoke, I detected what I guessed was a whiff of alcohol, which floated on his breath. It triggered a memory of our earlier, long and hot journey and created a desire to quaff a cool beer! Seizing the moment, I spoke a newly acquired word of the Zulu language.

"*Umgane*," (Friend) I uttered, "Where can I buy beer?"

He explained that he drank *Mageu* (a muntu beer) and that it cost twenty cents per litre. But since the local shops were now closed, he offered to bring me some from his personal store. We agreed upon a sale price and I gave him two beakers to be filled.

Sometime later, he returned with the *Mageu*. The liquid was quite different to any beer I was familiar with. But it did have a distinct beer-like odour. It was grey in colour and had a thin, porridge-like consistency. I later learned it was fermented maize and considered to be nutritious. But it was also virtually non-alcoholic, although if desired, some might be added. Unfortunately, my taste buds found the first mouthful to be erring on the side of being repugnant. However, to show gratitude I slowly drank the contents of my beaker. Sandra, for her part, was more discerning. She refused outright to drink any of it!

Our friendly muntu laughingly watched my act of bravado before pocketing the sale money and joyfully walked away.

After consuming my portion of the *Mageu*, the prospect of drinking Sandra's rejected share was a non-starter. You might say, "It wasn't my cup of tea!" So, following our meal, I offered to dispose of the strange brew.

On my way to the ablution block, whilst guided by the light from a distant street lamp, I was taken suddenly by surprise. A deep, male voice called to me from the semi-darkness.

"Good evening, Mister Farley".

The sound of the voice stopped me in my tracks. "Who on earth knows me here?" I thought. And like a scene from a mystery movie, a slimly built man, with a dark complexion, slowly emerged from the shadows. And to add to the mystique he was smoking a pipe.

"My name is Earle - Jaap Earle," he said. "The muntu has just taken my payment for the campsite. I saw your name in the ledger, and I noticed your destination is Isandhlwana?"

"Yes, that's right," I said, "We are heading there tomorrow".

Mister Earle explained that he and his young son had travelled from the city of Durban, in their Volkswagen camper. And next day they were to meet a party of people in the centre of Dundee. The people had travelled from Wales and represented the present-day military regiment, known as the South Wales Borderers. Their intention was to lay a memorial wreath on a monument at the Isandhlwana battlefield.

In the year 1879 the South Wales Borderers were known as the $1^{st}$ Battalion of the $24^{th}$ Regiment of Foot, the $2^{nd}$ Warwickshire, and had its barracks at Brecon, in South Wales. The regiment suffered a great loss at the Battle of Isandhlwana.

Jaap Earle motioned me to follow, as he walked towards his auto-camper. Pitched next to the vehicle was a two-man tent and at a safe distance, a small campfire was burning. We stood in the better light as he quizzed me about my interest in the Anglo-Zulu battles. I explained my plan was to visit Isandhlwana on the actual date of the battle - albeit one hundred years later.

My answers to the questions seemingly met with his approval, because he invited the Farley family to join his little group on the following morning. Considering I knew little about the battles and even less about how to get to the battlefields, I gratefully accepted. After all, the opportunity of having a personally conducted tour was something not to be missed. With the acceptance of his invitation, he presented me with another. Sandra and I were asked to join him for a glass of wine! Knowing that his son was sleeping inside the campervan and our girls were safely bedded down, we joined him at his little campfire.

As the flames of the burning fire merrily flickered, the wine relaxed our thoughts. And I have to say it tasted much better than the Bantu beer! Mister Earle entertained us with the fascinating story of his life. And I was amazed and felt humbled when I learnt he was a practising neurosurgeon!

Next morning, I awoke to the sound of what sounded like children's laughter. My wristwatch registered five-thirty. Poking my head outside the tent-flap, I saw the surrounding turf was covered with dew. It surprised me to see no children but simply a gaggle of wild geese!

They were flying overhead at the height of the nearby street lamps. Minutes later, I heard another mysterious sound. It was the clip-clopping of horse hoofs, along the nearby road. A horse-drawn milk float was on its way to supply its daily customers. At that moment, I mentally compared the sounds of camp life, to the city life of Johannesburg. All of the former seemed so peaceful!

With breakfast consumed, preparations were made to leave the campsite. And whilst Sandra and the girls were washing the dishes, I packed the folded tent into our car. It was then I noticed two men making their way towards me. One was a muntu, and the other his European overseer.

"Goeie môre meneer" said the European.

"Good morning," said I.

Realising I was English-speaking, the man's facial expression instantly changed. Looking slightly puzzled, he turned his head to face the muntu. Extending an arm, he pointed a forefinger at the man.

"Meneer" he said, "I need to know if last night, you remember seeing this man."

The muntu appeared nervous. Submissively, his head bowed towards the ground. In a sheepish manner, the white, bulging portions of his eyes turned towards me. I wasn't entirely sure if he *was* our friendly muntu. But rather than create an incident I answered:

"No, I don't think so." And as an afterthought, I added - "Anyway, they all look alike to me!"

The European's head turned sharply towards me.

Looking slightly annoyed, he stared in a silent questioning manner. It seemed as though he wasn't sure if I was telling the truth or merely joking.

Surreptitiously, I glanced at the muntu. A glimmer of a smile appeared on his nut-brown face. He apparently realised my answer had cleared him of any implication in a possible crime. The European's face changed expression. It suggested he had been cheated out of a likely conviction. But he was not for giving up.

He asked to see my receipt for the camp fees. Fortunately for me, and perhaps also the muntu, the receipt was clearly dated. With a tone of exasperation in his voice, the overseer snapped the words, "Dankie meneer!" They were the last to be spoken before the two men departed. I could only surmise that perhaps some money was unaccounted for, and the European was attempting to solve the mystery.

At eight o'clock that morning, Mister Earle's auto-camper led the way to the centre of Dundee. A gathering of people was waiting outside the George Hotel. In addition to the visitors from Wales, there were two well-known people from Natal. They were to act as our tour guides for the day. One was Mr. George A. Chadwick, who had written numerous articles for the South African Military History Society's Journal. He had also published a pamphlet, which was perhaps the first official guide to the Anglo-Zulu battlefields.

Our second guide was Mrs. Sheila Henderson, who was an authority on the local history of Northern Natal. She was also the daughter of Mr Donny Davies, a Manchester journalist, who had lost his life in the Munich Air Disaster of 1958.

In 1979, Mrs. Henderson was instrumental in founding the Dundee Museum. Four years later, it moved to its present site, at the foot of Talana Hill and was re-named the Talana Museum. Its main building, titled the *Henderson Hall*, was named in her honour.

It was a seventy-kilometre drive from Dundee to Isandhlwana. En route, our little convoy of seven cars passed through the hamlet of Nqutu. From there onwards signs of civilisation became depleted. An occasional cluster of mud huts could be seen from the road. For the most part, the national road was asphalt but the long, final stretch to Isandhlwana was of graded soil. After reaching the top of the Nqutu plateau, we could see the distant battlefield. The strangely shaped hill, known as Isandhlwana, appeared like a giant, crouching lion.

In the year 1879, at the base of this hill, a British military column was camped. Hundreds of troops had previously left Rorke's Drift and were slowly making their way to the Zulu King's Royal Kraal at Ulundi. They hoped to destroy the military power of the Zulu kingdom.

But in the mid-morning of January 22$^{nd}$ 1879, a force of Zulu warriors attacked the British camp. It is said 20,000 Zulus overwhelmed the soldiers and killed all except for a small number who managed to escape. For various reasons, the deceased was left unburied. Months later a burial party arrived. Wherever they found groups of skeletons, they gathered the bones together and placed stones over them. The numerous piles of stones, or *cairns*, as they are known, can be seen today standing on the open veld. Each year, the stones are white-washed to make them easily recognisable.

As our little convoy arrived at Isandhlwana on January 21$^{st}$ 1979, the sky was overcast. We parked the vehicles near a large pile of white-washed stones. The cairn stood a little higher than the roof of our car. The guide, Mrs Henderson, informed us that beneath the stones were said to be the bones of many soldiers. Commanded by Colonel Anthony Durnford, it was at this spot they had made a last stand against the Zulus.

To avoid any confusion, the reader is informed that the remains of Colonel Anthony Durnford were removed from the battlefield and interred in a military grave located in Natal.

Dotted about the extensive area of open ground and in every direction, stood white-washed cairns of varying sizes. Mrs Henderson said the size of the cairn related to the number of skeletons buried beneath them. She also stated the placement of the cairns gave an indication of the formation of the troops on that fateful day.

I found it remarkable that in the space of one hundred years, the battlefield had suffered little physical change. There was also a melancholy atmosphere which prevailed. But since then a number of crude dwellings have risen near the battlefield. And a hotel was built on the side of an escarpment, which overlooks the area. In addition, a number of monuments have been erected at significant places. But that being said, the actual battlefield is ring-fenced and preserved.

An old monument of substantial proportions stands closest to the Isandhlwana hill. Its blocks of dressed-stone act as a base for a brown-coloured granite obelisk.

Supporting the obelisk is a singular granite block which bears an inscription. It reads: 'To the memory of 29 officers and 590 non-commissioned officers and men, of the 1$^{st}$ and 2$^{nd}$ Battalion of the 24$^{th}$ Regiment, who fell in action on the field of Isandhlwana, 22$^{nd}$ January 1879'.

Attached to a face of the obelisk, high above the ground, are miniature replicas of a sphinx, a wreath, (which encloses the number '24') and above that, a Royal crown. Each small item stands out proudly on the smooth granite surface. Curiously, at a specific moment in time, lightning has struck the peak of the obelisk. Its mystical force has etched a grey-coloured, snake-like pattern on the granite's surface. Strangely, the lightning was interrupted along its journey from the sky to the ground. When it touched the top of the Royal crown it came to an abrupt stop!

During a sombre interlude of our conducted tour, the representatives of the Welsh regiment performed their official duty. Two men stood to attention at the base of the white-washed monument. Each stood to one side of some stone steps whilst a third, who was carrying a wreath, climbed to the top. At the foot of the obelisk, he stood to attention. Words of remembrance were spoken and followed by a brief silence. Thereafter, leaning forward, the third man placed the wreath against the obelisk's base. Standing to attention, he offered a final salute. His simple action thus fulfilled the official ceremony.

Before leaving Isandhlwana, I asked Sheila Henderson numerous questions. She sensed my interest in the Anglo-Zulu war was no fleeting affair. And afterwards, turning to Sandra remarked, "I can see your husband will be treading the battlefields for some time to come!"

Our little convoy moved on to visit the battle ground of Rorke's Drift. The original war-time buildings had long gone. And where the soldiers' hospital had once stood was now a museum.

Wearing a wide-brimmed canvas hat, Mr George Chadwick addressed the group. He gave a detailed explanation of the events which happened on that ground and almost to the day, one hundred years before. During the talk it seemed Sandra was intrigued by Mister Chadwick's hat. She whispered to me that it looked like a fisherman's hat but without any fishhooks attached to it. She quickly added, "I wouldn't mind so much, but the sky is cloudy, and the sun hasn't shown all day!" Sandra spoke the truth but we knew little of the ways of the African sun. In later weeks we would learn from our mistakes. The sun doesn't have to be visible to tan or to burn one's skin!

From Rorke's Drift, our cars pressed on towards the nearby Buffalo River. A short drive later, we reached the gravesite of Lieutenants Melville and Coghill. It was perched high on a hillside and looked down on the distant river bank. In 1879 the two young officers had managed to escape from the raging battle at Isandhlwana. They had crossed the Buffalo River only to be killed by some pursuing Zulus. Above their cement-covered grave, which faces towards the distant Buffalo River, stands a large stone cross. Whilst our group paid our respects, Mr. Chadwick related a story which happened some years before our visit.

"I was telling the story of the officers' escape to a party of tourists whilst some local Zulu boys were listening," he said.

"I happened to mention one of the officers carried a nickel-plated revolver. The Zulu boys misinterpreted my story and thought the revolver was made from *silver*. As a result, the grave was disturbed by them in an attempt to find the valuable item."

Due to the disturbance of the grave it was later covered in cement, and a memorial stone was placed over it. Curiously, an item from the grave was retained and is presently displayed at the South African Military Museum, Johannesburg. The item is the combined sole and heel of a boot, which had belonged to one of the Lieutenants.

At the end of a most enjoyable day, the Farley family returned to Dundee. Once more we pitched our tent at the Municipal camping site and bedded down for the night. Early the next morning, I awoke to yet another odd sound. It was a spasmodic knocking on the side of our canvas tent. Unable to contain my curiosity, I looked outside. Strewn about in all directions were large pine cones! They had fallen from the nearby trees.

Some distance away was the site vacated by Jaap Earle and his son. Today, we would revisit the battlefields and this time without the need for haste. After enjoying a leisurely breakfast, we set off for Isandhlwana. The drive was more pleasurable than before, due to us knowing the route and our expected time of arrival.

Whilst driving along the quiet approach road to Isandhlwana, I chanced to see a group of two men, two women and a young boy. As they walked in our direction, it didn't take me long to realise three of them were *sangomas*. For the benefit of the unknowing reader, a sangoma is the Zulu equivalent of the European doctor.

Their skills in treating bodily ailments and things of a psychic nature are questionable but nonetheless often successful.

Stopping the car, I quickly grabbed my camera and hailed the group. In the year 1979 the English language was not generally understood amongst the wider Zulu community. But I had prepared myself for such an occasion. Waving my camera towards them, I called out some recently memorised Zulu words.

"Ngi nga ku thatha isithombe sakho?"

(Can I take a photograph of you?)

Apparently understanding the request they silently awaited my approach. Whilst preparing to take the photo' the people watched my every movement. Digital photography was something for the future. And since my camera was loaded with roll colour film, I felt it necessary to use a hand-held light meter. My intention was to calculate the best camera settings for the occasion.

The older male member of the group was most interesting. He was of a slight build, with bird-like legs and large feet. A hat made from fabric, which resembled a kingly crown, was perched on his head. And protruding from the top of the hat was a large tuft of animal hair. Long, black, dreadlocks hung down each side of his head. They contrasted sharply with his red-ochre-painted face. It was a proud-looking face with chiselled features and it sported a thinly-grown beard and moustache. But his eyes presented an odd, piercing stare.

Stepping forward with an outstretched hand, I pointed my light meter directly towards him. His eyes momentarily widened and appeared to express an instance of fear.

I suppose his reaction to my piece of modern technology was to be expected - especially as it was being offered close to his face. By the same token, if he had pointed his fly-whisk close to *my* face, I too would have shuddered!

With my camera lifted, I was about to release its shutter, when the young woman, who stood next to the older man, reacted. She quickly yanked down her brassiere, which was improvised from animal skin. In so doing, she deliberately exposed her breasts! Why? I do not know. On reflection, there was a tradition of the early Zulu culture which required a married woman to cover her breasts. Conversely, for a single maiden, the opposite applied. I was left wondering if perhaps the lady in question was making it known to me that she was single! Or maybe, she was just repeating an act requested by a previous photographer.

What seemed like two small and under-inflated balloons were attached to the back of her head. They were, in fact, gall bladders taken from goats! She carried a wooden spearhead in one hand and in the other a wooden drum, covered with animal hide. The items were the hallmarks of a trainee sangoma. The beating of the drum is said to invoke spirits from the spirit world. Similarly, the two male sangomas wore a beaded headdress and a piece of patterned cloth, in the form of a kilt. They also carried a fly-whisk and a wooden stick. The second young woman, along with a boy, wore normal attire. They appeared to be clients of the sangomas and may well have requested their help. The photo shoot was successful, and shortly after our family pressed on with our journey.

*'Three of them were sangomas'*

Johannesburg Historical Society at Isandhlwana (1979)

It may interest the reader to learn, when I returned home, I set about processing my rolls of film; as I normally did. But the 'special' colour film, which I had used to 'capture' the sangomas met with a mishap. By an unfortunate error, I processed the roll of colour film using monochrome chemicals. The result was the glorious colours of the Zulu group turned out to be black and white. Meanwhile, I was left wondering if the wide-eyed sangoma had somehow worked his art!

After leaving the sangomas the campervan arrived at the foot of Isandhlwana Hill. Our family stood alone, absorbing the peaceful ambience. It was twelve noon on January 22$^{nd}$ 1979. By contrast, precisely one hundred years earlier, the area would have resounded to the firing of hundreds of rifles and the chants from thousands of Zulu warriors. It was a sobering thought!

Filled with curiosity, our family examined the various white-washed cairns. Inside ring-fenced enclosures stood dedicated memorial stones. Each bore silent witness to the interred. At one end of Isandhlwana hill is a rise of ground known as Black's Koppie. On its summit stood a stone and wood structure, which served as an observation post. Its copper-plated roof offered visitors some protection from the elements. Standing beneath it was a scale model of the battlefield. It presented a panoramic view of the two opposing armies, as they appeared at the time of the battle. Set into a stone wall were display cabinets, which held artefacts, found on the battlefield.

In the year 2020, due to progressive vandalism, the observation post was dismantled. Its copper-covered roof had been the prime target.

The displayed relics were transferred to the Tourist Information Centre, which now stands near St. Vincent's church.

Sometime later, I found myself walking around the upper slopes of Isandhlwana hill. I was looking for a way to access its summit. But before I could do so, I heard voices emanating from the battlefield below me. A few people had arrived without me noticing. Two men were slowly going over the ground with a metal detector. My curiosity got the better of me, and I made my way towards them. It transpired they had travelled from England especially for the centenary day.

We were standing in the area where the British army wagons would have stood. I watched in silence as their detector scanned the surface of the ground. Within a few minutes, the detector resounded with a bleeping noise. One man quickly began digging with a trowel. He unearthed what turned out to be a spent cartridge case. There was wild excitement. The two men reacted as though they had just won a major prize in the British National Lottery. They ran to their parked vehicle to show their patiently waiting wives. One of the men revealed to me, their tiny find had made their expensive visit totally worthwhile!

As the day progressed, vehicles arrived in increasing numbers. And by two o' clock that afternoon, I counted a total of nineteen! A similar number of local Zulu children gathered, along with two or three adults. Clothed in an assortment of well-worn cotton garments, they watched in awe as a group of ten European males climbed from their cars. The men, with an average age of around thirty years, wore a mix of bright, red tunics and white, pith-helmets.

Their clothing represented the uniforms of the 24<sup>th</sup> Regiment of Foot. The reader may remember it was soldiers of this regiment who had perished at Isandhlwana, a hundred years earlier. Seeing the colourful spectacle, one Zulu spectator was heard to say,
"Awu, they are beautiful!"

The uniformed men were members of the Johannesburg Military History Society. They had worn their uniforms as extras in the 1979 movie, titled *Zulu Dawn*. The movie, which starred Peter O'Toole and Burt Lancaster, told the epic story of the Isandhlwana disaster. Unfortunately, the making of the movie was plagued by legal difficulties. There was a protracted delay, before the movie was finally released, for viewing at cinemas. I can recall attending the premiere of the movie at a Johannesburg cinema. Before the start of the performance, a group of young 'Zulu warriors' arrived in traditional dress. Standing on the cinema's stage and in front of the 'big' screen, they performed a traditional dance to a packed audience.

The Military History Society members sought to add some meaning to their visit. Gathered at the base of Isandhlwana hill, they stood to attention. An appointed leader shouted instructions and the would-be soldiers responded by carrying out elementary drills. They marched back and forth in front of the large monument, on which the granite-obelisk stood. All the men wore tunics, but many were without other items of uniform. One was minus a helmet, whilst others had no webbing. In truth, they looked as if they had recently survived a battle! Nevertheless, all had a common interest in remembering the fateful battle of Isandhlwana. Finally, in bringing the event to a close, a group member placed a bugle to his lips and sounded the 'Last Post'.

# 16

## KYALAMI RANCH HOTEL

The Zulu word *Kyalami* means *home of my people*. It is also the name of South Africa's venue for international motorsport. On March 3rd 1979, Kyalami's two-and-a-half-mile race track played host to the third race of the year's Formula One season.

The Grand Prix event began in glorious South African sunshine. But later that day, the weather developed into a period of heavy rain. It made driving conditions treacherous. Drivers were compelled to have their dry tyres exchanged for the wet weather variety. The move caused some drivers to lose vital seconds during the race and thus rendered the end result less predictable.

The eventual winner of the race was the French-Canadian Gilles Villeneuve. His South African teammate, Jody Scheckter, finished in second place. Meanwhile Jean-Pierre Jarier managed third place, and the reigning World Champion, Mario Andretti, finished fourth. Carlos Reutemann came fifth and was closely followed by Niki Lauda - who had been World Champion in 1975 and 1977.

At the time of the Kyalami event, a certain South African magazine published a humorous cartoon strip. It depicted two vultures who sat side by side on the branch of a tree.

Each had their shoulders hunched and looked quite miserable, as vultures often do. Whilst perched together, one vulture turned his head sideways and asked the other a question.

"Who won the 1977 motor racing Grand Prix?"

With one word, the second vulture replied - "Lauda".

The first vulture took a deep breath and raised his voice a few decibels, then repeated the question.

"I SAID - Who WON the 1977 Grand Prix?"

Appearing a little confused, the second vulture repeated his answer, but this time with emphasis;

"LAUDA!"

The first vulture finally ran out of patience and responded by shouting the words:

"I SAID - WHO WON THE 1977 GRAND PRIX? - YOU DEAF BASTARD!"

---

A week prior to the Grand Prix event, arrangements were made to visit Kyalami, with our Scottish friends, Ken and Jean. We planned to enjoy a buffet lunch at the Kyalami Ranch Hotel. It was situated near the famous race track but we had no expectations of seeing any Grand Prix drivers. Or could we be mistaken?

Sunday, the 25$^{th}$ of February 1979, began like most South African days. A huge sun shone in a deep blue sky, which made the world seem beautiful. Forming a two-car convoy, our group left our home in Solheim and set off in the direction of Pretoria.

Twenty minutes later, we arrived at a sign-post directing us towards Kyalami. Gouged out of the rocky hills, a narrow road lay before us. It pointed the way to the Kyalami race track and the nearby Kyalami Ranch Hotel. The hotel comprised a reception area, a curio shop, and a large restaurant. Its single-storey structure featured a thatched roof of ample thickness. In the event of heavy rain, its smooth sloping sides - which towered high above the ground - were designed for maximum drainage. In those days, the Transvaal (Gauteng) was noted for its heavy downpours, and usually at around five o'clock each afternoon.

The hotel's restaurant afforded a splendid view of a large outdoor swimming pool. Growing alongside it was a row of tall, popular trees. Facing them - across the pool's sparkling water - were numerous palms. At one end of the pool was an area of turf. Dotted around it, like sprouting mushrooms, was a number of large umbrellas. Intended largely for the use of visitors, they were covered with blue or yellow cloth. Beneath them were small, iron-framed, circular tables and chairs. Moreover, a few umbrellas nearest the pool were covered in thatch, and placed beneath them were sun loungers. They were specifically intended for the relaxation of swimmers.

Set lower than the hotel was the pool area. It was accessed by large stone steps. Some nearby concrete pathways allowed people to wander around the hotel's sprawling grounds. A short distance from the pool was a number of rondavels, which served as accommodation for paying guests. And adding a finishing touch to the beautiful setting was the nearby Juskei River.

It flowed adjacent to the hotel complex, with enormous willow-trees growing along its banks. Their drooping branches seemed to stretch towards the water - as if seeking a drink.

Our little band of travellers traipsed through the hotel's foyer. Catching our attention was the large curio shop, which boasted a current sale of Africana. A lion's skin, spears, handbags, jewellery, and a host of other items were on offer, but it was too early for shopping.

Instead of buying lovely things - at least for the time being - we found ourselves facing the stone steps leading to the swimming pool. Having chosen one of the tables, with cushioned, wrought-iron chairs, we made ourselves comfortable. The seats were placed to afford an uninterrupted view of the large, oblong swimming pool. Acting like a mirror, its blue-tinted water reflected the diffused sunlight. And from time to time, young European ladies paraded around the pool's perimeter. Their clothing was such that it exposed their long, bare legs and to their best advantage! Occasionally, they stopped and posed as though they might be entering a beauty contest. But their actual job was to serve pre-ordered drinks at the tables.

When lunchtime arrived, we entered the three-star restaurant. For the sum of three Rand per person, we had access to a splendid buffet meal. For myself, I chose slices of chicken and kosher pork, which I covered with a host of delicacies. They included salmon chunks, salad, scotch eggs and boiled rice. And as if the main meal wasn't enough, it was followed by a fruit salad and later still, by cheese and biscuits.

During lunch, we heard a rumour that some of the Grand Prix racing drivers might be in the vicinity.

Thinking logically, the news seemed highly likely, since many had checked into the hotel a few days prior to the big race. Ken, my Scottish friend, and I decided to chance our luck and have a walk around the grounds. Leaving our ladies to talk and our children to play, we ambled along the river bank like a couple of average tourists.

After a while, we came upon some distant tennis courts. Two sun-tanned players were engaged in a game. One of them, with a shock of blond hair, must have been six feet tall. We speculated as to whether they were racing car drivers or merely visitors. But afterwards I discovered the tall one was Jean Pierre Jabouille. Later that year, he won the Formula One French Grand Prix. And it so happened he was the first Frenchman to win the French Grand Prix since 1948!

Away from the tennis court and some distance in front of us, was a square-shaped grassy area. We could see several people reposed on sun loungers who appeared to be reading magazines. As we walked closer, Ken unexpectedly nudged my arm. Pointing towards the people, he exclaimed:

"Hey! Isn't that Niki Lauda over there?"

My eyes quickly followed the direction of his extended finger.

"Wow! - You could be right!" I said.

The man was wearing a red-coloured jockey cap, which gave us a clue to his identity. Seconds later, I was standing next to a two-time World Champion Grand Prix driver. His red jockey cap had the defining word *PARMALAT* clearly printed along its brim. A side of his face bore the graphic reminders of his horrific car crash of 1976.

It was hard to believe that only three years had passed since this man was trapped inside a blazing car wreck.

Niki Lauda was reclined on a sun lounger. Along with his Parmalat cap, his only clothing was a pair of boxer shorts. His legs were raised in an arched manner, affording support for his hands; which in turn held a magazine. Two large oblong shapes were just visible on the surface of his broad thigh. Since they were lighter in colour than the surrounding flesh, they appeared like a discolouration of the skin. But it was most likely they were the result of a surgeon's knife, having harvested skin to perform skin-graft surgery on his face.

A young woman, who sported her hair in a Mary Quant style, was seated on a lounger next to him. She, too, was reading and appeared oblivious to her surroundings. Behind her was a man with his back towards us, who was simply relaxing. Mustering some courage, I stepped forward and asked a question.

"Could I have your autograph, please, Mister Lauda?"

My outstretched hand offered him a blank postcard and a pen. Naturally, I had taken the precaution of arming myself with such 'weapons.' After all, I *was* on a potential autograph hunting expedition! Thankfully, he gladly placed his magazine down and proceeded to write his name.

At this moment Ken had the brilliant idea to take hold of his Kodak Instamatic camera. He held it at eye level in readiness and followed his action with a question aimed at Niki.

"Hey, erm, do yoos mind if we takes yer phota?" he said with a polished Scottish accent.

Niki calmly looked at Ken and silently nodded, thus giving his permission. It was the green light for me, too. Putting the autograph into my pocket, I quickly got my camera focused. Within a few seconds, Ken and I were giving a fair impression of budding press photographers. The cameras were poised and ready for action. In expectation of his camera's clicking shutter, Niki Lauda looked steadily at Ken. But just as we were about to capture the moment, Ken voiced a vocal gem. Wearing a beaming smile, he called out:

"Hey Niki, smile for the camera please - we'll make yoos famous!"

Niki appeared amused by the remark and smiled openly. The lady sitting next to him lifted her head sharply from her magazine and looked to gauge his reaction. She too, then smiled. The anonymous man, who until now was faced away, turned to see who we were. First one, and then the other camera, clicked and captured the magical moment!

*Niki Lauda at Kyalami. (1979)*

The earlier mild tension, seemingly felt by all, had gone; like morning frost on a sun-kissed window pane.

After giving thanks, we turned away feeling elated. Ken and I triumphantly made tracks towards our wives. But we hadn't got far along a pathway before good fortune smiled upon us again. This time, it was me who spied a famous person. I spotted whom I thought was Mario Andretti - and he was heading in our direction! As the distance between us lessened I saw he was wearing a short-sleeved shirt and a pair of shorts. But it was his shock of thick, black, wavy-hair that confirmed he *was* Mario Andretti - the reigning Formula One World Champion!

Walking directly towards me, I saw his open shirt exposed his hairy chest. While around his neck was a thin chain, which carried a small medallion. Stopping him in mid-stride, I asked for his autograph. Without saying a word, he signed my offered postcard and was about to walk on. But I quickly asked if I could take his photograph. Standing motionless while remaining silent, he stared into the distance. I guessed he was giving me his unspoken approval.

Quickly lifting my camera, I hurriedly pressed the shutter-release button. There was an audible click. Instinctively, I wound the film onto the next frame, intending to make a second exposure. But just as I was about to release the camera's shutter, the reigning World Champion side-stepped me and silently walked away!

I wasn't given the opportunity to take another photograph or even to thank him. I expect people like him are frequently approached by autograph hunters, and I suppose it must become tedious. However, my mother used to say, "It costs nothing to be polite!"

# 17

## PRIMROSE GOLD MINE

My earlier visit to the Venterspost Gold Mine aroused my desire to produce more photographs of a working mine. The Primrose Gold Mine was close to my home and seemed like an obvious choice. I arrived there on a chilly, June morning, of 1979. While sporting a smile and carrying a camera, I entered the Mine Manager's office. A wall clock displayed a time of precisely seven a.m. A slimly built man, in his mid-forties and dressed in mining attire, greeted me. He introduced himself as the Mine Captain and was to be my guide on an underground tour. He asked me to sign a form exonerating the mine authorities of any injury I might receive.

As we entered a change-room, I noticed a makeshift fireplace standing in a corner. A length of large-diameter steel-pipe had been cleverly transformed into a heating unit. It stood on short legs, made from steel pipes and welded to its base. Let into its front face was a hinged, iron door, behind which was a heap of burning coal. The coal fumes mostly escaped through a pipe in the roof, but some leaked into the room, causing the air we breathed to smell like a passing steam engine.

"You'll need to put these on before we go underground", announced the Mine Captain.

Smiling pleasantly, he handed me a white boiler suit, along with a waist belt, a pair of heavy boots and a safety helmet. After quickly changing, we sat on a crude wooden-bench and waited. As if on cue, an African 'boy' entered the room bringing each of us a cup of hot, sweet tea. At that time, 'Boy' was a word widely used to address a muntu of almost any age and wasn't considered to be derogatory.

"That tasted baie lekker" (very good), said my guide and placed his empty teacup on the bench. Leaving the room, we drove to the mine entrance in his well-used bakkie. On arrival, I was handed a heavy battery. It was designed to hang from my waist belt and supply power to an electric-lamp, attached to my helmet.

"A new battery can supply power to the helmet's lamp, for up to twenty-four hours", explained my host. "Whereas" he continued, "An older battery, like yours, will last for up to sixteen hours!"

"That's good to know," I said, as I thanked him.

But silently, I thought, "Don't worry, mate, I don't intend to be underground anywhere near that length of time!"

Minutes later we stood at the mouth of the gold-mine. Warm air, carrying thousands of dust particles, issued from the opening of the inclined shaft. They sparkled briefly as they were caught by the rays of the morning sun. My imagination transformed them into micro-planets, each making their journey through a giant cosmos. "Come," said a voice, and I followed the Mine Captain, as he descended the steps of a rickety wooden stairway.

My imagined 'cosmos' was left behind, and the sun's rays were exchanged for battery-powered light. Our helmet-lamps seemed to shine brighter as we went deeper. Meanwhile, the width of the wooden steps narrowed. We descended in single file next to a side-wall of the inclined shaft. From time to time, protruding rocks momentarily slowed our progress. On our right was a handrail constructed from half-pieces of wooden-poles.

Adjacent to that was the 'floor' of the inclined shaft, which ran parallel to the stairs. Mounted on the 'floor' were steel rails, designed to allow a steel skip - when filled with gold-bearing rock - to be hauled to the surface. The skip measured six by five feet and was fitted with iron wheels. By means of a controlled, 'steel-rope', it was allowed free passage both up and down the shaft.

A narrow beam of light issued from my miner's lamp. It punched a way through the ever-present darkness. Flitting about, both here and there, the light beam chanced to fall on some stout wooden poles. They were 'pit props' and their job was to support the goldmine's rocky ceiling - or 'hanging wall', as it is known. But what surprised me were the patches of fungus, which grew on their surface. Its presence failed to enhance my level of confidence in the mine's safety!

Continuing our downward journey, the Mine Captain spotted a small light. Hardly discernible in the distance below us, it appeared to be stationary. The Mine Captain called out in the Fanakalo language. There was no reply. We descended deeper and drew closer to the anonymous light source. Slowly, the light beams from our helmets seemed to widen. From within the darkness, they picked out the shape of a human body.

Occupying three or four steps, it was hunched in a foetal position. Instantly I thought someone had fallen down the narrow and slippery stairway. The Mine Captain bellowed another sentence of Fanakalo. Suddenly, the mystery body sprang to life! It was that of a somnolent African 'boy'.

He had been assigned the job of repairing some loose steps. But unfortunately, we had audaciously disturbed him from his forty winks! Jumping quickly to his feet, he stood to attention. Any thought of guilt which he may have had was not to be seen. Instead, his face presented a beaming smile. It would have softened the hardest of hearts. His chirpy voice bade a hearty "Goeie môre Baas". (Good morning, boss) The Mine Captain replied by asking the 'boy' if he was making good progress.

"Awu, ja baas, baie goed" (Oh yes, boss, very good) was his polite and cheery reply.

The ever-descending stairway finally reached the first level of the mine. Here was to be the start of my tour. An open area, some fifteen feet in width and eight feet in height, lay before us. Facing the stairway and placed against a wall, was a wooden bench. I was invited to join my host to sit and rest a while. Light from my helmet flashed about as I surveyed our surroundings. Not far from us, the light beam picked out a darkened tunnel, which branched off to our left. Similarly, another darkened tunnel branched off to our right. Meanwhile running along the ground, in the centre of the tunnels, was a railway track. Wheeled trucks known as *cocopans* conveyed mined rock along the rails.

Close to our wooden bench was a steel-grille, which was about six feet square.

Constructed with steel round bars, each welded to the inside of a steel frame, it resembled a cattle grid. The complete item lay above a stationary steel-skip, which stood below ground level. Once filled with rock, from the cocopans, the skip would be hauled up the inclined rail track to the surface of the mine.

As the Mine Captain and I rested, we heard a mechanical rumbling sound coming from the mouth of a tunnel. It preceded the appearance of a large iron-cocopan. Two sweat-covered, brown-skinned bodies brought it to a halt, next to the steel grille. With great effort the miners managed to push the cocopan's body onto its side. A hinged arrangement allowed the body to swivel, whilst leaving the wheeled assembly firmly on the rail-track. The gold-bearing ore was emptied onto the top of the steel grille.

Almost at once, a third African miner used a spade to extract every trace of ore from the container. Most of the rock fell through the rungs of the grille and into the waiting skip below. But any piece that failed to drop was helped on its way by the miner's spade. Meanwhile the two operators righted the cocopan onto its wheeled assembly. Once in place, they proceeded to return it to its starting point. It rumbled slowly along the track and disappeared into the mouth of the darkened tunnel. Soon out of sight, the rumbling sound of the cocopan's wheels gradually faded away.

Within minutes, the sound of another cocopan announced its arrival. But this time, it was from the mouth of the opposite tunnel. Its noise grew progressively louder, as small round lights formed in the darkness. They appeared to be suspended above the rails. Slowly, they got closer, along with the growing intensity of the rumbling sound.

The lights belonged to the helmets of three sweating miners, who arrived pushing a large cocopan. They quickly brought its squealing wheels to a halt. Bathed in the light from the miners' helmets, the cocopan was emptied, in the same way as its predecessor. Once emptied, it was pushed back into its tunnel - leaving the site clear for the next arrival. As I watched the miners at work, the Mine Captain had something to say. He pointed to the wall next to the steel grille.

"Do you see that wooden board hanging on the wall?"

My gaze followed his pointing finger. "The board," said the Captain, is drilled with a number of small holes. After each cocopan is emptied, a short wooden peg is placed into a hole. It's a way of keeping count as to how many cocopans have been emptied, during a working shift."

"That's interesting", I quipped, "But why would you need to know that?"

"Ja, well," my host answered, while smiling as he spoke, "That's because the number of emptied cocopans gives an idea of how much gold to expect for that day. For example, one ounce of gold might be expected from ten ore-filled cocopans."

My host was silent for a moment and then added,

"Of course, the number of cocopans could vary due to the yield of the gold-bearing ore."

Together, we watched the miners for a few minutes before continuing the tour. With light shining from our helmet lamps, my guide led the way along a tunnel.

We took care to avoid tripping on the rail tracks or stepping on the odd piece of loose rock - which lay on the ground. We also avoided the shallow pools of water, which appeared at irregular intervals on either side of the tracks.

*'Small round lights formed in the darkness'*

*'As the Mine Captain crawled into an open crevice'*

Along the way, my attention was drawn towards two parallel steel pipes. They were attached to the wall along the length of the tunnel. One conveyed water, and the other compressed air. During the drilling process, water and air were used to dislodge the gold-bearing rock. I couldn't help noting how the pipes were roughly installed. Rusty wire loops, twisted around them, were hung from nails driven into the rock. And some sections of the water pipe showed signs of rust. In the case of the compressed-air pipe, some of the connection joints hissed like demented snakes - as leaking air escaped!

As the Mine Captain crawled into an open crevice, he motioned me to follow. Standing on the sloping floor, we watched two miners drill into a gold-bearing seam. A jackhammer rattled away into the rock face. Its drill bit formed one-inch diameter holes of around two feet deep. A pipe fed water over the drill bit, which helped to keep it cool. At the same time, it helped to keep the dust to a minimum. Powder, produced during the act of drilling, mixed with water and formed a thin paste. And as the miners drilled holes, the paste splattered over their hands and faces. When they turned away, after finishing their task, they appeared like walking statues! Much later, sticks of explosives would be placed into the drilled holes and made ready for blasting. The job of blasting was to be done at the end of the shift when all personnel were clear.

When the miners ceased their drilling, I scrambled behind the Mine Captain as he climbed out of the crevice. We continued our journey along the railway track, when suddenly; two small lights appeared in the distant darkness.

They were followed by what was now a familiar rumbling sound. As before, we found two men who were pushing a cocopan. We arrived where a blasting operation had taken place the day before. Men were busy clearing away the gold-bearing ore. One man used a sledgehammer to break up the larger pieces of rock, while two others spaded the broken rock onto a platform. A fourth man completed the tasks by shovelling the rock from the platform and into a waiting cocopan. Of course, I now knew the cocopan would be pushed along the rail-track.

Everything I saw that day was part of a tried and proven routine. It resulted in extracting the gold-bearing ore and getting it to the surface. But what I hadn't anticipated was a surprise ending to my tour. Together, my host and I reached the foot of the rickety wooden steps. They were the ones we had descended earlier that day. Looking first at their challenging ascent, my host turned his head towards me. In a sombre and serious tone of voice, he asked a question.

"Are you ready for the climb to the surface?"

In the light shed by my helmet's lamp, I gazed contemptuously at the wooden steps. My mind contemplated the gruelling task of making the climb. Turning towards my host, I was ready to give him my answer. But before I could speak, his face erupted into a smile, and then he laughed.

"I'm joking!" he exclaimed. "We'll take the easier way up!"

Within minutes, I was crouched inside the actual steel skip, which normally carried broken rock. Suddenly I heard the bellowed words.

"Keep your head DOWN!"

With the Mine Captain's words still ringing in my ears, the skip moved upwards at a moderate rate. And from my crouched position, my gaze fixed on the beam of light emitted by my helmet's lamp. It followed the irregular-shaped rocky surface of the 'hanging-wall'. Soon, the darkness gave way to the light of day, and I gave a secret sigh of relief, realising the skip had finally reached the surface.

During my time spent at Primrose Gold Mine, I was introduced to an English-speaking European gentleman. Answering to the name of Mister Davies, he was a semi-retired engineer who had considerable mining experience. He had connections with another gold mine named *Balmoral*. Following my request, he arranged for me to visit the mine and do a photo' shoot. As our friendship developed, (No pun intended) I'm pleased to say I was instrumental in resurrecting his interest in photography. And since he was the proud owner of a vintage Leica 35mm S.L.R. camera, it gave him a good start! During his earlier years of photography, he had accrued some money by selling his work. Close to where he lived stood a public hall, in which weekly bouts of wrestling took place. His forte was to visit the events and take photos of the contestants in action. Afterwards he always had a few willing buyers of his work.

One day he told me about an unfortunate incident which occurred at a certain gold mine. As an Engineer, he was requested to attend an official hearing. He said a certain electrician was required to supply electricity from ground level to an underground tunnel. The obvious route for a supply cable was down the vertical mine shaft.

Initially, the mine shaft was cut through the bare rock and made large enough to accommodate a cage. But the shaft's sidewalls were anything but smooth. Irregular shaped rocks could be seen to protrude everywhere. For the cage to be lowered down the shaft, without hindrance, thick, wooden runner-rails were affixed to the shaft walls. The cage could then be lowered whilst guided by the rails.

When planning the electrical installation, it seemed logical to attach a power cable to the side edge of a wooden rail. The cable consisted of insulated, thick copper conductors. Protected by stranded steel wire, the composite cable was finally covered with a thick, plastic outer sheath. One can imagine that even a short length of the cable would be heavy to lift.

As a means of transportation, the cable was wound onto a large, wooden cable-drum. With concerted effort, the drum was hoisted onto the roof of the cage. A steel axle was inserted into the core of the drum and the complete assembly suspended on a steel frame. The electric cable could now be pulled off the wooden cable-drum, as it was made to rotate around the axle.

During the installation, the electrician and a muntu assistant, stood on top of the cage and next to the cable-drum. A second muntu assistant stood inside the cage. His job was to communicate with the winch operator, who worked in the distant control room. Communication was by means of an electric bell. An agreed number of rings from the bell would signal the winch operator to raise or lower the cage. At the mine shaft, the three men worked as a team. From the top of the cage, the electrician would shout the necessary instructions to his second assistant. And all the while steady progress was made.

The cage was periodically lowered in response to the necessary number of rings from the bell. And each time the cage made a slow descent, the electrician and his immediate assistant, manually turned the cable-drum. The electric cable rolled off the drum and was systematically attached to the wooden guide-rail. Metal saddles were used at regular intervals to secure it. Each saddle was placed over the cable and held in place by woodscrews. For a while all was going to plan. But usually, when an 'incident' occurs, something has been overlooked.

At the surface of the mine-shaft, a length of loose cable had been left lying on the ground. Having been wound off the cable-drum, the electrician intended to terminate its end at a later time. Unfortunately for all concerned, the cable demonstrated a certain characteristic. Prior to being used, it was wound around the cable drum, but now it was stretched out on the ground. And due to its characteristics, the cable began to assume its previous shape. In so doing, it slowly rose from the ground like a writhing snake.

Forming a curve as it ascended, it attempted to resume its previous coiled shape around the wooden drum. The cable's end nudged closer to the mouth of the mineshaft. Within minutes, it reached the shaft opening and flopped over. While hanging into the mineshaft, the force of gravity came into play. The attendant weight of the cable's length had the effect of wrenching the top metal saddle - along with its woodscrews - free from the wooden rail! As this was happening at ground level, the electrician and his assistants below ground, were blissfully unaware of the ensuing catastrophe. With the release of the first metal saddle, another metre of heavy cable was made free. The additional weight continued the sequence of events.

A second metal saddle was torn from its fixing. The free cable was now even longer than before and its total weight was even heavier. As it systematically pulled the metal saddles from their fixings, it was unstoppable. Within seconds, an avalanche of heavy cable fell towards the top of the cage. The first to know of anything untoward was the electrician. At the last moment, he was alerted to the sound of something rushing towards him from above.

Instinctively looking up, he was smacked about his head with the first of the arriving cable. He was then knocked physically over the edge of the cage. Instantly unconscious, he fell into the gap between the side of the cage and the wall of the mineshaft. Fortunately for him, he was wearing a safety harness. The second assistant, who was inside the cage, could see nothing. He could only hear unfamiliar sounds. Puzzled, but only for a matter of seconds, he was instantly shocked to see the electrician. The man was hanging, upside-down by the chain from his safety harness.

Meanwhile, the first assistant was much less fortunate. He was buried under a heap of fallen cable and didn't survive. The second assistant, whilst exercising great effort, managed to pull the electrician inside the cage. He immediately operated the bell to instruct the winch operator to take the cage to the surface. But due to the falling cable the bell failed to function properly. The winch operator was receiving intermittent 'rings', which, to him, made no sense at all. Realising that something must be wrong, he slowly brought the cage to the surface.

# 18

## HILLBROW'S REVOLVING RESTAURANT

Hillbrow, or *Hillies* as it was affectionately known to the locals, is a suburb of Johannesburg. In the year 1978 it had numerous hotels and high-rise apartment blocks, as well as an abundance of mixed shops and restaurants. For entertainment there was a choice of theatres, cinemas and many public bars - some of which had discotheques. A number of private doctors and dentists chose to have their practices in Hillbrow, and all were within range of a couple of hospitals.

The diversity of amenities which a person might need was available within a short walking distance. It made Hillbrow the perfect place for retirement living. Was it any wonder that the area was said to have the densest population per square metre, in the whole of the southern hemisphere?

Included in all of the above is the Strijdom Tower, which was named after J.G. Srijdom, a former South African Prime Minister. The telecommunications tower is considered to be one of the tallest man-made structures in Africa. And following its completion in 1971, it became a major tourist attraction.

The tower stands some 269 metres above the ground. In essence, it is a hollow tube constructed from reinforced concrete. It supports four, upper circular-levels stacked on top of each other. At its top is perched a transmitter mast, which points skyward like an accusing finger. Electric elevators, installed in the central core of the tower, convey passengers and goods to the four levels.

In 1978, one level served as an observation base for up to two-hundred people. Along with a curio shop, it had several coin-operated telescopes, by which city life could be observed through a choice of twenty-four windows. On another level was the Grill Room, which catered for over a hundred people. After ordering a meal, it was a novelty to watch the food being cooked on an open grill. On a third level was a V.I.P. room, in which functions were held. This special room could accommodate fifty people seated or one hundred standing. Finally, the upper-most level was occupied by *Heinrich's Restaurant*. Aside from an excellent food menu, the dining area had the unique feature of a rotating floor!

Since it was our wedding anniversary, Sandra and I decided to celebrate at the famous restaurant. At the base of the Strijdom Tower, we looked up at its dizzy height. Reaching towards the clear night sky, the tower seemed to climb forever. The pantomime story of *Jack and the Beanstalk* sprang to mind. I imagined myself in the role of Jack, but fortunately there was no need for me to climb any beanstalk!

Travelling at six metres per second, an elevator delivered Sandra and me to the Heinrich's level. Stepping out, we found ourselves standing on a luxurious fitted-carpet. Tapestries depicting scenes of early Johannesburg festooned the walls.

A waiter approached extending a warm "Velkom". He escorted us to our pre-booked table. Placed herringbone fashion against the windows, was an arrangement of tables. They suggested the idea of being spokes in a giant wheel.

Thick glass windows, set in the curvature of the tower's outer wall, offered a panoramic view of the city. And from our allotted window, we enjoyed a glorious sight, which lay far below us. Ablaze with its myriad of electric lights, was the sprawling city of night-time Johannesburg. Meanwhile, the restaurant's lighting was turned low. Prominence was given to the singular burning candles, placed at the centre of each table. The flame of our candle reacted to the gentle breeze, from a distant air-conditioner. Like an exotic dancer, it swayed slowly, and cast a curvaceous shadow over the table cloth.

Polished silver knives and forks lay in front of us. Next to them was a small wicker basket. It contained freshly baked bread rolls and paper-wrapped squares of butter. And for the customary after-dinner cigarette, a silver ashtray lay in readiness. The overall romantic scene, reflected from the darkened glass of our adjacent window.

A smiling waiter brought us a wine list and quickly departed. Taking one look at the prices I nearly fainted!

"They are charging fourteen Rand for a bottle of wine!" I exclaimed. And with increasing indignation, I added "If they want fourteen Rand for the wine, how much is the meal going to cost?"

Sandra put my troubled mind at rest.

"Don't worry, love" she said, "You made a mistake. You opened the wine list at the *imported* wine section!"

Heaving a huge sigh of relief, I gave the list another look. A bottle of Nederburg Stein was more familiar to my discerning eye, and the cost of three Rand per litre was decidedly better!

Whilst quietly sipping the wine, I took note of our surroundings. In the central area was an adequately stocked cocktail bar. And seated at an adjacent piano, was a smartly dressed, grey-haired man. He was surrounded by his musical 'friends.' They consisted of an electric organ, a clarinet, a violin, a saxophone and a piano accordion. Throughout the evening the man played each 'friend' periodically and kept us entertained.

An affable waiter duly arrived and made a mental note of our chosen meal. Suddenly, our table gave a gentle lurch. The adjacent window appeared to slowly glide away from us. In a sense, it did, but in reality, the floor was actually moving! Meanwhile, the outer and inner shells of the tower were stationary. At first, as the floor slowly rotated in an anti-clockwise direction, I felt a peculiar sensation. But after a while, the feeling wore off, and the pace of one revolution per hour became quite comfortable. This arrangement caused the music man, while seated at his piano, to be seen to gradually approach us. Minutes later, he would be playing opposite to us. Then, after a few minutes more and as our table rounded the inner core of the tower, we would see him slowly disappear!

Another interesting aspect of the hourly revolution was to observe the outside 'Golden City'. The panoramic night-time view constantly changed; and with dramatic effect. In the distant suburb of Brixton we could see the Albert Hertzog Tower. Built in 1962, it was better known as the Brixton Tower, due to its location.

At the height of 240 metres, it stands slightly shorter than the Hillbrow Tower.

While the floor of the restaurant continued to rotate, the view of the Brixton Tower gave way to one of the Carlton Centre. The fifty-storey building was said to be the tallest office block in Africa. Sited in the heart of Johannesburg, it was completed in 1973. Shortly after, another famous landmark 'glided' into view. It was the cylindrical-shaped Ponte building, which served as an apartment block.

As we enjoyed watching the moving spectacle, our previously ordered food arrived. For a starter, Sandra had chosen the avocado salad, whilst I settled for the lobster soup. Before long, we were gazing with joyous eyes at the highly recommended main dish. *Springbok van die Lowveld* was its title. Slices of tenderly cooked springbok meat formed a base for a mixture of cooked mushrooms and black cherries. On one side of the plate was a helping of boiled red-cabbage. Whilst at the opposite side was a slice of orange, topped with a blob of chestnut cream and crowned with a singular red cherry. Finally, small portions of spätzle filled any gaps on the plate.

At dessert time, Sandra ordered a peach melba. Because I was feeling well-fed, I chose not to order. But little did I know what was to come. Placed in front of Sandra was a generous portion of ice cream, crowned with an upturned half of a large peach. A trickle of raspberry sauce covered the peach, and a sprinkling of crushed nuts was added. The delightful creation was made complete by surrounding the peach with a quantity of fresh cream. After observing this culinary temptation, was it any wonder I succumbed?

In rounding off a most memorable evening, coffee and tea was served. But then, out of the blue, the waiter surprised us both. He brought a plate of strawberries, each of which had a crisp candy coating! They were the perfect end to a perfect meal. But when the waiter presented us with the bill, it came as a final show-stopping surprise. The cost for everything was a modest twenty-two Rand!

As if a meal at the top of Africa's tallest communications tower wasn't enough for one night, something more awaited us. I held two tickets to see a play at the Andre Huguenet Theatre! Sandra and I dashed through the streets of upper Hillbrow and arrived at the theatre in the nick of time. Australian author Burton Graham had written a play called *Nightfall*. The idea for the play is said to have been carried in his mind for several years. It began when he first learned that Strindburgian was an ardent fan of Edgar Alan Poe.

The piece of information intrigued him. He began wrestling with the idea of creating two Strindburgian-type characters and casting them in a Poe-type scenario - albeit in the format of a play. The two-act play titled *Nightfall* was the result. It had its World Premiere at the Andre Huguenet Theatre on the seventh of June 1979, just two weeks before Sandra and I got there.

The stage served as the living room of one of Jonas Fordyce's Thames-side cottages, near England's city of Oxford. The role of Jonas Fordyce was played by the film star Richard Todd. He had performed in movies such as *The Dam Busters* (1955) and *The Longest Day* (1962). The role of the second, of only two actors in the play, was performed by Jack Hedley. He, too, had performed in movies.

One of which was titled *The Anniversary* (1968), in which he starred opposite Bette Davis. He also appeared in *The Longest Day* (1962).

Sandra and I agreed that we had found the story hard to understand. But our interest was kept alive by witnessing the two great actors at work. At the end of the evening's performance we waited in the theatre's foyer. I hoped to add to my autograph collection. The evening's patrons brushed past us and quickly left the theatre. Sandra and I found ourselves alone. Suddenly, a door opened, and the two casually dressed actors emerged from the doorway. What followed next was like a private mini-performance. Standing close together, both men wore tweed jackets and plain-flannel trousers.

As Jack Hedley autographed a page of our programme, Richard Todd turned to face us. With a cultured and deep theatrical voice, he asked a question.

"Did you both enjoy the show?"

We answered "Yes". But then I ventured to return a question.

"But what was the play's story actually about?"

Richard Todd was slightly taken aback by my unexpected inquiry. He paused to ponder, before turning his head towards Jack Hedley.

"What do you think, Jack?" he asked.

Both men thought about the question and, between them, produced a joint reply. Unfortunately, it didn't make our understanding of the play any clearer. And to this day my question remains unanswered!

# 19

# THE STERKFONTEIN CAVES

A few days after our celebratory meal, at Hillbrow's Strijdom Tower, Sandra arranged for us to visit the Sterkfontein caves. They are located some fifty kilometres north-west of Johannesburg and lie near the Magaliesberg range of hills.

Whilst working at the Transvaal Museum in Pretoria, a Scotsman named Robert Broom began a study of early hominids. In 1936, he and his students found fragments of six hominids at the Sterkfontein site. Since that time, thousands of fossils have been found. They show human evolution over the past three and a half million years. But one of the most significant discoveries was made in 1947, by Dr. Robert Broom and John Robinson. They discovered the most complete Australopithecus skull inside the caves. Dr Broom named the skull Paranthropus Robustus but later referred to it as *Mrs Ples*.

In the aftermath of finding *Mrs. Ples*, Dr. Broom published a monograph. It led to most scientists finally accepting the Australopithecines were, in fact, hominids and not apes. Since the year 1979 the Sterkfontein site has delivered about 90,000 fossil specimens. They contribute to make the caves one of the richest and most productive paleo-anthropological sites in the world. After years of research, Doctor Robert Broom died in 1951.

It was a hot Sunday morning when we greeted our friends, John and Patricia Ainsworth. Leaving Johannesburg behind, our cars passed concrete buildings, which gave way to open veld. The surrounding scenery constantly changed, and having passed Krugersdorp, the views became mountainous. Forty minutes later, we were within range of the Sterkfontein caves. Someone glanced at a watch and loudly declared: "It's time for us to have a braai!"

Packed in the boot of our car was a portable braai unit. Alongside it was a large cooler bag containing tee-bone steaks and some boere-wors. For the reader who is unfamiliar with *boerewors*, it is a long beef-sausage and usually sold in a coiled format, in the style of a Catherine-wheel. When un-coiled it can measure around a half-metre in length. And when cooked, the coil can be cut into pieces of suitable length for eating.

Regarding tee-bone steaks, Sandra and I had recently managed to buy two for the princely sum of R1-80. Considering the exchange rate at that time was R1-88 to the English Pound, we thought we had done fairly well.

As our cars approached Sterkfontein caves, one of our parties was lucky to spot a narrow cart track. Flanked by tall trees, it left the main asphalted road. Giving a cursory look everyone agreed it seemed like the perfect place to have the braai. After driving along the track, for about twenty metres, we encountered a five-bar gate. A loop of wire, hooked over a nearby post, held it closed. There seemed no point in driving any further. Parking the cars at the side of the track, everyone climbed out. A volunteer assembled the braai unit in readiness to cook the meat. Nearby was an old tree. Its dry and brittle branches was perfect for fuelling our braai and in no time at all, the meat was cooked.

Everyone sat on out-spread blankets eating their portions of steak, boere-wors and mixed salad.

Between bites of food, I noted how peaceful our surroundings were. Looking down the cart track, I could see the main asphalt road. Apart from an occasional muntu walking past the junction, nothing disturbed the tranquillity of the scene. However, as sometimes happens, nature calls. Nicola, our youngest daughter, made a request to relieve herself. Since I had almost finished my food, I volunteered to help. We plodded into the veld, and a few metres from our impromptu camp, we found a private spot. Rather than risk soiling her knickers, I offered to put them into my jacket-pocket. Holding her at a short distance above the ground, she did her business. Meanwhile, back at the camp, the others had finished their meals. John had tipped up the braai unit and emptied the glowing coals onto the ground.

But as fate would have it, at that moment, a large Land Rover appeared. Leaving the main road, it entered the cart-track and drove to where our group was gathered. I heard its arrival and frantically set about cleaning Nicola before quickly making our return. John made every effort to stamp out the smouldering coals, as the others stood embarrassingly to attention.

Sat inside the vehicle was a stout, bearded, middle-aged male. Wearing a wide-brimmed felt-hat, he appeared to be a farmer. Two middle-aged ladies sat next to him. Their pressed floral, cotton-dresses and floppy straw hats gave them a regal appearance. It occurred to me they were returning from a church service. Suddenly, everyone realised we had chosen the man's driveway to have our braai! Sensing that the Land Rover wanted to pass through, I reached for the gate and opened it.

A window wound down, and a dour-looking face peered at us. With a deep-sounding voice, the man said,

"Goeie More." (Good morning.)

John was quick to answer. "Good morning to you; it's a lovely day, isn't it?" he said. "We're sorry we didn't realise this was someone's driveway."

The man's countenance changed.

"Are you Engels?" he asked.

He heard John speak and must have realised by his accent that he was definitely a non-local.

"Yes, we are," said John.

"Ag okay - nee problem mense. Maar, please make sure you kill all those coals before you gaan. (Go) Ek have lots of cows in the veld, and the grass is baie droog. (Very dry) It could easily catch alight."

John assured him that we would. The farmer saw me standing next to the opened gate and drove forward. He gave me a half-wave as his vehicle passed through. But the look on the faces of the two ladies more than adequately conveyed their disgust!

With the gate closed and the coals extinguished, our camping paraphernalia was packed away.

It was then that Nicola called for my attention.

"Daddy," she said.

"Yes, Nicola, what is it?"

"Can I put my knickers on now?"

Instantly, all eyes focused on me. And judging by their accusing expressions, a brief (no pun intended) explanation was silently called for. When my strategy for Nicola's cleanliness had been divulged, everyone roared with laughter!

Having eaten some food and feeling in a happy frame of mind we continued our journey. Ahead of us, on the distant hillside, was a simple layout. It comprised a cave entrance, a small museum, and a café. Collectively they constituted the tourist attraction named *Sterkfontein Caves*. The cost of entry was seventy cents for adults and was free for children under six. Closing time was scheduled for five-thirty, which meant our tour was to be the last of the day.

Presenting our tickets to the muntu guide, we followed his group of tourists towards a gaping rocky hole. It appeared like a vacant eye socket in the rugged landscape. This was the entrance to the ancient caves. Carefully, we descended numerous stone steps. Within seconds, they gave way to an electrically illuminated tunnel. Upon reaching its end, we entered a large, dome-shaped cavern. Stumps of stalactites extended from its ceiling, while some distance ahead of us was a wall of natural stone. It was blackened by fires, made by people of long ago. Dozens of names were scratched onto the wall's sooty surface. But contrary to our thoughts, the names were made by visitors of modern times!

Crouching for most of the way, we shuffled through a twisting passage, before we came upon an underground lake. Here, we saw minute shrimps swimming in the water. According to our guide, the local Bantu considered the water to be therapeutic.

Shortly after moving along, I chanced to step on a dead bat. Recovering from the initial shock, I thought to myself, "So much for the therapeutic water!"

A few minutes later, Sandra excitedly drew my attention to another bat. But this one was alive and flying around the cavern at low level - whilst skilfully avoiding any collision with the throng of visitors. An American tourist standing nearby, heard Sandra's outburst and turned to look. As he observed the flying bat, somewhat dryly he said,

"It's probably the ventilation system!"

Much later, we entered an enormous chamber and viewed in awe, some fifteen-metre-high stalactite formations. When our tour finally came to an end, our group was obliged to climb some steep-steps, before reaching the surface. It was there we came face to face with a bronze bust of Dr. Robert Broom. It had been prominently placed there in recognition of his work. Wishing him a fond goodbye, our little band of visitors agreed to extend our visit a little longer. We all pledged to enjoy a freshly made pot of tea, at the on-site cafe.

# 20

# OUR CAMPERVAN EXPEDITION

Could it have been our journey to Zululand, with its thinly populated areas? Or the roads we had travelled, where we seldom saw another vehicle? Or was it perhaps sleeping under canvas and having a varied choice of location? Whatever it was we had been undeniably bitten by the proverbial travel bug!

Sandra had recently joined me in finding employment at the Siemens' Isando factory. Before long we had planned another adventurous trip. It was designed to visit most principal cities of South Africa. Starting in Johannesburg, we intended to motor down to Kimberley and from there, on to Cape Town. After that, we would travel the Garden Route to East London and then follow the coastal road to Durban. Our journey would continue along the east coast and eventually turn in-land to reach Piet Retief. From there, the final leg of the journey would return us to Johannesburg. The intention was to travel a total distance of around 5,000 miles in a period of three weeks.

In South Africa the seasons of the year are opposite to those of England. December is the hottest month and is when most South Africans take their annual leave.

When Christmas time arrived our employment at Siemens had been scarcely a few months. However, the kindly management agreed to let us take the required three weeks leave. But before we could travel, it would be necessary to arrange transport. Sandra and I decided the best option would be a Volkswagen transporter. It should be capable of carrying four adults and have reasonable comfort. Naturally, that kind of vehicle costs big money. But since I was somewhat frugal in my outlook, I looked for a cheaper option. Within a short time, I spotted a promising newspaper advertisement. For sale was a 1973 Volkswagen panelvan. It was advertised as being 'Off the road' and at a reasonable price. I soon discovered the reason for the low cost was because its engine was seized!

At the seller's house, the five-year-old vehicle was parked on a driveway. Its faded, pale-blue paint caused it to look drab but the bodywork was virtually rust-free. Mechanically, all was in good working order, except, of course, for the seized engine. The owner claimed the van had run well until the fatal day, when a resounding bang was heard from the engine. He decided not to have it repaired but rather to sell it 'As Is'. A sale price of 400 Rand was agreed upon, and the van was towed away. I must say that prior to the sale I had researched the price of a new engine. I discovered that even after paying for a replacement engine, the vehicle would still be a good buy.

Later that month, I managed to locate two German motor mechanics. And, like ourselves, they happened to be immigrants. As the vehicle was towed to their garage a relevant thought presented itself. What better choice of mechanic could there be, to work on a German Volkswagen?

An examination of the 1800cc engine revealed the cause of its present condition. For an inexplicable reason a loose steel nut had wedged itself between the engine's moving parts. It resulted in damage done to the valves and the pistons. Surprisingly, the Germans offered to repair the engine for the sum of 400 Rand! Purely by chance, the amount matched the price already paid for the actual van!

The prospect of having a fully functional campervan for less than a thousand Rand was delightful. For a few days, the mechanics worked diligently on the seized engine. Eventually, a welcomed 'phone call invited me to visit their garage. I was overjoyed at the prospect of collecting a driveable vehicle. However, sadly, on arrival a mechanic gave me some unexpected bad news.

"Vee are sorry to tell you, zat vee cannot complete zee job because of rrust!" (The man rolled his spoken 'r's.)

"What RUST?" I exclaimed in astonishment.

"Because das van has not been used for some time, der ist rrust inside der benzintank," he said.

"Excuse me - Rust in the what?" I quickly asked.

"Ah, sorry for mein Deutch, I mean der petrol-tank. Und if vee pour petrol into der petrol-tank it shall mix mitt der rrust. So, vee cannot start, or tune das engine vithout clean petrol."

Breathing a deep sigh, I asked a further question.

"So, what is the answer to the problem?"

"Vee shall have to remove der old petrol tank, und replace it mitt a new vone," said the mechanic.

"But to do zis vee shall have to take das engine out of das body. Und zen vee can exchange der tank for a new vone," he added.

The mechanic's revelation was a serious blow to my plan. In short, the Germans claimed there was rust inside the petrol tank. And if fresh petrol was poured into it, there was every chance it would become contaminated. It followed that the rust would then cause problems during the tuning and future running of the engine. Therefore, to eliminate short-term and potentially future problems, the fuel tank would have to be changed!

Unfortunately, the design of the panel van was such that when looking inwards from the rear bumper, the fuel tank was located immediately behind the engine. To access the fuel tank, with a view to replacing it, the engine would have to be removed! That could only result in substantially more expense. I informed the Germans I would let them know my answer in a day or two.

Sandra and I discussed the problem. It occurred to me the mechanics had done a good job of repair. They said they had fitted some new engine parts and I had no reason to doubt them. But I suspected that perhaps they had overspent on their quoted cost of repair. And now, they were trying to claw back some of their outlay. Maybe, just maybe, they were 'spinning me a yarn'. After several cups of hot tea and some equally hot words, we formulated an action plan. Near to our home was an automobile scrap yard. During a visit, I was very lucky to find a used but rust-free fuel tank. It seemed as though the wheel of fortune was turning again - and this time in our favour. Luckily for me, our panel van's body-work was designed with a 'shelf', which was directly above the engine compartment.

My plan was to place the scrap yard's petrol tank - containing some clean petrol - on top of the shelf. A suitable flexible pipe would couple the petrol tank to the engine's carburettors. The petrol could then gravity feed the engine. When all was in place, I believed the German mechanics could then complete their job!

A couple of days later, I boldly returned to the Germans' garage. With eyes agog, the mechanics watched as I placed the rust-free petrol tank above the panel van's engine compartment. Holding a container of clean petrol in one hand and a flexible pipe in the other, I explained my plan to them.

"Here are the items you need" I said. "Attach one end of the pipe to the petrol tank and the other to the carburettors. Pour the clean petrol into the tank and tune the engine. Once you have tuned it, I shall pay your invoice and take the van away!"

A look of incredulity appeared on their faces. Within seconds, the Germans were conversing in their mother tongue. "Shisse!" was one of the few German words I had learnt during my employment at the Siemens factory. And during the mechanics' heated conversation, it's possible I may have heard the word spoken more than once!

Finally, they agreed to my idea and asked me to return the following day. On my return visit, I saw the engine running nicely. It appeared my plan had worked. I promptly thanked the mechanics and paid them in cash. But as I was about to leave the garage, one mechanic called me aside. Speaking quietly, he said, "I can assure you that you have not been cheated!"Inwardly, I had to agree, and with the 'new' petrol tank perched above the engine, I carefully drove the van home.

But nagging questions raked my mind. Was the original fuel tank impregnated with rust as the Germans had claimed? Or had they simply spun me a line? Furthermore, could I really afford to take the chance of using the original suspect tank? After much deliberation, I decided to leave the engine in situ. However, I would remove the existing fuel-tank – but from *inside* the van!

Although it seemed possible to do the job, it would be a tricky operation. On the metal surface of the van's floor, under which lay the original petrol tank, I used a marking pen to scribe three sides of an oblong. The next step was long and laborious. Unable to obtain an angle grinder, I drilled a series of small holes along each of the three scribed lines. Once the final hole was drilled, each hole was caused to merge into the next. In this way, a three-sided oblong was formed. With great effort, the long side was forced out and bent downward. Once done, it resembled the flap of a giant, upside-down letterbox. At last, I could see the offending fuel tank. But then began my struggle to extricate the tank from its awkward location.

As time progressed, the existing fuel tank was finally removed and the 'new' one was installed. The 'flap' of the imaginary 'letter-box' was forced back into its original position. Wide strips of metal were riveted across the cut lines and held the flap in place. They resembled sticking plasters on the face of a mugging victim! But now, at least, the van was fully functional with its re-conditioned engine and replacement fuel tank. But wait a moment, a pertinent question remained unanswered. What about the original tank? Quantities of petrol were used to flush its interior and were visually inspected. In addition to this, the light from a torch conducted an internal inspection of the fuel-tank.

Finally, Sandra and I were able to answer the nagging question of "Was the fuel tank rusty inside?" The answer was a unanimous;"No; it was not!"

The seats fitted to our panel van were original and basic. Sitting in them was most uncomfortable. Thankfully, the scrap yard, from where I bought the replacement petrol tank, also had an old Volvo saloon. In exchange for a few Rand, I acquired its two front seats. What a difference they made. Compared to the panel van's seating, they could easily have belonged to the next century. Covered in light-brown leather and with fabric inlays, they were also fitted with headrests. Spurred on by the resultant improved look, I made further additions to the van's appearance. Designed to hold the spare wheel, I fitted a box-section bracket to the front bumper. And by putting the spare wheel outside the vehicle, extra internal space was gained.

Inside the van, I constructed a steel, box-section framework. Covered with sheets of chipboard, it supported a double sponge mattress. This meant our mobile home now had a double bed. The space created beneath the bed frame was used to store our cooking utensils and food supplies. A shallow, wood construct, designed to act as a wardrobe, was placed above a wheel arch. And a twenty-five-litre plastic water container was mounted on a corner of the bed frame.

When travelling, the floor space behind the two front seats was our daughters' play area. At bedtime it became their bedroom. There was even some room to keep their toys.

After taking everything into consideration, the 'old van' had now become our home from home!

Our epic journey began on the twenty-first of December, 1979. Just under six hours after leaving Johannesburg, we reached the city of Kimberley. We had knocked the first 297 miles off our five-thousand-mile journey. Interestingly, less than a hundred years before our arrival, diamonds had been discovered there. Of course, they lay under the ground and embedded in blue clay. Hundreds of would-be miners ultimately arrived. The small hill on which diamonds were first discovered rapidly became a large crater. More diggers arrived, and the crater became steadily deeper. By the year 1914, work finally ceased. It was estimated that up to 50,000 diggers had toiled at the site. Between them, they had produced 2,722 kg of diamonds.

The crater is known as the 'Kimberley Hole' and is 240 metres in depth. It has a width of 463 metres and its surface area is seventeen hectares. While standing on a viewing platform, above the opening of the 'hole', it offered an amazing sight. Densely coloured green water, which lay motionless many metres below, was simply awesome. The steep sides of the hole were inlaid with huge rocks and interspersed with numerous trees of various sizes. Above ground and not far from the 'hole', a makeshift town had been created. Comprising of various buildings from the previous century, it had been erected to form a living museum. Our family found it all so interesting.

A signpost on the road leading out of Kimberley, pointed the way to Cape Town. It also pointed to Magersfontein, which was our next place to visit. In the year 1899, during the second South African War of Independence, a major battle took place at Magersfontein. British military forces were advancing towards Kimberley when they were halted by their enemy.

The enemy was mainly farmers, known simply as *Boers*. They had entrenched themselves at the foot of a range of hills, in front of the British advance. Pressing forward in tight formation, the British came under fire from the 'invisible' Boers. Casualties were in the hundreds.

During our time spent at the site, we were the only visitors. Rock-strewn ground lay all around us, and a dusty, straight road stretched towards the hills. The Boers had been ensconced at the hills on that fateful day. We stopped to take in the view. Climbing out of the campervan, I picked my way through the rocks which lay on the battleground. I tried to imagine what it must have been like for an infantryman on the day of the battle. Dotted about wherever I looked were clumps of thorn bushes. They were covered with sharp thorns, each about an inch long. To the Afrikaans-speaking person, they were known as 'wag 'n bietjie' or 'wait a bit' bushes. The title was derived from the thorns' ability to cling relentlessly to a person's clothing. Once hooked, the victim was obliged to spend a time in disentanglement.

I didn't know if the bushes were present at the time of the battle but it was easy to mentally morph them into British troops. Suddenly, my imagination was brought back to reality. A singular thorn had pierced my finger. Thick drops of my blood fell to the ground. Wrapping my handkerchief around the wound, I pondered the thought that I had actually shed blood on the Magersfontein battlefield!

From Kimberley to Cape Town was a long slog of 968 miles and mostly through a region of South Africa called the *Karoo*. Consisting mainly of semi-desert it has the dubious distinction of occupying one-third of the total area of the country.

Before leaving Johannesburg, we had heard various yarns from our work colleagues. Some said they had done the journey from Jo'burg to Cape Town in twenty-four hours! Another story maintained that huge trucks frequently used the route. It was said that Volkswagen Beetles had been flipped over by the passing truck's slip-stream! Having listened to all the advice, we decided to do the journey in whatever time it took. And furthermore, I took comfort in the knowledge that we were not driving a Volkswagen Beetle!

Sandra and I took turns to drive the campervan. The shared driving was a good arrangement but meant having to stop the van periodically to swop over. Odd as it might sound, stopping and changing places every hour or two became tedious. But at some part of the journey an idea sprang to mind. Thinking to spice up the task, we agreed to change places - but this time whilst still travelling!

In retrospect, it was a totally insane idea, but nevertheless, we did it. Sandra was driving along a stretch of straight open road where no vehicles were to be seen. It was then the two of us performed a manoeuvre, which any professional contortionist might have applauded. Of course, our physical frames were slimmer at that time.

Sandra stood partially upright and leaned forward over the steering wheel. At the same time, we both kept eye contact with the road. My legs adopted a frog-like stance, as I slid my body between Sandra and the upright part of the seat. The vehicle was travelling at between thirty and forty miles per hour. I took hold of the steering wheel with my right hand and let my body slowly descend onto the driving seat.

On the word of command, Sandra quickly let go of the wheel and slid her body sideways towards the passenger seat. My left hand took hold of the steering wheel, and my right foot pressed on the accelerator pedal. Mission accomplished! We congratulated ourselves on a successful outcome - albeit one that could have gone terribly wrong!

When our vehicle approached Cape Town we quickly recognised *Table Mountain*. The iconic centrepiece was so called because of its level top. And like a tablecloth draped over a dining table, a gathering of clouds silently and gracefully swirled over it. Rising from sea level against a pale blue sky, the combination of mountain and cloud looked magnificent. At this point of the journey, our home on wheels had just completed a jaunt of almost one and a half thousand miles, or one-fifth of our total planned journey. Spurred on by a desire to see more, we motored towards Simonstown. Located at False Bay, on the eastern side of the Cape Peninsula, Simonstown has served as a naval base and a harbour for more than two centuries. It was there we found a camping site from which we would make excursions to the nearby places of interest.

A southern journey of a few miles took us to Cape Point. It was from its rocky out-crops where we saw two oceans collide. They were the Atlantic and the Indian. Saying goodbye to Cape Point our campervan travelled the narrow road which passed through the Table Mountain National Park. It was there we saw some wild tortoises slowly amble across our path. We stopped to watch, as their scaly shells moved silently along. Their steady progress caused me to think. It seemed as though we were much like each other, because we travelled with our home around us!

On the way to the seaside village of Scarborough, Elanor and Nicola spotted a deserted stretch of beach. We halted the campervan where only a short distance away, the Atlantic Ocean glittered. Sea waves broke on an outcrop of rocks, producing sprays of white. By carefully placing our camping table and chairs, we partially avoided the frequent mild gusts of wind. Leaving Sandra to finish her coffee, our daughters and I made our way to the water's edge. It was then we realised the silent power of the sun. So hot was the sandy beach, that it made our bare feet hop and skip, before finding solace at a nearby rocky outcrop. Standing like human sentinels, we watched the sea waves. They rolled relentlessly forward, until breaking on the rocks around us, in a fierce frenzy of froth. Naturally, we felt the urge to put our feet into the cooling seawater. But what a shock! The sea genuinely felt ice-cold, and my feet quickly reached the point of aching!

Later that day, I noticed the lily-white skin of my tender feet was badly sunburnt. After all, having lived in England for most of my life, it had been many years since my feet last saw the sun! And when I came to put on my shoes, I discovered my feet were swollen. For the next day or two, as a substitute for shoes, my feet were obliged to wear slippers! Oh yes, I had packed my slippers for the holiday - after all, the campervan was home from home, was it not? However, it may be appreciated that frequently worn slippers need to be washed. So, on the morning we planned to leave the camping site, I washed them. The sun was high in the sky when I placed the wet slippers on the panel van's broad front bumper. I presumed they would steadily dry while our family enjoyed a leisurely breakfast. Preparing for our planned trip to Cape Town took over an hour to pack everything away.

The journey to Cape Town provided some scintillating scenery along the route. Our destination was the cable car station on the side of Table Mountain. On the outskirts of the city, some stretches of road allowed us to make good time. But the city centre was busy with traffic, and the various robots we encountered hampered our progress. Somehow, they managed to regularly show their red lights. Eventually, after negotiating the various twists and turns along the route, we arrived at the cable car's parking facility. Opening the door of the driver's cab, I climbed out. It was then I saw a sight which made my eyes pop. Sitting next to the spare wheel, on the van's front bumper-bar, was my pair of slippers! They had remained in situ throughout the whole journey! As a 'footnote' to this story (pardon the pun), the slippers were perfectly dry and ready to wear!

The next leg of our journey was the 670 miles from Cape Town to East London. Along the way, we would pass through the city of Port Elizabeth. [5] Ever in the shadow of mountains and craggy cliffs, a portion of the National Road from Cape Town to Port Elizabeth is known as the Garden Route. It derives its title from the indigenous Fynbos, which makes it the world's smallest and most diverse of all the floral kingdoms. On one side of it are the Outeniqua Mountains and on the other lies the Indian Ocean. Between the mountains and the ocean lies the famed Tsitsikamma Forest. It is cleft by lush, green kloofs and woven through with clear babbling streams. Exquisite fungi are to be found, and tree ferns which grow over three metres tall. The forest has over one hundred species of indigenous trees. Some of them provide rare and beautiful hardwoods, such as the stinkwood. But perhaps the best known is the yellowwood, whose honey-coloured timber is popular for the making of furniture and floorings.

Bird life around these trees is spectacular and rare. Not limited to the Cape Parrot, there is the Knysna Turaco and African pigeon. These indigenous birds live off the yellowwoods for food and shelter. Mammals are also found around the trees, which include monkeys, bush pigs, bats and rodents.

Standing guard over the tree-top canopy, in the heart of the forest, is the *Big Tree*. It is a yellowwood tree which is believed to be around eight hundred years old! This majestic tree stands over thirty-six metres tall, with a trunk circumference of around nine metres. In 1979, tourists had fun holding hands, whilst stretching around the nine-metre circumference of its trunk. Unfortunately, today, it is surrounded by protective fencing!

During our visit to the *Big Tree*, the guide told us an amusing anecdote. But before he began, he asked everyone a question.

"Who can tell me which part of the tree is the FRONT?"

Looks of puzzlement appeared on the faces of the many tourists as they spoke amongst themselves. Eventually, one brave soul returned a question.

"Excuse me" he said, "But just to be sure what you mean. Are you asking us to tell you where the front of the tree is located?"

"Ja - that's right", the guide replied. "Or, in other words, which part of the tree is its front?"

The tourists discussed the puzzling question amongst themselves. Now and then, looks of enlightenment appeared on some faces, but they quickly changed into doubtful expressions. Finally, in the end, the guide spoke.

"All right, I'll tell you the answer" he said. "A few weeks ago, I asked a group of tourists the same question. Before long, a little Irishman offered an answer."

"Sor," said the Irishman, "Oi tink oi 'ave der answer to yor question".

"Okay," said I, "What is it?"

The Irishman walked slowly around the tree, twice before stopping. Then, he casually pointed to the base of the tree. Everyone looked in the direction he was pointing. On the ground was a piece of crumpled paper. Beneath it, and partially out of sight, was a small mound of human excrement.

"Der is where der *back* of der tree is!" exclaimed the Irishman.

"The BACK of the tree and not the FRONT?" said I inquiringly.

"Dat's roit sor!" affirmed the Irishman. "Dat is the BACK of the tree!"

"Okay," said I. "And why do you say that?"

"Well, you see sor; no one ever shits at der FRONT of a tree!"

———◇———

Driving along the main highway towards Port Elizabeth, we caught sight of the famous *Apple Express*. The Class NG G16 Garratt steam engine was pulling a series of green-coloured carriages. It travelled the railway track, which covers a length of 177 miles, from Avontuur to Port Elizabeth. It claims to be the world's longest, narrow-gauge railway line and because it crosses the Van Stadens Railway Bridge, it is also the highest.

. The area's numerous apple farmers affectionately named the train service the *Apple-Express*. They employed the railway to transport the produce of their fruit industry, intended for export, to the Port Elizabeth harbour. Workers in the Gamtoos Valley copied their example by sending limestone from their quarries to the city's cement factory.

Our camper-van was parked at the side of the main road as we watched the Apple Express steam merrily on its way. For the most part, it travelled along a lush green valley against a backdrop of a tall mountainous ridge - which appeared to dwarf the iconic engine. About the same time, I noticed a stack of recently cut tree branches, which lay a short distance from us. An opportunity to gather some readily available firewood was not to be missed. The thought of having an evening braai also sprang to mind. Without hesitation, I picked up a few pieces and placed them on the floor of the camper. But as I placed a final piece onto the heap, I wasn't sure if I saw a slight movement. It came from under the bark, which had partially parted from the tree branch.

Giving the branch a quick, sharp rap on the ground, I distinctly saw the movement of a black-coloured object beneath the bark. When I gave the branch another and more determined rap, I got a big surprise. A sizeable black scorpion jumped to the ground! It instantly scurried away into the nearby scrub. Sandra and I wasted no time in double-checking the other branches. Breathing a huge sigh of relief, we were pleased not to find any more would-be passengers. Afterwards we discussed the whys and wherefores of scorpions. And much later discovered the black variety is quite dangerous, and reputed to have an aggressive nature.

It is a kind which can both sting and spray its kurtoxin venom. That night, after thanking my lucky stars, I rested easy, knowing we had escaped a potential tragedy.

Leaving Port Elizabeth behind, our next destination was to be the port city of East London. The vast area of land in-between them is known as the Eastern Cape and is home to a tribal group of people known as the Xhosa. Along the way, I caught sight of two Xhosa youths. Each with a woollen-blanket wrapped around their body and white-clay daubed on their face. Their appearance was part of a tribal ritual. My natural curiosity caused me to bring our campervan to a halt. After persuading the lads to pose for a photograph, I was given an impromptu surprise. As both youths smiled nicely, a sudden gust of wind blew a blanket to one side. The resultant view exposed more than the camera's film!

In the year of 1979, traditional rites and customs still had meaning in the lives of the Bantu. For Xhosa boys, circumcision and its attendant rites proclaimed their manhood. For a time, the initiates entered a spiritual no-man's land between boyhood and adulthood. Their state of being was symbolically reinforced through their physical seclusion in special huts – which were set aside from their village. During this time of their life, they were instructed in the ways of being men and would learn about their obligations to society. The high point of the initiation ritual was the circumcision ceremony. Many years ago, an assegai blade would have been used, but today, the boy had to face a knife. It was expected of the boy to show no fear, and if his courage failed him, he would bring dishonour to himself and his family. A further period of seclusion follows the ceremony, which gives the wound time to heal.

It is during this time the young men are smeared with white-clay. Realising our two friends were experiencing the necessary ritual, we wished them well and continued our journey.

After reaching East London, we visited its recommended museum. It contained a couple of very interesting objects. One of them had been acquired in 1935 by Marjorie Courtenay-Latimer, the then Curator of the museum. It is an egg of the Raphus cucullatus, which is a flightless bird and is believed to belong to the pigeon family. Its more popular name is the Dodo!

The Curator received the dodo egg from her great-aunt, Lavinia Bean, who had kept it as a valued family possession for many years. A cast was made of the egg, and along with a model of the dodo, they are displayed inside the museum for all to see. Meanwhile, on account of its value, the original egg is stored in a museum strong-room.

The second object is a Coelacanth. One morning in 1938, when the Curator received a telephone call, it turned out to be the start of an exciting day. A voice urged her to see a recent catch of fish, which was sitting at the dock-side. She could hardly believe her eyes when she saw a fish, which was considered to be extinct for 340 million years! The fish was carefully preserved and today is a major attraction at the museum.

My family saw the Coelacanth suspended inside a cabinet and looking quite miserable. Perhaps that was to be expected after having its innards removed and its remains treated with formalin! Originally, the five-foot-long fish was coloured 'a pale mauvy-blue, with faint white flecks of whitish spots.' But now, due to the formalin and the years spent at the museum, it has a drab golden-brown appearance.

Setting it apart from other fish are its 'hard scales' and its four, 'limb-like' fins; along with a strange 'puppy-dog tail'. It is because of the four 'limb-like fins' that the fish has been dubbed *Old Fourlegs*, and it is widely known by that name.

A few miles after leaving East London, we crossed the Great Kei River. The river provided a natural boundary between the areas of land, then known as the Ciskei and the Transkei. Once across the road bridge, we entered the independent homeland of Transkei. At that time, it was necessary for us to have our passports stamped; because technically we were leaving South Africa and entering another country!

In 1976 Transkei had been declared independent of South Africa. Throughout its limited existence, it was an internationally unrecognised and diplomatically isolated, one-party state. At one time, it actually broke relations with South Africa, which was the only country that acknowledged it as a legal entity. But in 1994, it was reintegrated into its larger neighbour and became part of the Eastern Cape Province.

From East London to Durban we clocked 418 miles, and after arriving in Durban, we had travelled more than half our planned route. Continuing our journey we took the coastal road from Durban, in Natal, to Mtunzini, in Zululand. The road edged the Indian Ocean, with its long stretches of unfettered beach. The rich golden sand reached out to the north and south of Zululand, as far as the eye could see.

A short distance from Mtunzini, the main highway took us away from the coast and headed inland. On the remaining homeward journey, we passed through eMpangeni, Piet Retief and Ermelo, before finally reaching Pretoria.

It was January 16$^{th}$ 1979, when we arrived home and parked the camper on our driveway. All too soon, the expedition had drawn to a close. It felt good to be home and to be surrounded by our familiar comforts. After living in a camper-van for three weeks, the use of a fully equipped kitchen, and some comfortable chairs to sit on, seemed wonderful. But above all, having a soft and luxurious bed to sleep on seemed heavenly. However, aside from all of this, something appeared to be different. Before we commenced our expedition, there had been a change of neighbours. The elderly Portuguese people, who lived behind our rear garden wall, had moved away. The newcomers, who were young Afrikaans-speaking people, immediately made changes to their habitat.

Our previous neighbours' delightful grape vines had been chopped down and in their place was a swimming pool! Soil from the digging was banked up against the neighbours' side of the dividing wall. It provided a platform from where spectators could stand and survey the pool. Unfortunately for us, they were also able to peer at our rear lawn. From then onwards, our privacy was compromised. The weekends, which had been previously quiet, were now disturbed by weekly braai and swim sessions. Of course, their many friends were often invited to join them. And considering the amount of litter we regularly lifted from our lawn, it seemed as though they had a shortage of refuse bins!

Nevertheless, we managed the situation, that is, until one particular day. Whilst doing my regular chore of mowing the lawn, I made a surprising discovery. Against the dividing wall, at its mid-way point, was a small bush. It was growing normally, except the grass, which lay immediately around its base, had turned white!

A careful inspection revealed a hole, which had been knocked through the wall at ground level. Backwash from our neighbours' swimming pool was allowed to flow onto our lawn. And chemicals in the pool's water caused discolouration of the grass. To avoid any argument with our neighbour I called the local municipality.

In due course, an Afrikaans-speaking, Government inspector called at our house. The slim-waisted, eagle-eyed man, wore a safari suit. It comprised a short-sleeved jacket and knee-length shorts. He also wore long woollen stockings. Displayed in one of them was a plastic hair comb, which poked a regulatory two inches above the stocking top. In those days, the practice was considered to be traditional amongst such officials. And for English speaking people, it was cause for some amusement. The inspector carried a clip-board and smoked a cigarette as he walked to the offending area. Deep in thought, he stroked his sleeked-back hair and peered through his black, thick-rimmed glasses at the discoloured grass.

Within a minute or two, the man turned to me and spoke.

"Jammer meneer, maar (sorry, mister but) because your land is lower than your neighbours' property, you are obliged to accept their storm water."

I made the inspector aware that it was not storm water but wastewater from their swimming pool. He thought some more before giving me a reply.

"Ja meneer that may be so, maar as the law states, you must still provide a means to accept the storm water". He quickly added, "However, you can decide where it may flow. And I think one corner of the lawn would be good."

The two properties were, in fact, built on a gradient, and it wasn't hard to see that our property was set lower than the other. But at one corner of the lawn, where it met the dividing wall, our daughters had a sand-filled play pit. With this in mind I chose to have the hole made at the other corner. The inspector agreed to tell our neighbours what must be done. But of course, because of our Cape Town expedition, we were not around to see his instructions carried out. It was only on returning home when the outcome was apparent.

An eight-inch diameter plastic pipe protruded almost a foot through a hole made in the concrete wall. And unfortunately for our daughters, the end of the pipe was just above their sand pit! It naturally followed that it provided passage for storm water, plus the swimming pool's back-wash! But it was too late to argue.

As it happened, the people with the swimming pool were not our only worry. Our neighbour to one side of our house had a young boy. He became the chief suspect when a series of eggs were smashed outside our kitchen door. Over a number of days, they were thrown individually, and each left a sticky mess. Later in the month, another incident occurred, which proved to be the proverbial 'last straw'. During our recent expedition I used a cine camera to record our progress. The camera used small reels of Kodak 8mm cine film. Once exposed, the reels of film were sent to a Kodak laboratory for processing. A bespoke, yellow-coloured postal packet was provided for the purpose. Some days later, the processed film would be returned to our home and placed in the letter box. The reader may recall that our letterbox was perched on a pole next to the front gate of our house.

As a point of interest, the postmen at that time wore a uniform of a khaki, short-sleeved shirt, and shorts, together with a white topee helmet. For transport, they rode a red-painted bicycle, and attached above its front wheel was a wire basket. The basket of course, held the mail items to be delivered. Overall, the postman presented a pleasing sight but sadly, I would say the helmets ceased to be used after the mid-1980s.

One day, long after our expedition, I was shocked to find an empty Kodak cine-film-packet, which lay on the ground and next to our letter-box. Presumably, someone had taken the roll of film and dropped the empty packet where it could be easily seen. Surely, the traditional thief would have taken both film and packet together? I believed that leaving the *empty packet* was deliberate and the thief was adding insult to injury. Sandra and I discussed the matter and jointly reached a verdict. Logically speaking, it seemed prudent for us to find a less troublesome area in which to live.

# 21

## A MOVE TO THE WEST RAND

A few weeks after finding the empty Kodak cine-film packet, Sandra presented me with a copy of the Johannesburg *Star* newspaper. Her finger pointed to a column on the *Property for Sale* page. Excitedly, she asked the question,

"Have you seen this?"

Four lines of type described a property for sale. It was an eight roomed house, along with a double garage and other smaller units. In addition to the property, was a plot of land measuring two and a half hectares. Remarkably, the asking price was 19,000 Rand!

This seemed like a Heaven-sent opportunity. It meant we could be free from troublesome neighbours and have the option to maybe take up a little farming! However, there was a downside to the idea. The property was near the town called Randfontein, which was on the West Rand. It was a considerable distance from the Siemens' factory. But following a lengthy discussion, we both agreed it wouldn't do us any harm to have a look; now would it?

A telephone call confirmed our appointment with an estate agent. The agent's building stood on the outskirts of Randfontein. Arriving in good time, we entered a rustic-looking office. Standing next to an antique desk was the estate agent.

His friendly but gravelly sounding voice welcomed us.

"Goeie môre mense" (Good morning, people), he said. "My name is Piet."

We exchanged a few pleasantries, but when offered a cup of tea, we politely declined. A glance at the tea-cups and their state of cleanliness had influenced our choice! Affable as he was, the agent fell short of my idea of a salesperson. He was no suave, smooth-talking city-slicker. Instead, he portrayed, let's say, a certain casual style. A two-piece suit hung limply on his body. A small patch on a jacket pocket suggested it had seen better days. A weather-beaten, bucket-style, sun-hat was perched on his head. Meanwhile, hanging from a corner of his mouth was a burning Lexington cigarette. Its smoke rose lazily, causing one eye to squint. And his partially closed lips made it difficult for him to speak.

"Would you like to see the property now?" he mumbled.

Nodding our heads approvingly, he proceeded to usher us out of the office. Pointing to a vacant parking place, the estate agent made a suggestion.

"Why not leave your car here, and I'll take you to the plot?"

With three or four miles to travel, we crammed into the agent's old Chevrolet saloon. The car's scratched and dented paintwork, and its tired upholstery, seemed to complement its driver! For a few minutes, we drove along the main Carletonville road before reaching a district called *Hillside*. Turning into *Road No. 1* the car continued until it met a tee-junction, where it joined a graded-road named *Pemberthy*. Driving a short distance along Pemberthy, we arrived at a gate opening.

The Chevrolet attempted to climb an ill-defined thoroughfare which lay before us. Impregnated with partially submerged, irregular-shaped stones, it resembled a war-time battlefield, with its attendant landmines. Two shallow ruts spaced evenly apart, flanked a ridge of higher ground which stood between them. It induced any reasonable motorist to proceed with caution. Looking to the left of the driveway was a low, barbed-wire fence. It marked the boundary between two plots of land.

Over the fence, the land was cultivated and played host to a profusion of growing vegetables. But the land to our right was somewhat different. Its unkempt state contrasted sharply with its neighbour. Large furrows from earlier farming activity were overgrown with sun-bleached, coarse grass. Patches of khaki-bos grew in clumps of up to three feet in height. At the far side of this aberration of nature stood the remnants of a brick-built, water-storage tank. Portions of its circular wall were visible, but much of it extended beneath ground level. Abandoned long ago, it was partially filled with all kinds of detritus.

The sun was high in the sky as the old Chevrolet slowly clawed its way up the track. Occasionally, its chassis scraped the higher ground. At those moments, Piet's lips quivered, as he faintly muttered words of contempt! Reaching the top of the drive, stalks of torn grass involuntarily festooned the saloon's front bumper bar. The surrounding ground levelled off and formed a wide plateau. It stretched from one side of the plot to the other. A large tree with spreading branches became an instant car-port for the agent's car. Standing a short distance away was a single-storey house. Its structure reminded me of a Swiss chalet.

Producing a bunch of keys from his jacket pocket, Piet invited us to follow him. Unlocking a door at one end of the house, he revealed a primitive looking kitchen. A cast-iron, wood-burning stove stood against a wall. Although designed specifically for cooking, it also served as a means of heating the house. Fortunately, South Africa's winter period is usually quite mild. And in this part of the Transvaal (Gauteng), the worst of winter usually amounts to little more than a few mornings of light frost.

Standing against an adjacent wall was an unsteady wooden frame. It supported a well-used stainless-steel sink. While in a corner of the room, mounted horizontally against the ceiling, was a modern water cylinder. In England, it would be known as an 'immersion heater', but in South Africa, it was simply called a 'geyser'. Either way, with the use of electrical power it provided the house with hot water. The bathroom was nothing special but it did have the essentials. Altogether, including the kitchen and bathroom, were eight rooms. None were furnished, and all were without floor covering.

Meanwhile, standing a few yards from the house was a quaint but essential feature. It was a wind-powered water-pump. Standing proudly against the backdrop of a blue, sun-filled sky, its wind-vanes squeaked as they slowly turned. All the while, water was pumped from under the ground and into a catchment tank, adjacent to the house. As I gazed at the turning wind-vanes, the estate agent interrupted my fleeting thoughts.

"Ja, well nee, meneer" he said, taking a smoking cigarette from his mouth. "This plek (place) is worth every penny of the price. And let me tell you this, for every cent you put into this plek, it will be doubled!"

His words prompted me to think of the future. I glanced across the short stretch of land towards Sandra and our girls. Standing not far from the house, they were discussing a large, brick-built water tank. Its circular wall stood four feet above the ground, while a further six feet visibly extended beneath ground level. It was filled, for the most part, with clear water. In South African parlance, it is called a *dam*, and the water is normally used to irrigate arable land. But the ladies were discussing how the dam and its contents would make a suitable swimming pool!

Midway, between the wind-pump and the dam, was a *rondavel*. Such buildings were a popular form of dwelling place for the Bantu. Cylindrical in shape and eight feet in height, its brick-built wall had a singular window and doorway. Both the doorframe and its door were made of strengthened tin. The choice of metal was a necessary precaution against the infestation of termites. However, the roof structure was a skeletal framework of wooden poles. Assembled in the shape of an umbrella, they were covered with thatch.

Noticing my discerning look, the agent took the opportunity to spin a little more sales talk. Pointing towards the far side of the plot, he began.

"Ja, well nee, meneer, daar (there) is many fruit trees. Daar is peach, and fig, and even prickly pear. They produce fruit every year, and your vrou (wife) can make some lekker (nice) jam from them all."

Intrigued by the mention of 'prickly pear', I asked Piet to tell me more. Before answering, he took a box of *Lion* matches from his jacket pocket. A finger and thumb fumbled inside the opened box.

Moving about with a seeming will of their own, the tiny sticks of wood evaded their fleshy predators. Finally, one was captured and struck. Its burning flame was held against the end of yet another cigarette. Piet took several long draws before it glowed red and hung from his closed lips.

"Ja, well nee, meneer," said Piet after drawing hard again on the newly lit cigarette. Gesturing towards a brick-built enclosure he added, "Can you see the pigsty over daar?" My eyes followed the direction of his pointing finger.

"If you look to one side of the sty, you may see a large cactus bush".

Sure enough, I saw one with its spade-like branches spread outwards in a haphazard fashion.

"Ja well, nee meneer. If you look at the ends of the branches, you may see fruit growing. They are shaped like pears but have tiny, sharp hairs covering their skin. The hairs look like beard stubble on an ou toppie's (old man's) face. But passop, (take care) if you get those goeters (things) in your fingers - yerr, they itch like hell!"

I was tempted to laugh at his explanation, but I needed to know more.

"So, tell me, Piet, can you eat the prickly pears?"

My sudden question caused him to interrupt his incessant smoking. Having taken a long draw from his latest Lexington, he swallowed the smoke. "Ja, meneer, jy can", he said, as the cigarette smoke began to wisp from his nose and mouth. "Maar, it's best to put them in a fridge overnight. The next day, you can strip off the outer skin".

"But be sure to wear gloves. Inside is a soft fruit with a lekker (nice) taste. Maar (but) in the middle is baie (many) seeds, so passop for them. You don't want to eat them."

At this juncture, I caught sight of a small brick outhouse, which stood at a far corner of the plot. At its entrance was an elderly Bantu couple who were watching our movements. Realising I had seen them, the agent offered some advice.

"Ja, well nee, meneer, monie (don't) worry about those mense (people). They are from the previous owner and will soon be gone."

Accepting his promise I wandered over to the circular dam.

"So, what do you think, young ladies?"

Filled with excitement, Elanor and Nicola replied.

"Ooh, daddy, we think its lekker!"

Sandra looked towards me and gave a smile. At that moment the agent spoke his closing piece.

"Ja well, nee mense, I can assure you of one thing. Hierdie plek (this place) is good value for money. And it's got lots of potential."

Little did we know those words would return to haunt us in the months which followed.

That night, Sandra and I discussed the events of the day. We both agreed a pertinent question needed to be answered. "Do we, or don't we, buy the plot?" During much deliberation, we considered what needed to be done. Firstly, our house would have to be sold.

Then, there was the required deposit for the sale of the plot. Sadly, in order to provide the cash, our car, with less than 4000 kilometres on its odometer, would have to be sold. But in the grand scheme of things, it was considered a small sacrifice to make for such an epic gain. Finally, we decided to make an offer. As we retired for the night, we looked at each other and laughingly repeated the estate agent's words:

"It's got lots of potential!"

*"It reminded me of a Swiss chalet"*

*The dam, rondavel and wind-pump*

# 22

# SPION KOP AND BOSJESSPRUIT COLLIERY

Our work colleagues were astonished to learn we were moving to Randfontein. One of them even tried to dissuade us.

"So, you're going to boere territory?" he said. "Are you mad? They hate the English, you know!"

His words were reminiscent of the ones spoken in England before our journey of adventure began. Didn't someone say I would get an assegai in my back? So far, my body had remained un-punctured, but I did consider the latest advice.

The West Rand was noted for its population of mainly Afrikaans speaking people. They were the descendants of European settlers who had experienced historic conflicts with the British authority. The Anglo-Boer War of 1899 - 1902 was the most recent and less than a hundred years prior to our arrival in the country. Many people who had witnessed something of the war were still living. For them and, in many cases, their descendants, the actions of the British during that conflict were very much on their minds. As a result of the past, the English and Afrikaans speaking populace tended to favour living in segregated areas.

Unfortunately, knowing very little about the Anglo-Boer conflict, we blissfully went ahead with our plans.

Along with negotiating the sales of both our car and house, I searched for a suitable job vacancy. It was thought that employment nearer to the plot's location would make our daily life easier. Good fortune favoured me again. I found an English company named Laurence, Scott, and Electromotors, or L.S.E. for short. It manufactured a range of bespoke electric motors - or "drives" as they were called. The company was represented in Johannesburg and advertised the vacancy for a *Service Engineer*. The job entailed travel within South Africa and offered the personal use of a company car.

The Rand Water Board was the authority responsible for supplying potable water to the populace of the Transvaal (Gauteng) Province. For that purpose, some powerful variable-speed 'drives' were purchased from L.S.E. They were installed at various water pumping stations, to drive huge mechanical water pumps. In addition to the Rand Water Board, L.S.E. supplied electric drives to the newly constructed Sasol II coal liquefaction plant. Sited at the town of Secunda, the plant processed coal to produce a range of liquid fuels.

A few days after attending the L.S.E. job interview, I received a letter offering me the post. Like the prize-winning rollers of a slot machine, everything suddenly fell into place. My position at L.S.E. was confirmed, and my notice at the Siemens factory was served. Our Opel Ascona was sold and the money was used to pay a deposit for the sale of the plot. With some cash left over, we bought a used Volkswagen Beetle. Sandra took charge of the beetle, while I had the use of the company car.

Meanwhile, our beloved campervan transported all our belongings from Solheim to the West Rand. It took several journeys of seventy kilometres before we finally settled into our new home. Eventually, with some time to spare, Sandra and I wandered around our extensive estate; all 2.5 hectares of it!

Giving it a leisurely inspection, we stopped to share our opinions. "Well" I announced, "I suppose it could do with a touch of tender loving care."

"A touch!" Sandra exclaimed, "Surely, a *huge shove* would be more appropriate?"

During our tour of inspection, I suddenly remembered the Bantu who resided at the top corner of our plot. The estate agent who had assured me they would be gone, was mistaken! Gingerly I approached them. Silently, they stood there with expressionless faces. Their eyes looked at me with a cold blank stare. With an uneasy feeling I asked them to leave. I wasn't sure if they understood my words, but ultimately, there was little doubt they grasped the meaning of my hand gestures!

Days later, whilst inspecting their abandoned dwelling place, a disembodied male voice hailed me. It sounded from over the adjoining neighbour's fence. Speaking English, with a pronounced Afrikaans accent, the voice stated the Bantu were now living there. The revelation caused me to feel like an ogre. But reason had me think I had never agreed to employ anyone. After all, the main object of leaving our previous home was to find some privacy.

Weekends were spent with my family, when we shared the many jobs to help improve the standard of our new home.

While during the week I would drive into Johannesburg and attend the L.S.E. offices, based at Braamfontein. My job entailed a fair amount of office work, such as writing reports or organising spare parts for client's machines. On occasions, I was sent to remote locations to investigate faults with certain L.S.E. drives.

An example was a water pumping station named Zuikerbosch. Located near the town of Vereeniging, the station employed a number of variable-speed machines. They drove huge water pumps, which supplied the townsfolk with drinking water. Since the demand for the supply of water varied, the speed of the pumps needed to be regulated.

One day, a seasoned L.S.E. engineer arrived in Johannesburg from England. I was requested to accompany him to the province of Natal. We were to visit the Jagersrust water-pumping station, at the foot of the Drakensberg mountain range. An unusual problem had occurred associated with a bespoke water-pump drive. The two of us climbed into my company car and set off. The Mark III - Ford Cortina Estate, with its 2.5-litre engine, proved to be admirable when making long journeys.

Heading in the direction of Jagersrust, during the final leg of our travel, the main asphalt road joined one of compacted soil. Its surface was baked by the Natalian sun and appeared like corrugated sheeting. Previous torrents of rain water had created its shallow undulations. They caused the car's suspension to react violently. The wheels jumped up and down like drumsticks beating a retreat. While inside the car, the noise was deafening. Coupled with that, choking dust found its way through the tiny gaps around the ill-fitting doors.

However, from a distance, it must have been a spectacular sight. Against the backdrop of the Drakensberg Mountain range and overshadowed by a clear blue sky, the car produced a rooster's tail of rising, red-coloured dust. Putting aside our discomfort the senior engineer turned to me. Above the constant noise he gleefully shouted,

"I've always wanted to do this!"

Our mission was to inspect a fault with a synchronous induction motor, which was vertically coupled to a water-pump. Standing at floor level, the engineer and I gazed at its lofty height. When viewed from a distance, we must have appeared like dwarfs!

Like most electric drives, it was supplied with voltage, and its output was rated in horsepower. As it was, this monstrous machine was energised by eleven thousand volts and rated at 1035 horsepower! Imagine for a moment the collective power of over a thousand live horses!

Earlier, on our journey to Jagersrust, I noticed a road sign which pointed the way to *Spion Kop*. The name was given to a hill where, during the Anglo-Boer War of 1899-1902, a battle had taken place. The Afrikaans spelling is 'Spieon Kopp' which means a hill to lookout from. Many soldiers from England's county of Lancashire had died there. Having completed our task, the engineer and I agreed to visit the site. We drove to the hill's lower slope and parked the car. It was an arduous walk up the hillside in the heat of the day. Almost reaching the hill's summit, we came across a long, narrow grave. It was about the length of two single-deck buses and almost the width of one. In the year 1900, British soldiers had climbed the route we had taken.

Making the climb during the night, they reached what they thought was the summit of the hill. And for their protection, they dug, as best they could, a shallow trench. But when daylight came, they sadly realised there was some way to walk before reaching the actual summit. And unfortunately for them, their enemy lay in waiting. An exchange of rifle fire began and was soon joined by shelling from distant artillery. By the end of the day, there were many dead and wounded. The British dead were gathered and the trench, which they had previously dug, became their grave!

During the 1960s the South African Government came under pressure from external forces. Cuban troops in their thousands occupied Angola and posed a threat. Ultimately, conflict broke out and continued into the 1990s. It was known as *The Border War*. In addition to this, the United States of America and Great Britain instituted sanctions against the South African Government. Their intention was to bring about the end of Apartheid and, ultimately, a change of Government. But contrary to expectations, and in the face of all adversity, the stoic resolve of South Africa's leaders, steered their country on a course for survival. National service was introduced for all its citizens and technologically advanced weapons were developed.

Fuel used to propel military vehicles was home-produced. To achieve this, a process of obtaining petroleum from coal was copied from German scientists, who had developed the method during World War II. Fortunately for South Africa it has huge coal reserves and ample space to build factories.

Sited in the province of Mpumalanga, a little over a hundred kilometres south-east of Johannesburg, two coal liquefaction plants were built. Operated by the Sasol Mining Company, they were named Sasol I and Sasol II. Construction of the second plant commenced in the year 1976. To cater for the thousands of Sasol employees, a new town was built and named *Secunda*.

At the Sasol II plant, coal was processed to produce petroleum, diesel and jet fuel, as well as a variety of phenols, ethylene, propylene and ammonic. To this day, Sasol fuel is available for sale at most of the country's filling stations. It is supplied from a bespoke pump which stands alongside the regular ones. However, Sasol fuel usually costs more to buy than the regular brands.

To provide coal for the Sasol plants, a coal mine was created. It was named *Bosjesspruit Colliery* and was said to be the biggest coal mine in the southern hemisphere. Towards the end of 1979, I was instructed to visit the colliery to investigate a problem with an L.S.E. electric drive.

Whilst driving to the Bosjesspruit coalmine, I witnessed the construction of a power station's cooling-tower. Mesmerized by its enormity, I stopped briefly to watch the progress. A powered winch hoisted a large steel bucket to the top of the tower. The bucket carried tonnes of ready-mixed concrete. Ascending slowly, it took a few minutes for the attached steel cable to do its job. Unfortunately, when it reached the top, the bucket snagged. And instead of the concrete emptying onto the tower, it was sent plummeting towards the ground! I watched in awe as the mass of concrete, which initially appeared as the size of a small car, cascaded earthwards.

During the descent it steadily broke into smaller portions. And by the time the load had reached the tower's halfway point, there was nothing left to be seen! I can only imagine if anyone was standing at ground level and beneath the bucket, they might have experienced light 'rain' in the form of damp particles of cement!

Bosjesspruit Colliery used a 'long-wall' method of mining. This means a solid seam of coal, or 'long wall', is mined. Using sophisticated technology, the coal can be cut in a single slice of up to a metre in thickness. And the slice may be up to a kilometre in length.

Before making the descent to the working coal mine, I was kitted out with protective clothing. Clad in overalls and protective boots, together with a safety helmet and its battery-powered lamp, I looked every bit like a working coalminer. Minutes later, I was many feet underground. Stepping out of the hoist, I was directed towards the working area known as the 'long-wall'. Stretched in front of me was an oblong-shaped tunnel. Its length disappeared into the distant darkness. Known as 'the gallery', it was cut out of the coal seam.

Sidewalls of solid coal rose above me. The width of the tunnel was similar to that of a narrow two-lane road. Covering the ground was a thin layer of coal dust, into which my protective boots plodded. Walking was relatively easy, except for the occasional shallow depression - for which I kept a sharp lookout. Guiding my way was a narrow beam of light, which shone from my helmet's battery-powered lamp. It was the only light present. Within the dark but dry surroundings, a continuous cool stream of ventilation air pushed gently against me.

After walking for a few minutes, with the heavy battery pack tugging on my waist-belt, I heard the ominous sound of a machine. It was some distance away but seemed to be heading towards me. As the rumbling sound grew progressively louder, whatever was responsible remained indiscernible.

After a little while, two large, shining discs mysteriously materialised in the darkness. They seemed to be floating about three feet above the ground. As they moved at a steady pace towards me, I soon realised they were a vehicle's headlights. Drawing ever closer, the sound grew louder. It was time for me to move out of its way. Fortunately, sheltering points were formed in the sidewalls of the tunnel. Made at regular intervals, they were large enough for a person seeking refuge to stand upright.

I made a bee-line for the nearest one and waited inside. The headlights grew progressively larger. Steadily, the machine got within a few feet of my refuge. As it trundled past me, the narrow beam of light from my helmet's lamp picked out portions of its form. For a second or two, I saw it clearly. It was a motorised vehicle - or rather the chassis of one - looking like a montage on a black screen. Its driver, exposed to his surroundings, sat motionless with a fixed, forward stare.

The vehicle's wheels disturbed the layer of coal dust which lay on the ground. It rose upward, acting like a billowing swarm of microscopic locusts. Just as quickly, the rising coal-dust appeared to gobble up the light from my helmet's lamp. I had no way of escaping. Slowly and inevitably, the light beam disappeared before my very eyes!

Within seconds, I was standing in total darkness! Thankfully, the situation was brief. Almost without delay, a reversal of the experience occurred. The beam of light, whilst still shining from my helmet, slowly reappeared before my eyes. A little time passed before reaching its full potential and I was able to continue my journey.

Eventually, I reached the end of the darkened gallery, where it converged with a lateral tunnel. At that point it formed a tee-junction and I had reached the 'long wall'. The area was brightly illuminated by floodlights, which allowed me to see a marvel of engineering. Standing against the face of a solid wall of coal, was specialised machinery. A long row of hydraulic steel rods, known as 'chocks,' were attached to steel plates. Placed side by side, they pressed against the ceiling of coal and held it in place. Each section was about two metres in width, and collectively, they stretched for about four hundred metres.

From ground to ceiling measured five or six metres. Located beneath the steel ceiling-plates was a huge mechanical 'arm'. It carried a circular steel disc. Fitted with cutting teeth, the disc rotated at a controlled speed and traversed the wall of coal. Acting like a giant bacon slicer, the disc's cutting teeth continuously sliced chunks of coal off the wall. And waiting beneath the falling coal, was a motorised conveyor belt, which continually carried the coal away. The whole spectacle demonstrated automation in action.

A small number of Bantu operators performed various tasks, while a male European stood watching. Because he was tall and thick-set, it occurred to me that he might be an Afrikaner. Gingerly, I approached him.

As I introduced myself I managed to utter a few words of greetings in the Afrikaans language. They were ones I had recently memorised. But imagine my surprise when he let me know - and in no uncertain terms - that he was from Scotland!

We chatted for a while and I soon discovered he had lived in South Africa only a few months longer than me. Considering the radical change of his environment, that is, from Scotland to South Africa, a question occurred to me.

"How do you like working with the Bantu?" I asked.

"Well, laddie", he replied, "To tell yoos the trooth, I'd rather work wi' a muntu than an Afrikaner."

"Why is that?"

Lowering his head, he leaned closer to me.

"Because"- he said, "at least yoos knows which ways the fookin' knife's cumin'!"

The man offered to show me the electric-drive which presented a problem. An inspection revealed that condensation was forming inside its electrical connection box. Needless to say, water and high-voltage electricity don't get along together. The problem needed to be resolved. I duly made some notes and bade my Scottish friend farewell, before returning to Johannesburg.

# 23

# WIND-PUMP AND WATER

One important feature of our Hillside plot was the tall, wind-powered water-pump. Many is the time I watched its lofty wind-vanes, as they turned gracefully in the gentle breeze of a sun-filled day. The movement filled me with admiration. Perhaps it was to be expected since our family depended upon its rotation to provide us with potable water.

When we first arrived at our new home, the machine worked efficiently. Pumping water from an underground source produced an abundant supply. But a few weeks later the delivery had noticeably reduced. I soon discovered the pump had certain mechanical parts which required periodic renewal. Luckily for me, a tradesman who was able to help lived up the road from our residence and I decided to pay him a visit.

Leaving our property, I walked a short distance along *Pemberthy road* before joining *Road No. 1*. Following the gradual slope of the hillside, *Road No 1* bordered one side of our neighbours' plot. During my walk I was able to view the surrounding countryside. In every direction barbed-wire fencing demarcated the land into individual plots. Plodding up the hill, I caught sight of the entrance to my neighbours' land. An open gate leaned awkwardly against the barbed wire of the perimeter fencing.

A short driveway led to a bizarre-looking house. Occupying a top corner of the plot, the house was dark in appearance. It had a roof of rusty, corrugated iron sheets, and its walls were a mix of wood and brick. Window frames made from wood, appeared in desperate need of paint. Hessian sacking, draped across two windows, hung apologetically in the absence of curtains. Distributed haphazardly around the front of the house were items of farming equipment. Stacks of thin, wooden seed boxes stood in rows. And due to their height, they leaned precariously to one side. They gave the impression of miniature towers of Pisa.

A large dog presented himself as a bull-mastiff. Like a sentry on guard duty, he ambled around the house frontage, sniffing the ground as if searching for something. A short distance from him was a muntu. Dressed in a dirty white shirt and a pair of worn corduroy trousers, he tended to some chickens. Rolled up shirt sleeves exposed dark-brown arms, while a tattered sombrero shielded his head from the searing sun.

Immediately behind the house was a tall, breeze-block wall. It marked the boundary of the two plots. At a distance of about thirty feet from the other side of the wall was *our* house. The positioning of both properties was deliberate. It allowed for maximum use of the land. On our side of the wall was a large tree. Beneath its leafy branches is where we normally parked our vehicles. It was a natural shelter from the sun's baking rays.

Before continuing up the hillside, I caught sight of my neighbours' dam. The circular, brick-built structure stood near the driveway. And not unlike others I had seen it was part above and part below ground. Except that this one was filled to the brim with irrigation water.

Contrasting sharply with our plot, the neighbours' land appeared well cultivated. Regularly watered crops of various vegetables grew along demarcated furrows.

A few minutes later, I was chatting with the friendly wind-pump mechanic. Mister Nicholaiessen and his wife welcomed me to their home, as seven dogs and two cats wandered freely in and out of the main room. The man's body was thick-set and sturdily built. A noticeable feature was his bulbous nose, which protruded below his close-set eyes. His leather-like skin suggested much time had been spent in the sunlight.

Their house was well furnished and almost to the point of being cluttered. A large, antique pedal-organ stood against a wall. Numerous old clocks of various sizes faced me from different directions. Aside from repairing wind-pumps, I guessed that fixing clocks was the mechanic's hobby. Standing against another wall was a very old refrigerator. It was the kind in which a large block of ice was placed in a top-most compartment. I surmised it hadn't been used for its original purpose in many years.

The ceiling looked deceivingly modern. It was constructed from lengths of tongue and grooved, knotty pine wood lathes. Set aside at the rear of the house was a large garage. It was filled with all manner of steel pipes and what appeared to be scrap iron. And in keeping with the house - as might be expected - was a large tract of land. Two cows looked at me lazily, with their half-closed eyes, while near them stood some grazing sheep. Mister Nicholaiessen noticed me looking at the cows. Suddenly, he was reminded to ask a question.

"How would you like to buy some fresh milk?" he asked. "It's just two Rand for five litres!"

How could I refuse?

Eventually, we discussed the need for my wind-pump and arranged for him to renew the worn parts.

Earlier that day, as I approached his house, I had noticed something unusual. The land behind both my own and that of my neighbours' plot was vacant. It was fenced off and demarcated into two plots of equal area. On the land immediately behind my neighbour's plot is where I saw the unusual sight. Dug in the ground, a few feet from the edge of Road No. 1, were four clearly defined graves. And contrary to the usual oblong shape - which would normally accept a coffin - these were the shape of a body. They had a head and shoulders and the straight, full-length of a person. The graves were dug to around two feet in depth and lay adjacent to each other in a lateral line. I wasn't overly interested at the time, but my curiosity caused me to mention them.

"What are those graves for?" I asked Mister Nicholaiessen.

"What graves?" he blurted, appearing taken aback.

"The ones in the veld, across the road," I said. "All four are empty dug-outs."

A look of displeasure appeared on his face.

"Empty, you say? There will be serious trouble if they've been moved."

I think he was aware of them and maybe knew their history, but I didn't pursue the matter. That was all that was said on the subject, and I didn't give it any further thought. But in retrospect, I wish I had.

When I consider the string of events which happened during our tenure at the plot, I think that possibly there may have been a connection. They *were* clearly gravesites, but the question "Who had been buried in them?" remained unanswered. Perhaps a clue lay in the history of South Africa. In the early pioneering days, it was not uncommon for people to bury their relatives on their farmland. When considering the number of plots which constitute the district of Hillside, it is likely that collectively they were once a large farm. But other questions sprang to mind. Were the graves old, or were they modern? And, if they had been used, what had happened to the occupiers? Sadly, I never found out.

Some days later, the friendly Mister Nicholaiessen arrived at our plot. He got busy with his experienced hands, and within an hour or two, the wind-pump was refurbished. Once more, its vanes turned briskly, and our water supply was plentiful.

Standing proudly next to the wind-pump was our thatched rondavel. The reader may remember my earlier description. Sadly, its appearance was destined to be altered. Returning home from work one afternoon, the wheels of my car cautiously picked their way along the rough driveway. As the car neared the house, I instantly noticed a change to the nearby, sun-bleached grass. Normally, at this time of year, it forms a natural golden carpet. However, on this occasion, its colour had changed from golden to burnt - black, and in the space of just a few hours!

But seconds later, a much worse sight became apparent. The blackened grass stretched from the driveway and up to the base of the rondavel. And when the car was in line with the structure, I stopped and looked aghast.

The rondavel's thatched roof - which was satisfactory at my early morning departure - was now no more! All that remained were the smouldering stumps of the roof trusses!

Unknown to me, my neighbours' muntu had seen my car arriving home. Surreptitiously, he climbed over the perimeter fence. Meanwhile, standing in front of the rondavel, I was part in shock and part in disbelief. The whole scene was like a bad dream. Seemingly from nowhere, the neighbours' muntu appeared and greeted me with the words: "Ola baas." His unexpected presence had the effect of jolting me back to reality.

"Sorry, baas," he said as he nervously fingered his sombrero. "Me burning rubbish - de wind blew fire to grass - de fire jump fence and burn de grass - de fire jump high and burn rondavel - Sorry baas!"

What could I say or do? Inside the rondavel, burnt pieces of wood lay strewn about its concrete floor. Its glass window panes had shattered due to the heat. An electrical distribution box - containing wiring and circuit breakers - was destroyed. It was obvious the overall damage would cost a lot to repair. Much later, when Sandra arrived home she too was shocked by what she saw. But the practical side of her nature quickly thought of a solution to the problem.

"We have house insurance, don't we?" she asked.

It was a light-bulb moment.

"Why yes, we do," said I. "I'd forgotten about that. That could be the answer to our troubles. We can claim on our insurance! Good thinking, my dear!"

Following some lengthy negotiation, the insurance company paid us a sum of money. Of course, it would have been preferable to have the insurer reinstate the roof, but as it happened, the cash proved to be more beneficial. As it was, Sandra had the use of our old Volkswagen beetle, so it followed that the money would enable us to upgrade. The re-roofing was put on hold and we began a search for a replacement car.

Within a week or two, I answered a promising newspaper advertisement. A Johannesburg Jewish accountant was retiring from work and selling his MK3 Ford Escort. He planned to buy a new car - which he intended to be his last. The Ford Escort was pale blue in colour and registered a modest 29,000 Km 'on the clock'. Its condition was very good, save for a medium-size dent on the rear wing. The seller explained it had been sustained whilst reversing from his driveway. He was asking a sum of 800 Rand for the car. By an odd coincidence, the figure exactly matched the sum we received from the insurer! Sandra became the proud driver of a relatively new Ford Escort. And as for the dent in the rear wing - well - I thought it gave the car some character!

# 24

## CHILDREN SEE GHOSTLY FIGURES

Sandra and I often took turns reading a bedtime story to our daughters. Afterwards, their bedroom light was switched off, and they usually drifted off to sleep fairly quickly. One book I tirelessly enjoyed reading was the classic story of 'Little Red Riding Hood'.

"Grandma, what big *eyes* you have", said Little Red Riding Hood.

"All the better to see you with my dear" was the wolf's reply.

Of course, I embellished the story-telling by using improvised voices. And for effect, I would growl while slowly uttering the wolf's spoken words. The girls would listen without interruption until I read the most familiar lines. At that moment they happily joined in.

But when I read the words: "Grandma, what *big* teeth you have," the girls would duck their heads under their bed-clothes and wait excitedly for the wolf's reply. The wolf finally answered with a growl,

"All the better to EAT YOU WITH MY DEAR!"

Instantly, I would lightly grab the girls' enshrouded shoulders. And at that moment they would respond with a light scream, followed with a few giggles. It was all harmless fun!

At the breakfast table one morning, Elanor announced she had a story of her *own* to tell *us*. But this one was seriously different. She said that the night before, she and her sister had seen ghosts! Sharing the same bedroom, the girls' single beds were placed side by side, about a metre apart. The headboards leaned against a wall, which faced the two previously mentioned plots of land. One of which had the vacated grave sites.

"Sometime after going to sleep", Elanor said, "I was awakened by a strong feeling that someone was in our bedroom. I sat up in bed and looked at the far side of the room. There, I saw a string of short people at the foot of our beds and walking across the room. The person leading the group of three or four was wearing clothing like that of a ringmaster at a circus. He wore a kind of top-hat, with a jacket which had tails."

Elanor does not clearly remember the others because the sighting was a scary experience. And soon after seeing the apparitions, she ducked under the bedclothes. A second or two later, she heard Nicola quietly call her.

"Elanor - Do you see those people?" she asked.

Apparently, Nicola was awake and was watching the same spectacle as her sister. Elanor pulled the bedclothes from her face and answered Nicola.

"Yes, I do" she admitted.

At that moment, the ghostly people changed direction and passed in-between the two beds. Both girls saw the ghostly figures seemingly walk through the outside wall of their bedroom! Once again, they ducked under their bedclothes.

Seconds later, when they mustered the courage to look, the ghostly figures were gone!

More than forty years later my daughters still remember the visitation. But what had they seen? Had they hallucinated? Or could the ghosts have been historically related to something which happened within our house? Or were they perhaps connected with the empty graves dug in the nearby veld? Fortunately, our daughters were unperturbed by their nocturnal encounter and next day, pursued their normal activities.

Near the corner of the plot, where our 'inherited' Bantu had lived, was a medium-sized tree. Attached to one of its few strong branches was a length of sturdy rope. Its loose end was tied to an old car tyre. What better form of swing could a girl wish for? And before anyone could say, "Be careful", the two sisters were having fun. Sitting with legs dangling from the tyre's centre and arms wrapped around its outer rim, each girl took turns pushing the other. Hours of fun were had in this way.

Another makeshift form of entertainment was a see-saw. One-half of an old oil drum, with its open half faced down, was placed on the ground. Its curved upper surface provided a base for a plank of wood. The plank's mid-way point pivoted on the half-drum. A folded blanket placed at each end of the plank served as make-shift seats for the young playmates. Giggles of joy from the two sisters could be heard on the wind, as they repeatedly see-sawed up and down.

Of course, it wasn't all fun and laughter for Elanor and Nicola. Perhaps inevitably, there was the occasional spat. In addition to the swing and the see-saw, the girls had the use of a 'Wendy-house'.

This was a common form of dwelling place for young South African girls in which to play. Rather like an over-sized doll's house it was knocked together using various pieces of scrap wood. The girls' small dwelling had the approximate shape of a house - given a good imagination! But it did have a lockable door and a fair-sized window - although the window frame was without glass! Undeniably, the property would never be sought after and probably never given a second glance. But to the fertile imagination of two fledgling adventurers, it possibly seemed like a Royal palace.

One day, inside the Wendy house an argument ensued over the use of a ball of string.

"I want that!" demanded Nicola.

"You can't have it!" Elanor retorted.

A few heated words were exchanged before Nicola finally declared,

"All right - If that's your answer!"

And having uttered those parting words, she stormed outside their little house. Elanor was left sitting on the floor. Once outside Nicola decided to punish her sister. Using an improvised 'lock' Nicola promptly fastened the door. Elanor jumped to her feet. She tried to open the door but without success. Instantly, the 'Royal palace' had become a maximum-security prison.

"Let me out!" was Elanor's plea - as she realised she was now an unwilling prisoner.

"No - I won't!"

"Oh, please let me out, Nicola."

"No - You can jolly-well climb through the window if you want to get out!"

"I can't" was the response. "The window is too small!"

"Oh no, it jolly-well isn't", Nicola insisted.

Elanor knew the window was big enough for her to climb through but wasn't there a point of principle to be made here?

"All right then", she hollered, "I'll show you!"

The internal walls of the house were covered with cut-out pictures from their mother's magazines. Each sister had a personal wall and decorated it with their choice of pictures. They ranged from images of fluffy kittens to ostentatious ladies wearing expensive dresses.

Elanor thought to teach her sister a lesson. She began tearing the pictures from Nicola's wall. The ominous sounds of tearing paper reached Nicola's ears. Adopting a calm attitude, Nicola quietly asked a rhetorical question.

"Elanor, what are you doing?"

Smirking triumphantly, Elanor replied.

"Open the door, and you'll see."

Not wishing to be defeated, Nicola rushed to the window frame and peered into the house. Her fears were confirmed. Elanor *was* performing the act of tearing pictures from *her* wall.

With tears welling in her eyes, Nicola screamed "Stop it!"

In a panic, she scampered towards the door and quickly unlocked it. Elanor's ruse had worked.

Entering the house, the shock of seeing her torn pictures, which now littered the floor, caused Nicola to freeze in suspended animation. Seizing the moment, Elanor darted through the open doorway. She ran swiftly across the veld and towards the house. Moments later, Nicola regained her senses and chased after her sister, shouting loudly,

"I'll get you for this, Elanor!"

Elanor pushes Nicola on their swing

# 25

## JIMMY THE DOG

Our daughters were delighted when Sandra and I decided to buy a dog. And when it came to selecting a breed, a Walt Disney movie titled *One Hundred and One Dalmatians* influenced our choice. Thankfully, just *one* Dalmatian puppy was enough for our girls! Delighted with their new friend, they decided to call him *Jimmy*. But since *Jimmy* was their grandfather's name it created some confusion. Fortunately, the matter was resolved when they chose to call their four-legged friend *Jimmy-the-dog*. When spoken quickly the words merged into one and became the dog's actual name. No one seemed to mind and least of all, the dog!

Elanor, Jimmy-the-dog with the author and Nicola.

In time the puppy grew to become a large and independent dog. With two and a half hectares of land for him to explore, it must have seemed like a canine Utopia. Curiously though, Jimmy-the-dog confined his activities close to the house. But he quickly changed his allegiance each time I left home. As my car descended the driveway, the dog made a point of following. He would frolic to and fro, whilst keeping a short distance behind the moving vehicle. These were early days in our life at the plot. A large gate had yet to be attached to the security fencing, which surrounded the house.

Consequently, to enable me to make a departure, I was obliged to ask Sandra to escort our pet indoors. The procedure worked for a while, although I often ran the gauntlet of disturbing Sandra's sleep. In due course, an iron gate was fitted to the security fencing. Unfortunately, it had to be fully opened when driving the car to or from the house. Jimmy the dog was quick to take advantage of the situation. And as soon as the gate was opened he would dash to the driveway, in anticipation of following the car. It took considerable patience to coax him back again - before finally driving away.

For a time, all went well, until the fateful day, when he emphatically refused to return to the house. Darting passed me, he stood defiantly awaiting my departure. Each time I tried to catch hold of him, he would duck and dive and prance about - like a contesting boxer in a ring!

With a regular swift action, his four legs lifted him - like a kangaroo - high into the air. Only to plummet to the ground again some distance away. And not unlike a child on a 'bouncy castle', he was having fun!

I made several attempts to restrain him before requesting Sandra to help. She was feeling a little indifferent at that moment and voiced her preference to stay in bed. Boisterous as ever, Jimmy-the-dog refused to co-operate. He simply wanted to follow the car. Desperation grabbed me and caused me to slowly drive away. It was my hope that before reaching the end of the drive, Jimmy the dog would give up the chase and return home. But instead, he continued to follow.

Entering Pemberthy road, I was surprised to see two anonymous dogs, playing together. They hardly noticed as my car edged passed them. Looking in my rear-view mirror, whilst slowly driving on, I saw that Jimmy-the-dog had lost interest in my car and had joined the playful dogs.

"Surely," I thought, "he would return home again when he was done playing?"

Later that day, I received a 'phone call at my workplace.

"Hi, it's me," Sandra began. "There's been an accident and Jimmy-the-dog is at the vet's."

"What!" I blurted, "What happened?"

"Earlier today, our neighbours' muntu called at our house. He told me he had seen a car hit Jimmy-the-dog."

As the story unfolded, I learned that our dog had been hit by a grey-coloured car. He was left in the middle of the road, unable to walk. The long, straight road began in a cul-de-sac and skirted the entrance to just four plots of land. And one of them was ours. At that time of day, the chance of a car passing the group of dogs was slim, to say the least.

Sandra and our neighbours' helpful muntu put our dog into her car, before driving him to the vet.

That evening, I called at the vet's surgery to collect him. A wagging tail and a face, which appeared to be smiling, showed he was pleased to see me. But that was as much as he could manage. The vet informed me that our pet had a fractured pelvis. Everything had been done to make him comfortable. Jimmy-the-dog's hind quarters were encapsulated within plaster-of-Paris. He appeared as if wearing an oversized nappy. With as much care as possible, the patient was carried to my car.

When we arrived home, I pondered the best way of taking him inside the house. For fear of hurting him, I avoided holding the lower half of his body. Instead, I held him by his front elbows and allowed his body to hang free. It was a short distance from car to house but undoubtedly a long way for Jimmy-the-dog. His pain must have been severe. In an attempt to limit his bodily movement, I held him close to mine. Moving quickly along, I felt a gradual pain in my right shoulder. Jimmy-the-dog was slowly sinking his teeth into my flesh. He behaved like a wounded soldier, biting the proverbial bullet. At that moment, I empathised with his pain, but was unable to put him down until we entered the house.

Sandra and I cared for him as best we could and within a day or two, he seemed to be improving. He even managed a few steps outside the house to relieve himself. However, around the third or fourth day, he released a torrent of blood-red urine. It seemed obvious he had some serious internal damage.

The next day was the start of the weekend.

It was early in the morning when I stepped out of the house. Sandra and the children were still sleeping. Leaving the kitchen door open in case our dog wished to follow, I set about repairing a part of the fencing. Later, when I returned to the house, Jimmy-the-dog, was not there. In his condition, I was sure he couldn't have gone far. Having looked inside and outside the house, I searched farther afield.

At that time of year, the tall grass surrounding the area was a uniform brown-colour. Striding through its lengthy stalks, I suddenly caught sight of something coloured black and white. Feeling apprehensive, I approached it with caution. When I got within a metre or two, I was shocked to see... Jimmy-the-dog!

He lay on his side perfectly still. Unblinking eyes, framed with tiny eyelashes, stared from his motionless head. A stiffened tongue protruded from his mouth. A few seconds elapsed as I wrestled with my grief. But I soon realised something had to be done - and especially *before* the children woke up. I ventured to tell Sandra. She was never in the best of moods early in the morning. Keeping a rein on my emotions, I gently woke her and quietly announced, "Jimmy is gone."

Slowly rubbing her eyes, she snapped, "What do you mean 'gone'!?"

Raising my voice, a tone, I blurted - "He's dead!"

Her face instantly changed expression. Silently, she appeared to mentally rationalize my news. In the interim, I had already formulated a plan of action.

"We need to bury him before the girls wake up!" I insisted.

Sandra dressed and followed me outside. Pointing her in the direction of our pet, I went to fetch a spade and a wheelbarrow. When I re-joined Sandra her gaze was transfixed on the dog's lifeless form. I realized it was time for action.

"Okay! Take hold of his back legs! I'll take the front ones! We must lift him into the wheelbarrow!"

As though acting in a trance, Sandra silently nodded.

"Okay, lift now!" I commanded.

As though released from an unseen shackle, Sandra responded. We stooped to take hold of Jimmy's legs. With one swift movement his limp body was lying in the 'barrow. A far corner of the plot, where the unwanted Bantu had previously lived, became Jimmy-the-dog's last resting place. He was laid in the soft ground and covered with stones. Later that morning, we told the girls our sad news. It was an emotional weekend for us all.

Monday morning arrived. My working hours were filled with nagging thoughts of the weekend's trauma. Something needed to be done, and I decided to act. Arriving home at the end of the day, I parked my car at the lower end of our driveway. Inside the car's boot I opened my tool box. Producing a two-pound hammer, I pushed its wooden shaft down the belt of my trousers. Hastily fastening my jacket's buttons, I strode slowly along the narrow Pemberthy road. My eyes peered like a sharp-eyed eagle looking for its prey. Three houses stood ahead. Logic suggested one of them must be the home of a *grey*-coloured car.

Clothed in a jacket and pressed trousers, with white shirt and tie, I must have looked conspicuous in that urban environment.

But as it was, there was no one about to see me. Except, as it happened, the driver of a car, which surreptitiously approached me from behind. The sound of tyres rolling slowly on a gravel surface reached my ears. Less than six feet from me, a car came to a gradual halt. Turning around, I saw a red-coloured Peugeot 504. The driver was a squat male of around thirty years of age. He struggled to wind down a door window and then shouted.

"Are you looking for someone?"

The sound of spoken English was unusual in that neighbourhood. But was his inquiry founded on a knowing guilty conscience?

Edging my way towards the car, I saw the man's piggy eyes staring at me from behind the windscreen.

"Ja", I answered, "I'm looking for a *grey car.*"

His face instantly displayed a look of surprise.

"Oh, well, that must be me!" he said.

"So, you are the one who ran over my dog?" I announced with an accusing tone of voice. And before the man could answer, I exclaimed, "But this is a red car!"

"Ja, that's right", he confirmed. "But hell, man, it was my wife's car that hit the dog; I was following behind her."

The man flailed his hands above his chest to emphasise his words.

"It was a hell of a thing, man - the dog just ran in front of her."

"I can understand that happening", I admitted, "But why did you not tell someone at the house? Instead, you left the injured dog in the middle of the road!"

"Why, hell man, we would have been late for work!"

That short and unsympathetic reason brought my temper to breaking point.

"So, you left a poor animal to writhe in agony on the ground; and simply because you would be late for work? You disgust me!"

A bewildered expression formed on the man's face. Inside my jacket, I felt a hand grip the hammer and slowly pull it away from the belt. My attention was focused on the oblong-shaped headlamp, of the car's offside wing. What came next was the manifestation of a dream-like sequence.

Seemingly in slow motion, and like a tennis racket in action, the hammer swung through the air. A resounding crash followed. The sound of exploding glass reached my ears. The impact shocked me to my senses, and in an instant, I realised what I had done. But I think the man got a greater shock than me. His jaw fell open in astonishment and his piggy eyes instantly grew bigger! Returning the hammer to my belt I admonished him with my words.

"I hope that gives you some inconvenience; like the way you have caused me!"

With those parting words, I strode off towards my house. Almost reaching the driveway, I heard the man's car engine rev-up. Hurriedly performing a three-point turn, the car's tyres sent dirt and gravel flying into the air. I was about to walk up the driveway when the car slid to a halt alongside me. The window of the driver's car-door was open. Turning to face the driver, I was surprised to see a military-styled pistol - which rested on his lap.

"So that's your answer, is it?" I asked.

"Ja, well, I do feel like blowing your head off!" the man admitted.

"Well, that's not going to change anything," was my response.

"So, you took the law into your own hands,"

"Don't talk to me about the law!" I barked.

The man tightened his grip on the pistol. At that moment, I vividly remembered an incident from a few evenings earlier. It was when I sat in the study room at one end of our house. From over the boundary wall, next to our neighbours' property, I heard the rattle of an automatic weapon. There was a silent pause, and then another burst followed. It was an unnerving sound, to say the least. With the thought that terrorism was the vogue, I decided to inform the police. When the local police station answered my call, I asked a question.

"Do you allow people to fire automatic weapons in this part of the country?"

"Certainly not, sir!" was the immediate and curt answer.

I explained what had happened and gave my details to a policeman.

"Okay," said the voice, "We'll send a policeman to visit you within the next hour."

It was early evening when I made the call. Unfortunately, after midnight, I was still waiting for the police to arrive! Next day, I called at the local police station. A young European police officer listened intently to my complaint. Within minutes I was ushered into an office, where a middle-aged officer was seated behind a large desk

A strip of medal-ribbons worn over a tunic pocket added to his demeanour of authority. Smiling, and offering to shake my hand, he introduced himself in a friendly manner.

"I'm sorry no one responded to your call last night" he said "The truth of the matter is, at the time you phoned, the officer on desk duty was about to finish his shift. And before he handed over to the next officer he failed to enter the incident in the report book. As a result, no action was taken."

Shuffling some papers which lay before him, he asked a question.

"Did you see the person who fired the weapon?"

"Afraid not" said I, "It was dark, and there is a tall wall between the two properties."

"Ah well, if there *is* a next time, if you could look over the wall, to see if you can recognise the culprit, that would help us."

I looked at him blankly and wondered if he was making a joke. Then, in a seemingly apologetic way, he continued.

"You know, for the most part, my staff is young men who are only interested in their pay cheques and their girlfriends."

A widening smile spread across his face, as he concluded by saying,

"I'll send my Sergeant there today; I can rely on him to investigate."

My mental scenario slowly faded, and my attention returned to the driver with the piggy eyes.

"This is a company car!" he exclaimed. "What if I was to damage *your* car?" he asked.

"Mine's a company car too!" I retorted. "So that's not going to help any."

"Couldn't we go to my house to discuss this?" he asked.

"I don't think so. Anyway, as far as I'm concerned, it's over now. There's nothing more to be done."

The man with the piggy eyes appeared to agree, and we parted company.

Later that evening, a questioning thought occurred to me. What if I *had* gone with the man to his house? He may well have shot me as an intruder! Furthermore, he could have buried my body on his land, and who was to know?

A few days later, a strange-looking fellow appeared at the top of our driveway. I happened to see him from the dining room window. His face expressed a look of bewilderment. It was as if he wasn't sure of what to expect. His bushy, grey-hair and a large, full beard caused me to think of the literary Robinson Crusoe. His clothes suggested a partial military style. They were a long-sleeved khaki shirt with double breast-pockets and a pair of shabby corduroy trousers.

Stepping out from the kitchen doorway, I called out,

"Can I help you?"

The man answered with a pronounced Afrikaans accent.

"Ja Meneer, asseblief. I am looking for a Meneer Van Tonder."

The man stood waiting for an answer. Running the name through my head - 'Van Tonder' meant nothing to me.

"Nobody of that name lives here", I explained.

"Oh, ja, ek sien. Jammer meneer. (Oh, yes, I see. Sorry mister.)

But what is *your* name?" he asked.

"Farley", I swiftly answered.

He looked slightly puzzled. Making sure he had heard me correctly, he quickly added, "How do you spell that?"

Without thinking of any possible consequences, I recited the spelling. Seemingly satisfied with the information, the pseudo-Crusoe turned about and wandered down the driveway.

When I told Sandra what had happened, we both puzzled over the incident. But we needn't have wasted much time wondering. A day or two later, all was made clear. A uniformed policeman appeared at our opened security gate. He made his way towards Sandra and me. Quietly, I flippantly remarked,

"It's becoming overpopulated around these parts!"

The words "Can I help you?" had hardly left my mouth when I experienced a feeling of de ja vu. As the policeman approached us he unbuttoned a pocket of his tunic.

"Ja Meneer" he answered.

Producing a small notebook, he flipped over the pages. Scrutinising some written words, he spoke with uncertainty.

"I'm looking for a Meneer FARLEY." he said.

Keeping his eyes on the book, he carefully repeated the sentence.

"That's me" I retorted.

"Ah, good" he said. "And do you live here, sir?"

"Yes, I do", I quickly replied.

Looking around, he saw my company's car. It was parked in the shade of our large tree. Stretching out an arm, he pointed in its direction.

"And is that your car, sir?" he inquired.

"Yes, it is," was my reply, and quickly added, "It's my company's car."

"Ah, that's good sir. Then I must give you these papers."

Feeling slightly flummoxed, I took a sealed envelope from the policeman's outstretched hand. Instantly, he turned on his heels and walked away. And before I could respond in any way, the policeman was heading down the drive. Inside the envelope was an official-looking letter. I read its type-written words. They said I was officially summoned to appear at the Magistrate's courtroom in central Randfontein. I was to answer to a charge of *malicious damage to property*. The name and address of the complainant were clearly stated. It was the man with the piggy-eyes!

My South African lawyer was of the Jewish faith and had an office in Johannesburg. He was friendly enough but was a straight-talking person. At the outset, he stated the charge for his service was eight hundred Rand. At that time, I thought his fee was a lot of money.

The day of my 'hearing' duly arrived. All concerned were present and seated inside the Magistrate's courtroom. Collectively, the people and the surroundings had the appearance of a theatrical performance and this one was about to begin.

The courtroom was arranged with rows of seats, resembling church pews. They faced a raised, centrally placed desk. Seated at the desk was the judge. Contrary to what I was expecting, he wore no wig or robes – just a plain two-piece suit. From the desk's elevated position, the judge had a commanding view. He was a mature-looking individual with grey-hair and a slim frame. His sullen-looking face was slightly intimidating.

Centrally placed in front of the 'pews' was a raised, enclosed platform, on which I stood. It faced the judge who read out the charge laid against me. Standing next to the platform was a muntu court official. His head was level with my waist. In keeping with all present, he wore a two-piece suit - with collar and tie.

The plaintiff was asked to take the stand. Passing to the right of me, he entered another raised and enclosed platform. It completed a triangular arrangement of the three wooden structures. The plaintiff looked resplendent, wearing a two-piece suit, with a shirt and tie and his hair neatly groomed. He appeared quite different from when I last saw him. But I couldn't mistake his piggy-eyes. The judge asked him to relate his experience in connection with the accused.

His verbal story of the past event unfolded. The man's tone of voice often changed. It rose and fell with dramatic effect. At times, his oratory was heated, but at all times, it was spoken in the Afrikaans language. I had little idea of what was said, and for the most part, I was left confused. However, it was the muntu court official's job to translate for me. But I could see by his face that he was enthralled by the plaintiff's testimony. More than once, I had to tap him on his shoulder to gain his attention.

"What is the man saying?" I quietly asked.

The muntu seemed at pains to take his eyes off the plaintiff. He half turned towards me while proceeding to voice an edited account. His attention vacillated between me and the man. And since he spoke with a deep African accent, I had difficulty understanding his English. In addition to this, his breath was heavily tainted with the smell of alcohol, which caused me some discomfort. Considering the time of day, I could only hope that his condition was the result of the night before!

When the judge was satisfied with the plaintiff's statement, he allowed my lawyer to question him. From the outset, my English-speaking lawyer, who was fully bi-lingual, spoke in Afrikaans. But he made a subtle point by asking the plaintiff a simple question.

"Is it true you speak and understand English perfectly well?"

"Ja, dit is," (Yes, it is) the plaintiff proudly acknowledged.

"But you chose to speak Afrikaans here today?"

"Ja, ek doen." (Yes, I do).

I later asked the lawyer if the man was making some kind of political statement. He admitted it might be so but added that the man had the legal right to speak in the language of his choice.

However, his choice of language had unwittingly given me a certain advantage. During the cross-examination, the plaintiff had used the Afrikaans word 'Mal' to describe my actions. My wily lawyer, who realised the significance of the word, grasped an opportunity. He presented the plaintiff with a number of questions which encouraged the man to use the word 'Mal'. How this was to my advantage would be revealed later in the outcome of the trial.

When the plaintiff was asked to stand down I was instructed to take his place. From my fresh viewpoint I could observe the whole of the courtroom. The plaintiff stood facing the judge and for the first time that morning, I saw Sandra. She was sitting in the pews behind the plaintiff's platform. I wondered what she must be thinking.

The judge began questioning me about my actions on the day of the misdemeanour. He made a comment about me being an engineer. There was a veiled inference in his remark. It seemed to suggest that because I was an engineer, I would have a certain level of intelligence. And that certain level might help me to weave a web of deceit. From my point of view, all I hoped to do was to tell, and with honesty, how I had reacted.

During my address, I explained that Sandra and I had two daughters but no son. And in the hope of having a son, we had suffered two miscarriages. Odd as it might sound, Jimmy-the-dog was playing the pseudo-role of our wanted son. To us, this made his loss seem much greater than that of a pet. My words were tainted with emotion as I spoke. The judge looked genuinely concerned. His previous dour demeanour morphed into a partial look of empathy. (Had he experienced a similar loss?)

Following my testimony, there was a brief recess. When everyone returned to the court room, the judge stated that a verdict would be given at a later date. A feeling of surprise was shared by all present. Outside the courtroom, my lawyer complimented me on my testimony.

"It was very touching and equally convincing!" he said.

"I was only telling the truth," I insisted.

After confirming the date of the next court appearance, we said our farewells. The lawyer climbed into his car and attempted to start its engine. There was a brief whirr of the starter motor and nothing else. He repeated the action three or four times. Standing nearby, I could hear the sound. It was familiar to me and I quickly recognised the problem. Turning around I walked back and reached the lawyer as he was climbing out of his car.

"Is your battery dead?" I asked.

Breathing a deep sigh, he answered, "Yes" - "It's been acting up for a while."

Knowing I always kept basic tools in the boot of my car, I confidently announced "I believe I can help you".

He had another appointment that day, and time was pressing. For him to get official roadside assistance would be fairly difficult. When he heard my offer of help, his face brightened.

Sounding surprised, he asked, "How can you help me?"

"I'll show you," I said. "Lift your car's bonnet, please".

At that moment, my knowledge of car mechanics came to the fore. I spent a little time removing *my* car's battery. When I carried it to the lawyer's car, I found him waiting. The bonnet of his car was open, and he was looking agitated.

"Relax," I said reassuringly. "Please, just sit in your car and wait for me to tell you when to start the engine."

His face reflected a doubtful expression as he followed my request. My next move was to remove *his* car's battery and replace it with my own.

"Okay, you can start the engine now!"

A quick turn of the key and the engine fired immediately. I was pleasantly relieved. Instantly, the lawyer's face erupted into a triumphant smile. However, the best trick was yet to come.

"Would you stay inside your car?" I said to the lawyer. "And keep your foot resting *lightly* on the accelerator pedal."

With the lawyer's car engine running at a slightly faster than idle speed, I disconnected my battery. The lawyer's eyes watched my every action. At the moment when I removed my battery, he was amazed to see his car's engine was still running. In truth, the car's alternator was now powering the engine! I quickly replaced the lawyer's original battery, and his car engine continued to run normally.

"There", I said, "That should charge nicely and get you home. But be sure to get a new battery soonest."

The lawyer was pleased, and he thanked me. But as I said earlier in this story, he was 'direct.' My good deed hadn't changed his business outlook. I realised this as he gave me some parting words.

"You know," he said, "I fully expected the judge to give us his verdict today. However, since I have to make another journey from Johannesburg to Randfontein, I shall have to charge you an additional fee!"

I froze with surprise and only managed to ask, "How much?"

His face reflected a dead-pan look as, without hesitation, he announced, "Three hundred Rand will do it!"

I was still pondering his words as his car roared away.

Some days later, at the Randfontein Magistrate's courthouse, the judge gave his verdict. His face reflected a familiar dour expression as he was heard to say,

"I find the defendant NOT guilty on the grounds of being temporarily insane."

For me, the verdict was tantamount to winning the National Lottery. I glanced at Sandra sitting across the room; the look on her face expressed the utmost relief. By way of contrast, the man with the piggy eyes looked dejected. However, my lawyer was not surprised by the outcome and explained his reason why.

"It was when the plaintiff described your facial appearance that tipped the scales".

"What do you mean?" I asked.

"The plaintiff said, as you were about to strike his car's headlamp, you looked *Mal*. It was a key word in the description which made all the difference to the outcome".

"Why? What does *Mal* mean?" I asked.

"The Afrikaans word *Mal* translated to English means – 'Mad'. But to be more precise, it means mentally unhinged. The man was actually admitting that you were, INSANE!"

Sandra and I were elated with the result and so too was our lawyer. But the man with the piggy eyes was otherwise. However, in retrospect, when thinking about the verdict, I believe justice had been done. In one way or another, all guilty parties were made to *pay* for their actions. Of course, in a monetary sense, my lawyer was very well paid!

# 26

## THE 'BULL NASTY'

The move to our new home had caused me to ponder a few questions. "What are our new neighbours like? Are they young or old? Are they approachable or not?" The answers came to me in an unexpected way.

A week or two after my Randfontein Magistrate's court hearing, Elanor, our first daughter, walked into the house carrying a kitten. She explained how the neighbours' muntu saw her playing near the boundary fence. He had called her over and gave her the kitten as a present. Perhaps he, or maybe his employer, thought the kitten might take the place of Jimmy-the-dog. With the passage of time, the kitten made herself quite at home. And unwittingly, she paved the way for us to eventually acquire five more cats - albeit not from the same source. And as it happened, the arrival of Elanor's feline friend set into motion a string of events.

When I arrived home a day or two later, I was greeted by Sandra, who shared some important news.

"We've been invited to visit our neighbours' house to enjoy a cheese and wine evening."

"Oh, really?" said I, "How did that happen?"

"Well, it turns out that our neighbours have two little girls of a similar age to ours. They saw each other over the boundary fence and got talking. A short time later, Elanor came to me to say that the lady next door wanted to speak with me. So, I went along to the fence and had a chat."

"So, what did she say? - And what is she like?" I asked.

"Well, she and her husband are Portuguese and something similar in age to us. She asked if it would be all right for the girls to play together. And then she invited us around to their house for a cheese and wine evening."

My imagination instantly pictured an array of various cheeses, with a collection of different flavoured wines and together forming a veritable canvas of colour.

"Cheese and wine sound like a good idea" I admitted, "So what are the arrangements?"

"We are expected to be there tomorrow evening at six o'clock."

The following evening, we walked along the short driveway towards our neighbours' house. Some weeks had passed since I last saw it. The lay of the land was much the same, except that it was now teeming with growing vegetables. As for the house, it looked as before. The tatty curtains still adorned the paint-worn window frame; while the roof covering continued to rust. Next to the front door was the familiar stack of wooden seed trays, which remained in imminent danger of toppling over. The large bull-mastiff - aka security dog - was present too! He prowled about outside the house as before. But catching sight of our approach he stopped. His broad head turned and pointed in our direction.

A second later, the flabby lips of his huge canine mouth quivered. With his mouth partially opened, the lips vibrated as the beast produced a deep-throated growl. It sounded like the roll of distant thunder. Following the growl was a loud and gruff bark. It was repeated two or three times. Sandra and I froze. Our two daughters moved closer to us and gripped our hands tightly. Fortunately, the barking of the dog was quickly followed by a human voice. Words of the Portuguese language were shouted from the house.

"Quieto! Brento quieto! Esta tudo bem!"

(Quiet! Brento quiet! Everything is okay!)

The familiarity of the voice shocked the animal into submission. Its head instantly turned to face the caller. A young woman suddenly appeared next to him and shouted across to us. This time, her spoken words were English.

"Hello! - It's okay now, - You can come to me."

Sandra recognised the lady.

"Hi, Maria", called Sandra, "Nice to see you again".

The bull-mastiff stood obediently to attention, as saliva slowly dripped from his wide jaw. Quietly, and with heavily lidded eyes, he suspiciously watched our approach. Maria's two little girls ran forward to greet our daughters, and soon, they were all playing together.

Making us most welcome, our hosts invited Sandra and me to enter their home. We gathered in the kitchen area, where the surroundings were, to say the least, basic!

A large, pine-wood table dominated the floor space. Littering its top-surface was an assortment of various-size drinking glasses. And standing next to them was an array of oddly shaped bottles. Filled with different coloured wines, each carried a hand-written label, which described their intriguing content.

Besides the familiar names of apple and potato, there were some exotic ones to choose from. Banana, prickly-pear and even pomegranate, were there to try. I never knew so many flavours of wine existed. Thinking it prudent to drink something familiar, I accepted a glass of peach wine. Sandra, on the other hand, was more adventurous. She chose a glass filled with the pomegranate variety. Not long afterwards, we were given some cheese and biscuits to chew on.

As the evening progressed, I discovered we and our neighbours shared a common interest in agriculture. It was also good to learn that our collective daughters were of a similar age. As a result of these joint interests, our conversation flowed freely. The host's wine also flowed freely and fortunately, not as fast as the conversation!

Fairly soon, the wine caused me to feel a warm glow from within. On the outside, I think my face must have looked a little flush. Sandra also showed unmistakable signs of enjoying the occasion. But just as things were running smoothly, a short and sharp scream was heard!

Maria stopped talking in mid-sentence and darted through the kitchen doorway. Before Sandra and I realised what was happening, Maria returned and was holding Nicola in her arms.

The poor child was crying loudly. Maria put her mothering skills into action. Cradling Nicola with one arm, her outstretched free hand grabbed a bar of soap from the kitchen sink-top. Helplessly, I watched as she rubbed the soap over a cheek of Nicola's tearful face.

Four or five bloody marks were visible on one side of her mouth. They were consistent with dog's teeth having scraped skin from the flesh. Fortunately, the soap managed to stop the minor bleeding. Sandra took hold of Nicola and as her crying gradually eased, she managed to gurgle some words.

"The... big... nasty... doggy... bite... me!"

Naturally, Maria was more than sorry for the canine's misdemeanour. She quickly assured us that it was an unusual occurrence. What could we do?

From that moment, the wine's intoxicating effect quickly subsided. Nicola was in shock and refused to leave Sandra. We thought it best to return home. Standing at their front door, Maria and her husband waved us goodbye. Their dog, with his big eyes and salivating mouth, stood passively watching every step we took.

With the passage of time the incident was largely forgotten, except for the name of the dog. Soon after the fateful meeting, our children aptly called him the *Bull-nasty*.

Sandra kept on friendly terms with Maria, and from time to time, the four girls played together. Sadly, however, the peaceful state of affairs was not destined to last.

At my place of work, late one afternoon, I received a phone call from Sandra. Hesitantly, she explained her reason for calling.

"I'm sorry to tell you our neighbour's dog has bitten Elanor."

"What!" I exclaimed. "What happened? Is she hurt?"

Sandra struggled to answer.

"The children were playing next door, and the dog bit Elanor on her face! I took her to Krugersdorp hospital, where she had stitches to her cheek".

Confusion instantly gripped my tormented mind. My reaction was to ask more pertinent questions.

"Is she all right? - Is Nicola all right? - Are you okay?"

"Yes," said Sandra reassuringly. "Everything is fine. It's just that, as a precaution, they'll have to keep Elanor at the hospital overnight."

I didn't like the sound of things.

"All right," I said, "I'll come home first and collect you. Then we can visit the hospital together." Sandra was in agreement.

Later that day, I set off from my workplace and headed for home. The Main Reef road, from Johannesburg to Randfontein, is long and straight. When it reaches the Randfontein end, it forms a tee-junction. A left turn takes the driver into Randfontein, whilst a right turn points towards Krugersdorp. It was at this tee-junction where a strange thing happened.

Making a left turn, I clearly saw what I thought was Sandra's car. Travelling in the opposite direction, towards Krugersdorp, there was no mistaking a yellow-coloured Volkswagen beetle. What's more, Sandra appeared to be driving it.

As we passed each other, I gave her a quick wave. From behind the driver's wheel, she looked directly at me and smiled. Unfortunately, separating our two driving lanes was a metal crash-barrier. It started at the tee-junction and continued some distance towards Randfontein. At that moment, it crossed my mind that Sandra was making her way to the hospital without me. Perhaps there was some urgent reason for her to do that.

Because of the crash barrier, I was obliged to drive to the next junction before I could do a U-turn. Only then would I be able to drive after her. Completing a U-turn, I drove as fast as I could towards Krugersdorp. At any moment, I expected to see Sandra's car. No turn-offs, or other junctions appeared along the route. Surely, I thought, her car could not out-pace my own? All the way to the hospital, I expected to see a yellow beetle, but that didn't happen. Finally, I arrived at the hospital's small but adequate car park.

At a glance, I could see every car that was parked there. But there was no Volkswagen beetle to be seen. Suddenly, I realised I had something else to worry about.

Inside the hospital, Elanor shared a room. When I entered, another young girl occupied an adjacent bed. An elderly man was chatting with her. I spent some time with Elanor, trying my best to comfort her and listen to her explanation of what had happened.

"I was playing with the little girls from next door," she said. "There was a swing near the house. It was one their daddy had made. We took it in turns to have a swing. The big girl was pushing me, as her sister and Nicola watched."

"My swing-time came to an end, and the big girl brought the swing to a halt. It was then the bull-nasty wandered over towards me. As I leaned forward to get off the swing, the dog was standing in front of me. He looked so nice. I stretched out my arm to give him a pat, and his mouth suddenly grabbed my face!"

One side of Elanor's face was heavily bruised and swollen. She had received twelve stitches! It wasn't a pretty sight. After saying our goodbyes for the night, the elderly man called me to one side. Wearing a small trilby hat and dressed in a well-worn suit, he stood an inch or two shorter than me. His kindly eyes looked up from his wrinkled face.

"What happened to your daughter?" he inquired.

When I finished explaining, he looked at me with a pitiful expression.

"Are you going to have the dog put down?" he quietly asked.

"I don't know" I answered. "It's not my dog."

Looking at me in a kind but challenging way, he said,

"What if it had been her eye?"

Whilst driving home, the man's words echoed in my mind. His question prompted me to have a serious talk with Sandra. Of course, first of all, I would have to find her. She hadn't been to the hospital, of that, I was certain. On my way home the roads were void of traffic, which allowed me to travel quickly. Arriving at the plot, I was surprised to see Sandra's car parked under the large tree. My probing hand felt the engine to be cold. It suggested the car had been there for some time. Furthermore, inside the house, I found Sandra fast asleep!

Next day, I quizzed her about her yellow beetle and how she had smiled at me from the driving seat. She chuckled saying I was 'seeing things'. Sandra was adamant she had remained home the whole evening. I was puzzled by her admission and wondered if I *had* seen her and the car, or maybe I was simply mistaken.

Later that morning, after discussing the previous day's incident, we agreed that our daughters should stay away from our neighbours' home. At least until they got rid of their dog. Subsequently, I paid the neighbours a visit. When I suggested their dog should be put down, Maria's husband gave an emphatic shake of his head. Regrettably, at that moment, our newfound friendship came to an untimely end. Days passed without us seeing our neighbours, or for that matter, even their dog!

But weeks later something peculiar happened. Whilst driving in the direction of Randfontein, I had an unfettered view of the road ahead. Suddenly, at a distance of about a hundred yards, I caught sight of the lifeless form of a large dog. It lay on a wide grass verge, at the side of the road. Its bloated body lay on its back, with legs stiffened and pointing skywards. Without any doubt, it was a bull-mastiff. Its size and colour looked so much like the presumed-missing *Bull-nasty*. However, I have to agree there are countless bull-mastiffs in the world, and it is perfectly possible the corpse was not the guilty dog. But by the same token, it appeared to be a very strange coincidence.

But assuming it *was* the actual dog, is it possible that Providence could have deliberately placed it there for me to see? And perhaps to let me know that karma had been at work. Either way, I was certain that particular dog, would never bite any little girl's face in the future!

# 27
## TOPSY AND TIM

When travelling through the rural areas of South Africa, *farm stalls* were often seen by the roadside. A *farm stall* is an impromptu shop where people sell home-grown produce. Items such as fresh eggs, jams, fruit or vegetables may be purchased. The produce is usually fresher and cheaper to buy than the supermarket equivalent.

One day, whilst driving through the hamlet of Finsbury - which is not far from our Hillside home - I saw a farm stall with a difference. Scrawled across a makeshift sign and written in the Afrikaans language were the words: SKAAP TE KOOP (Sheep for sale). Taking a closer look, I saw the sheep were Swartkoppersie or Blackhead Persian. This particular breed of sheep has a white-coloured body and a distinctive black-coloured head. Curiously, their body grows hair and not wool. This makes them best suited to the hot conditions found in some countries - in this case, South Africa.

Sandra agreed that a couple of sheep could make a difference to the plot's overgrown grass. At any rate, they might take some of the hard work out of keeping the land in good shape. Furthermore, it seemed logical that, given enough time, maybe the two could produce a healthy flock. A few days later, the stall owner was pleased to sell me a male and a female sheep.

Two willing muntus lifted Mister and Missus Sheep into our V.W. panel van. By carefully driving the short distance to our plot, the sheep arrived unscathed. But now I was faced with the task of getting them from the van and onto the ground. Necessity being the mother of invention, a couple of wooden planks placed against the van's doorway, provided an improvised ramp. Sensing a way of escape, the sheep wasted no time in scampering down them. Glancing around in a bewildered state, they began to investigate their new home. (I was about to write 'they looked about *sheepishly*' but thought again!) Our extended family, aka the cats, grouped together at a distance.

Looking on with discerning eyes, they watched the newcomers enter *their* world. The felines appeared to hold an impromptu meeting. Appearing doubtful of the sheep's' integrity, they quickly dispersed. By way of contrast, Nicola and Elanor were delighted with their newfound friends.

"Ooh goody-we've got two goats!" cried Elanor.

"Sorry", said I. "They're actually sheep."

"Well, they look like goats!" shouted Nicola.

After giving the animals a longer look, I had to admit that the children were right.

"Do you know something? They actually do. But I'll tell you what."

"What's that?" the children asked.

"How about calling them SHOATS? That would be a mix of the words sheep and goats?"

Elanor and Nicola laughingly agreed.

Of course, all friends have names, and the sheep were not to be excluded. Sandra and the girls quickly chatted. After careful consideration, they decided to call the sheep *Topsy* and *Tim*. The names were derived from characters that featured in a school book. In the story book, *Topsy* is the name of a little girl, and Tim is a little boy. They made perfect names for the two sheep...oops - I mean shoats!

It wasn't long before the shoats and our daughters became friends. And from time to time the girls were only too happy to share their snacks of bread-slices and jam. They made a tasty supplement to the shoat's grassy food. And not forgetting our pet cats, they too contributed *their* food - although not by choice! The shoats were regular visitors to the felines' feeding bowl and helped themselves to whatever was there.

Aside from the above, Sandra and I were unaware that sheep should be fed on grass of a high quality. And we should have known it was not advisable to feed them bread! Sometimes, as the saying goes, ignorance is bliss. Flowers, too, were a no, no. But as far as that particular requirement was concerned, we were okay. Because at the early stage of our tenure, no flowers were to be seen anywhere on the whole two-and-a-half hectares of land! Surprisingly, having fed the sheep with the occasional carrot or apple, we discovered it was the right thing to do. Apparently, both foodstuffs are considered to be a treat!

Another snippet of knowledge we would eventually learn, was the gestation period for a sheep. It happened to be five months. When the next five months passed and Topsy appeared much fatter, in all honesty I thought it was due to our generous feeding programme.

But as it turned out one weekend morning, I discovered Topsy was actually giving birth!

My initial awareness was due to Tim, who was standing near the wind-pump. Bellowing at regular intervals, his blackhead pointed towards a clump of tall, coarse grass, which grew amongst a few scattered stones. He sounded as if he was calling for help. Hot footing our way from the house, Sandra and I approached the stones and were surprised to see a heap of white hair. Initially, I thought Topsy had stumbled and fallen over. But it soon became evident she was in the throes of giving birth.

Sandra and I knelt down to offer her comfort. We didn't know what else to do. Briefly, I looked up and saw Tim at a distance. He hadn't moved from where I first saw him. But now, standing quietly, like an expectant father-to-be, he simply looked on. My attention returned to Topsy. A small bulge protruded from her rear end and didn't move. Topsy gave a few short, quick gasps, as if to take in air and her life ended!

The event reminded me of when Jimmy-the-dog had died. Fortunately, this time, Elanor and Nicola were away for the day on a school outing. Once again, Sandra and I were galvanized into action. The previously used wheelbarrow conveyed Topsy to her final resting place. A large hole was dug alongside Jimmy-the-dog. Medium-size stones were placed on the mound of earth, which covered her. All the while Tim watched from a short distance and I could only empathise with his loss.

For the next few days, Tim wandered about dejectedly near the house. He was heard to frequently bleat with a forlorn sound as though calling out for his lost mate.

As it happened, our neighbour, who lived near to where our animals were buried, had a couple of cows. They were regularly seen wandering about his land and often near the dividing fence. At certain times of day, Tim stood next to the fence. It was as if he knew when the cows would appear. I began to wonder if he actually communicated with them. A week or so later, I was more than surprised to see that Tim had somehow breached the fence. He had joined company with the cows and was happily following them about. The expression, 'A cow in sheep's clothing,' crossed my mind.

Sandra and I decided to leave matters as they were. After all, Tim seemed happy enough, and our girls were in agreement. During the days that followed, I made regular visits to the fence. It was reassuring to see Tim happily trailing after his four-legged friends. Then one day, I approached the fence and as usual, saw the two marauding cows. But this time, Tim was not to be seen. Minutes later a gruff voice called out. It was the one which spoke some months earlier, following the departure of the Bantu. Speaking brashly, it asked a question.

"Are you lookin' for your fokken sheep?"

Turning to face the voice, I saw the tall figure of a man. From a distance he brandished a farming implement.

"Yes, I am" was my polite reply.

Without delay the man lifted the implement and pointed it towards a nearby building.

"Then you'd better come an' get it," he shouted. "It's cut-up - an' it's 'anging in the fokken shed!"

# 28

# A TALE OF TWO HERBALISTS

The town of Randfontein lies thirty kilometres to the west of Johannesburg. Like most towns on the West Rand, it owes its foundation to the discovery of gold. In 1978, its prosperity was reflected in the gold price, which fluctuated between $165 and $243 in American dollars. Amazingly, by the middle of 1979, it was pushing the $400 mark! Collectively, the gold mines in the vicinity of Randfontein employed some 13,000 men - which included 12,000 Bantu. To accommodate the mineworkers, scores of new houses and hostels were built. [4]

Most of the Bantu employees had travelled from distant rural societies. And while their medical needs were met by the mining establishments, large numbers still held traditional beliefs. Their needs, which included medical and psychological support, were provided by herbalists or sangomas. Such people could be found to offer a service, either from their home or a bona fide shop.

Not far from where the main Krugersdorp road enters Randfontein, stands a flour-processing mill. It is owned by the Tiger Milling Company. Facing the mill is a group of shops, and in 1979, one of them was occupied by a Zulu sangoma. A similar shop, situated nearer my Hillside home, was run by the sangoma's brother. Each time I drove passed his shop, I glanced at its main front window.

My imagination was fired by the strange items displayed there. Flattened skins of snakes and animals - the origin of which I knew not - were festooned across the inside length of the window frame. They reminded me of drying clothes on a washing line.

For weeks, I nurtured the idea of making some photographs of the shop interior. Eventually, carrying a camera and flashgun, I mustered the courage to enter. It was more spacious than I had imagined. Multi-tiered, chrome-plated steel-frames, with glass-shelves, were attached to the walls. They supported a multitude of different-shaped bottles. Some appeared to be recycled whisky bottles, filled with pastel-coloured liquids. Others held oddly shaped dried roots, taken from wild plants.

Another collection of smaller bottles contained brightly coloured tablets. I presumed all had certain therapeutic qualities. Sitting next to the bottles, in an upright position, were a number of pinecones. I remembered as a child, how my mother had used a pinecone to forecast the weather. The hard scales of the cone reacted to ambient weather conditions. If the scales were closed, it signified rain was imminent. But perhaps the doctor had a different use for them.

Clad in a Swazi-patterned, wrap-around cloth, a young African lady stepped forward. She politely asked if I needed assistance. Hastily, I explained my interest in the shop and expressed my desire to make photographs. Projecting a thoughtful smile, she nodded her head lightly.

Courteously she asked, "Would you like to see the Doctor?"

Instantly, I imagined someone from the early Hollywood Tarzan movies.

A strange-looking wretch, adorned with animal skins and a bone through his nose. And one who might work his African magic on me - when, I might be transformed into a frog!

The smiling lady had large, brown eyes, and looked at me intently as she awaited my answer.

"Err, yes, please," I nervously replied.

Before I could change my mind, the lady walked behind a partition. Standing at the end of the oblong-shaped room, it formed part of an enclosed area. Seconds later, a short male muntu walked into view. His appearance betrayed my mental image of a 'Doctor'. I was taken aback to see him wearing a knee-length laboratory coat. But what surprised me more, was the crocheted white-cotton Muslim kufi, perched on his head.

"Hello!" he chirped, as he approached me in an excited and friendly manner. His white, pearly-teeth gleamed behind his smiling lips - which opened on his dark-brown face. With words spoken in staccato, the doctor asked me a question.

"How can I help you?"

I explained my interest in his profession and asked to make some photos of him, along with the items displayed in his shop.

"Sure, why not?" was his immediate and positive response.

Just then, I sensed a pleasant rapport developing between us. For a moment, he paused for thought and then exclaimed,

"Come with me! Let me show you my treatment room!"

Motioning me to follow, we walked towards the partition. Suddenly, my mind became engulfed with doubt.

"Is this the moment I had dreaded?" I asked myself, "Would I ever leave the shop again in human form?"

We stood together behind the wood partition. The ambient lighting was low - which added a dramatic effect to the overall scene. The floor space was loosely carpeted with wild animal pelts. Placed upon them was a cluster of mysterious objects. In a corner stood some gourds of various sizes. Each was partly decorated with multi-coloured beadwork. Randomly fixed around the walls hung the horns of various wild animals. Propped up in a darkened corner was what appeared to be a stuffed monkey! Its facial expression looked decidedly forlorn, as it blankly gazed at the assortment of bric-a-brac.

Meanwhile, a faint and intermittent musical sound, floated on the surrounding air. It stemmed from a number of short bamboo canes suspended from the ceiling. Loosely strung together in the form of a circle, they swung gently from side to side. A steady stream of air - from a distant ceiling-fan - was the motivating cause. Periodically, they touched each other and created soft and mysterious musical notes. But something attached to the top of the arrangement gave me a chill. Two eerie-looking wooden-eyes seemed to watch my every movement!

More bottles of odd shapes and different sizes stood upright on the floor. All were filled with liquids of varying quantities and different colours. Some were corked, and others capped, but all seemed to invite being opened. Continuing my visual inspection, I suddenly caught sight of something which challenged credulity.

Although hard to believe, it was a full-size chicken! There was no doubt it was not alive, but in the dim light I couldn't be sure if it was real or artificial. Either way, it gave me the shivers. At that moment, the doctor observed my roaming eyes and hastened to offer a little explanation.

"Ja, Mister", he briskly chirped, "This is where my patients come to me for help. What you see are the things which I use during the treatment process."

Apart from the hanging bamboo canes, there was another item of particular interest. Suspended from the ceiling was a length of twine, which almost reached the floor. Strung with multi-coloured glass-beads, its lower end was attached to a small gourd. Below that was a bulbous piece of polished wood and a vertically-placed porcupine quill. Collectively, the pieces resembled a large fishing float. But somehow, the whole arrangement put me in mind of a pendulum. And when I offered my thoughts to the doctor, surprisingly, he agreed with me.

He explained how the device was used in his divination practice.

"What do you mean by 'divination practice'?" I asked.

Speaking in his usual staccato manner, he took the trouble to explain.

"Well - you see, Mister - people come to me with their problems. For example, they may have troubles with their love life. Or they may have lost some valuable possession. Well, in most cases, I am able to help."

"Oh, really!" I exclaimed. Intrigued by his statement, I asked, "And how are you able to help?"

"Well, Mister, it all depends on how the 'pendulum' responds to my request. Firstly, I speak to the spirit world and present my question. It is from the spirit world that answers are given."

At that moment, I couldn't resist asking another question.

"Sorry!" I said, "But what do you mean by the *spirit world*?"

The doctor smiled broadly. "Ah!" he shouted and drew a long breath. Speaking slowly and deliberately, he answered.

"That is the place where the spirits of people go when they die. All spirits live together in *their* own world. Zulu people believe the spirits communicate with the living and offer guidance and reassurance."

Studying my facial expression, the doctor's searching eyes looked for clues, which might betray my lack of understanding. Presumably, since none were detected, he continued.

"Part of my job is to act as a communicator between the living and the dead. I ask the spirits questions, and the pendulum is used to give me their answers. It may swing from left to right or swing away from me or towards me. And depending on the way the pendulum swings, I am given an answer of 'Yes' or 'No' to my question."

Making sure I fully understood the doctor's explanation, I quizzed him some more.

"So, am I right in thinking the spirits from *their* world control the swinging of the pendulum?"

The doctor's face erupted into a smile of appreciation.

"Ja Mister! That is correct! You have got it!"

It was then the doctor had a flash of inspiration. Excitedly, he announced his next move.

"Mister! Come with me! - I want to show you something."

As we returned to the shop, his lady assistant watched us as from a distance. Reaching a central table, the doctor stopped. Placed upon it was a mix of plants and vegetables. Quickly looking over the assembly, his hand reached out and grabbed an item. Covered with layers of brown-crinkly skin, it resembled a giant onion. At its top, thick leaves sprouted, which resembled those of a pineapple. Without any introduction, the doctor revealed himself to be something of a showman. Holding the vegetable in front of his chest, he appeared as though performing to an audience.

Turning to face me he voiced some instructions.

"Come, Mister; Roll back your shirt sleeve and let me see your bare arm."

Perhaps seeking some reassurance, I shot a quick glance at the lady assistant. Her face returned a look of concern. Mustering some courage, I complied with the doctor's instruction and pushed back my unbuttoned shirt sleeve.

"Okay," said the doctor, "Now hold your arm out straight in front of you."

Like a hypnotised subject, I complied. My action prompted the doctor's free hand to clench its fingers. And in a flamboyant manner, he motioned it through the air in an exaggerated arc. He brought the hand to rest on the vegetable's surface. Everyone's eyes focused on the bunched fingers as they gradually unfurled.

Free again to move, the fingers tore a medium-sized piece of skin from the vegetable's top layer. With the piece tightly held, the hand swung around and stopped above my arm. For a second or two it hovered - motionless - in mid-air. Without warning, the doctor's hand plunged quickly onto my arm. Instantly his fingers rubbed the piece of vegetable firmly over my bare skin. Feeling unable to move my arm, I watched the doctor's actions in astonishment and wonder.

Taking a step backwards, the doctor gauged my reaction. At that moment, paranoid thoughts returned to plague me. My mind pondered some pertinent questions.

"Is my arm about to turn green?" and "Was this to be the first stage of my transformation into a frog?"

Within the space of a minute, my questions were set to be answered. I felt a burning sensation on my arm. The heat slowly intensified as the seconds ticked away. It caused me to verbalise my concern.

"Whoa!" I quietly hollered. "What's happening?" I asked in a surprised tone of voice.

"Ha!" exclaimed the doctor loudly. And then he said, "Now I've got the white man!" before dancing a short, triumphant jig.

Inwardly, I finally conceded that after all I *was* about to become a frog.

From a distance the lady assistant was openly smiling at the spectacle. As for the doctor, he enjoyed seeing the look of apprehension which grew increasingly on my face.

Fortunately, the heat reached a climax and gradually subsided. Within a couple of minutes, the feeling in my arm returned to normal.

In truth, what I experienced was medicine at work in its natural state! The piece of the plant had produced a rudimentary form of treatment. It was intended to alleviate the effects of rheumatism or arthritis. The experience left me suitably impressed. Furthermore, I realised the doctor had a keen sense of humour!

After regaining my composure, time was spent completing my photographic mission. The images I captured, were mainly of the doctor at work inside his 'treatment room'. And before leaving the shop, I promised to return with some complimentary photographic prints.

A little over a week passed before I set foot again in the doctor's shop. This time I harboured no more amphibious fears. When I gave the doctor my promised photos he was delighted with the result. Smiling broadly, he caught me by surprise when he announced he had a brother. He said his brother's name was *Adam* and he too was a doctor. It transpired that *Doctor Adam* ran a business, opposite the Tiger Milling Company's flour mill, in Randfontein. The brothers had spoken together about my photography, and Doctor Adam asked to see me.

Days later, I stood facing Doctor Adam. He was a tall, thick-set man. His rounded face sported a neatly trimmed moustache with a Van Dyke beard. During a brief introduction I learned that he and his brother were Zulus. They had been raised in Durban, and both followed the Islamic faith. It surprised me to hear they were Muslims but I chose not to question it.

Having seen my photography, the doctor commissioned me to produce some photographs of *him* at work. He wanted them framed to display in his shop. Feeling flattered and anxious to please, I readily agreed. On my return visit, I carried my camera and equipment. Doctor Adam's shop and that of his brother were a similar size and each had a partitioned treatment room. But aside from providing herbal remedies, and divination by using a pendulum, Doctor Adam also *'threw the bones'*.

My understanding of divination was clear, but the throwing of bones was something new. The doctor explained how it was done. He held a small canvas bag filled with fragments of various animal bones. Traditionally, they would have been from wild beasts, such as hyenas or lions. However, I suspect the ones used by Dr Adam were from a more common species of animal.

Before 'throwing the bones', the doctor maintained he would chew on a portion of a selected medicine. The choice of which was dependent on the service to be performed. He would then open the bag and 'puff' his bated breath onto the contents. The bones would then be emptied onto the floor. A few would be gathered up and held. With both hands clasped together, the bones would be given a brisk shake and thrown to the floor again. Each bone had a different shape and how it fell to the floor would determine how it appeared. It was believed the influence on the falling bones, came from the spirit world.

The doctor had the 'gift' of interpreting the meaning of the fallen bones, where it was believed the answer to a patient's problem was contained. Satisfied with the doctor's explanation, I set to work on making some photographs.

Doctor Adam had definite ideas of the poses he wanted me to capture. One of which had him standing in the shop with his two lady assistants. Both squatted on the floor at his feet. For the pose he wore a hat made from the pelt of a genet and complete with its tail. Draped over his shoulders was an elaborate cape made from jackal pelts. Festooned around his neck was a necklace of coloured glass-beads, with a small animal horn attached to it. In one hand, the doctor carried a fly-whisk, whilst in the other he held a gourd. Each was decorated with coloured glass-beads. The Zulus attach importance to decorating certain items with coloured glass-beads. In some instances, the meticulous arrangement of the beads may convey messages to the eye of the beholder!

During my time spent with the doctor, we built a level of mutual trust. And on one occasion, a European woman of around forty years of age entered the shop. She and the doctor had a short private talk. Afterwards I was asked to wait aside for a little while. The two of them entered into the treatment room. Sounds of voices and the tinkling of glassware floated on the air.

As the consultation progressed I couldn't help hearing the dialogue between them. The poor lady was having trouble with her love life. Judging by the doctor's probing questions and his follow-up advice, it seemed evident he was offering some psychological help. But whatever he said must have had a positive affect because the lady left the shop happily smiling.

Of the many questions I asked Doctor Adam, was one which was vaguely linked to my daughter's condition.

"Is it possible to get rid of scars using your muti?" (Medicine)

The doctor appeared to sense some purpose in my question and quickly followed it with one of his own.

"Why do you ask?" he said.

I cautiously mentioned my daughter had been bitten by a dog and how the bite had left a noticeable scar on her right cheek. A studious look fell across his rounded face. After hearing my explanation and with it, the inclusion of an indirect request for help, he gave me his answer. Slowly and studiously, he replied.

"It may be possible. Bring her to me so that I may see the scar!"

Later that day, I explained to Elanor that a doctor wished to see her face. But this doctor was different to others she had seen. He was a Zulu doctor, and he 'threw bones'! Her little face beamed with delight - she was thrilled at the prospect. After all it's not every day an invitation like that comes along. Of course, when her sister realised there was an adventure pending, she too wanted to tag along. I have to say Elanor's mother was not keen on the idea. Understandably, I suppose, since we had previously taken Elanor to an up-market Sandton clinic, where she had seen a specialist plastic surgeon.

Standing proud of the skin's surface was a scar - about two and a half inches long. On each side of it were small round lumps, the result of a needle, which had been used to make the original stitching. The Sandton surgeon had explained that little could be done. He suggested the scar might be re-cut and then re-stitched, but that would need to be done from inside the mouth. However, there was a possibility the re-stitching might cause the side of Elanor's face to droop. Sandra and I decided to leave it be.

*Doctor Adam's brother*

*Doctor Adam with Elanor*

Fortunately, however, Doctor Adam had given us fresh hope, although Sandra was not convinced. She wondered how a Zulu doctor - and one who throws bones - could make a positive difference. And especially after a top Sandton surgeon had offered little chance of success!

When my daughters and I arrived at Doctor Adam's shop, he greeted us warmly. During our visit, he pleasantly explained about the numerous mysterious items which occupied his treatment room. He even consented to me making a group photograph of himself and his assistants; together with my daughters. But after a while the meeting took on a serious tone. He offered to examine Elanor's face. It didn't take long for him to reach a prognosis. But before continuing he took time to explain about the Zulu belief in a spirit world.

The doctor said the spirit world is a place where there is a spiritual existence after human death. Departed spirits are said to be in communion with the living. And as a result of influences from that world, illness and misfortune may come about in the lives of the living. He maintained the causation of the dog bite was due to a negative influence extending from the spirit world. Furthermore, that negative influence was present within the dwelling quarters of the victim. And in order to expel the intangible influence, a cleansing procedure must be followed.

Before I learnt the rudiments of the cleansing procedure Doctor Adam prepared the necessary requirements. He spent minutes looking at containers. His eyes searched for specific types. Reaching towards a nearby shelf, he took hold of a small, round glass-jar. It was no bigger than a salt shaker and had a metal screw-on cap.

In the Zulu language its contents was known as 'Umfatu'. When translated to English it meant 'Fat', but in this instance, it might be called 'Ointment'. The Umfatu appeared as a dark and moody paste. Essentially, it appeared to be harmless, but the odour it gave off was almost indescribably bad. It exceeded the most repugnant smell I can imagine!

The next item the doctor chose was an irregular-shaped substance. Grey in colour and about the size of a chicken's egg, it had the appearance of rock but easily crumbled. Doctor Adam told me that it had come from 'Bethlehem' and that's all he said. Apparently, there is a town called Bethlehem located in South Africa, from where it may have been derived. But I wasn't sure of that. Or, had he perhaps meant the Bethlehem of the Holy Bible? The inference being that because of its origin, it must have certain spiritual powers.

Added to the collection of items was a packet containing charcoal discs. Each of them was about one inch in diameter and a quarter of an inch thick. Finally, some pink-coloured powder, which had a sugar-like consistency, was taken from a large jar. Enough was measured to fill two egg-cups and then wrapped in a scrap of clean paper.

Everything needed was now ready but before leaving for home, I was informed how the items should be used. The doctor explained how a ritual is performed by first cleansing the house from any negative influence. To do this a domestic sweeping broom may be used to sweep every inch of floor space in one's home. The sweeping process begins in the room farthest away from the last exit door.

It is to be done in one continuous movement; from the first room to the last. All the dust and any detritus are collected in one final heap at the exit door and swept outside.

The next stage of the ritual is to place a charcoal disc on top of a ceramic saucer. Touched by the flame of a burning match, the disc starts to sparkle and begins to burn. No flames are given off but the charcoal generates lots of heat. This is followed by breaking a piece off the lump of grey-coloured rock from Bethlehem. As soon as possible the piece is placed on top of the charcoal disc. Heat from the disc melts the rock, which in turn gives off a cleansing smoke. The smoke is not repugnant or disruptive and smells every bit like the incense, often used in certain Christian churches. As the smoke is produced, the saucer is to be taken into and moved around every room in the house. The action is done to replicate the sweeping function of the broom.

The final part of the ritual is perhaps best described after my daughters and I had returned home.

It was late in the day. The sun had sunk below the distant horizon, and darkness had consumed the surrounding land. Sandra, who chose not to join us that day, was sitting in bed and reading a book. With my guidance the girls took long brushes and began sweeping the floors of the house. Following their given directions, they began at the far end of the house and steadily moved towards the exit door of the kitchen. The collected dust was swept outside. At this time, it was necessary to introduce the cleansing smoke.

Holding a ceramic saucer, on which was placed an ignited charcoal disc, I added a piece of grey rock. As it melted and produced slowly rising smoke, I worked my way through the house. Passing from room to room, Elanor and Nicola followed in my footsteps. Excitedly, they watched, and, as might be expected, occasionally giggled. When Sandra saw us enter the bedroom, she immediately ducked under the bedclothes. The smoke from the saucer did its job and the air in the bedroom quickly smelt of incense. But not content with the room being cleaned, I thought the bed should be given the same treatment. Under the bed-frame went the smoke-emitting saucer. And for a grand finale, as quick as a flash, I pulled back the bedclothes and thrust forward the smoking item. Sandra shrieked with fright and, whilst clutching a bed sheet close to her nightdress, loudly expressed her displeasure. The children howled with laughter!

It was time for the final part of the ceremony. The girls followed me into the bathroom. Nicola jumped to the task of filling the sink with water. Meanwhile, taking the pink-coloured powder, I poured some into the palm of my hand. Holding it over the sink, I gently blew onto the powder. It quickly left my hand and flew through the air before falling onto the water's surface. Elanor watched closely as the powder floated, like a pink-coloured coral island.

In keeping with Doctor Adam's instructions, she dipped her hands into the floating powder and rubbed them over her face - paying particular attention to her scared cheek. After a minute or two of washing, she took a towel and dried herself. It was all part of the cleansing ritual.

Finally, it was necessary to smear some Umfatu onto the facial scar. The small round jar was opened. A nauseous odour was released, which permeated the surrounding air. It was far worse than any smell which had previously spent time in the bathroom!

Elanor gazed at a mirror, which hung on the wall above the sink. She smeared some Umfatu over the scar tissue. Much later, she confided that during the procedure, she had seen faint smoke rising from the scar. And over forty years later, she still maintains it happened! However, Nicola and I admit to seeing nothing. Nevertheless, the rituals of sweeping floors and the washing of Elanor's face were repeated twice more during the following days.

At the end of two weeks, there was an incredible difference. The prominent scar, along with the small round lumps, had receded. They had flattened out against her face. A scar was still visible but was by no means obvious. In later years, a dab of make-up might cover any trace. Sandra was obliged to admit, albeit reluctantly, that the Zulu treatment had worked. And I - for one - was ever grateful to Doctor Adam!

# 29

## SPIDER AND SERPENT

Our house had an oblong-shaped lounge. One of its long walls faced the outside sprawl of land. It was fitted with a composite of steel-framed doors and windows. Somehow, the room's limited space managed to accommodate our collection of furniture. Three brown-leather armchairs and a polished wood coffee table fitted perfectly. An armchair was carefully positioned to afford a commanding view of the external scene. Unfortunately, the view was restricted by the close proximity of the rondavel and circular water-dam. Wild kikuyu grass, with the texture of a thick worsted carpet, grew freely around the buildings. While maintaining a satisfactory height, it added a touch of pale-green colour to the scene.

One hot and sunny day, whilst seated in the armchair, I sipped steaming tea from a favourite mug. With mug in hand, my gaze passed idly through a steel-framed lounge window. On the outside of the window and in one bottom corner, I chanced to notice a vacant spider's web. Suddenly, and taking me completely by surprise, an airborne hornet appeared. On an unwavering flight-path, it flew directly into the web! The action might be compared to that of a Kamikaze pilot! The hornet was instantly entangled in the strands of the web.

Frantically, its tiny wings flapped as it fought to extricate itself. But quick as a flash, a previously hidden spider appeared from out of the corner. Bounding forward, it pounced on the back of its would-be victim. And as the spider was about to administer its death-inducing bite, the hornet's struggle paid dividends. It managed to break free from the web's gossamer grip. Both the hornet and its piggy-backed passenger became instantly airborne! And like a witch astride a broomstick, they flew off into the sky! Thus, in one momentous action, the captive became the captor and both were flying high! It was an amazing sight to witness.

On yet another hot and sunny day - but much later in time - I discovered a hornet's nest. About the size of an average pineapple, it was attached to the rondavel's doorframe. Surrounding the nest, the hornets were numerous and very active.

Regrettably, and purely in the interest of child safety, I decided they would have to go. A can of *Doom* sprang to mind. It was the one used to expel cockroaches at our old apartment. Clasping the can, I stealthily edged forward. The buzzing sounds of multiple hornets reached my ears. Stopping short of the rondavel, my senses bade me not to tarry. With an outstretched arm, I gingerly pointed the can's nozzle towards the nest. My fingers tightened their grip and pressed a button. It caused a gaseous cloud to enshroud the winged victims. Many reacted by shuffling around. But half a dozen became instantly airborne and flew towards me. Turning on my heels, I dashed to the house! Still holding the can, my sleeveless arm received two sharp pricks from the pursuers. I had been stung! Fortunately, I was inside the house before their friends decided to follow.

Next day, thankfully, the unwanted visitors were gone - but they had left behind a couple of *signatures* on my arm!

During the summer months, evenings spent at our Hillside plot were mostly pleasant. The irregular outline of distant hills stood steadfast - as though painted on a blue, canvas sky. Late in the afternoon when the sun slowly set, the sky changed colour. The surrounding land and its attendant buildings appeared to take on a different hue. Silhouettes of nearby trees and the occasional wind-pump acquired a temporary prominence. And when the sun finally disappeared behind the hills, a cooling breeze swept briefly across the land.

Soon after, hundreds of tiny winged insects mysteriously took to the air. Within minutes low, black clouds formed above them. Numerous small, flying bats had arrived. And like squadrons of jetfighters, they swooped and soared. Their mission was to voraciously consume the air-borne food source. Whilst the minutes ticked away, the sky drew steadily darker. And as if on cue, the bats flew off to some nocturnal retreat. In their wake, stars appeared to twinkle in the darkened sky. Another gentle, cooling breeze quickly followed and all was generally quiet. But now and then, the peace was interrupted by the distant spasmodic barking, of one dog and then another!

On certain evenings, the cacophony of invisible croaking frogs could be heard. Inhabiting a rocky stream between two faraway hills, they were a living portent of rain - which would undoubtedly arrive a day or two later. How the frogs knew rain was coming was a mystery to me. Sometimes, the rain would fall with gusto and strikes of lightning would often follow.

I remember one evening when a storm was in progress. With a view to making a drink of tea, I stood in the kitchen holding a kettle. Reaching to turn on the cold-water tap, I looked through the kitchen window. About a hundred yards away, forked lightning struck the ground. At the same instant, my hand received a mild electric shock from the metal water tap!

Living at the plot had certain benefits, but now and again, it presented challenges. After the previous night's thunderstorm, I found our telephone to be out of action. Its supply cable entered the house and ran along the upper-wall of the study room. Glancing at the wall, two small black smudges, about a metre apart, caught my attention. The 'smudges' were actually gaps in the cable. For an inexplicable reason the lightning strike had vaporized the cable in the two places. Fortunately, when I bridged the offending gaps - by attaching pieces of fresh cable - the telephone worked again!

There was another time when I was sitting in the 'chosen armchair' and drinking a mug of tea. On this occasion, whilst gazing through the lounge window, I pondered how I would complete the next household chore. The sun was high in the bright blue sky, and there was a general stillness about the scene - in fact, nothing was moving. Even the vanes of the wind-pump were stationary. Between gulps of tea, my eyes lazily scanned the area near the rondavel. Just as I was beginning to doze, I noticed a small movement. It came from the thick grass which grew next to the water-dam. Soon after, I saw what I thought was a snake! It was rapidly disappearing down a small hole in the ground.

Approaching the hole, I saw what I thought was an old belt, which lay on the ground. But on closer inspection, it was a discarded snakeskin! The sight filled me with fear and dread. With children around and not least our pet cats, the potential presence of a snake was a major cause for concern. There and then, I decided drastic action must be taken. Later that day, Sandra listened intently as I explained my intended plan.

"If I should see a snake again", I announced, "I'll call out loudly and let you know. And to limit its chance of escape, I'll keep my eyes trained on it."

"Okay, hawk-eye and then what?" asked Sandra flippantly.

"So then, wherever you happen to be, make a move towards the garage and bring me the spade."

"Is that all baas?" asked Sandra - sounding a little taunt.

"YES; I'll do the rest!"

"And what is the rest? Oh, hero of mine?"

"Just wait and see" said I, displaying a look which conveyed doubt as to her sincerity.

With my plans in place, we didn't have long to wait for the action to begin. A day or two later, as I left the dining room to enter the kitchen, I dallied. The two rooms were built on different levels and were connected by a singular stone-step. Facing the kitchen whilst standing on the step, I instinctively peeked through the opposite window. It was possible to see the garage, which stood a short distance from the house.

Between the two lay our concrete stoep and a flat stretch of turf. It so happened I dallied longer than a casual glance. My recent sighting of the serpent had caused me to be more alert.

Unexpectedly, I thought I saw something move in front of the garage. It was a slight but unmistakable movement at ground level. Another careful look and I suddenly realised it *was* a snake! Instantly, I froze with shock. But a moment or two later, my thoughts were galvanised into action. Remembering Sandra was in the lounge and reading a book and the children were playing in their bedroom - I hollered; "SANDRA!"

"What is it?" she asked.

"SNAKE!" I shrieked. "QUICK; GET THE SPADE!"

Keeping my eyes firmly fixed on the snake, I watched it slowly zigzag along the grassy turf. It was moving towards the kitchen and me!

Sandra rushed from the lounge and stood behind me. She tried to see the intruder. I suspect she may have thought I was joking. The children had heard my call and rallied around their mother as she assessed the situation.

"Sandra!" - I barked. "Go out through the lounge doors and move cautiously towards the garage. And bring me the spade!"

Having moved between the garage and the house, the reptile was in full view. Its two-metre-long body was stout, and its skin colour a mix of grey and brown. Sandra headed through the dining room and into the lounge, with the children in hot pursuit. As I watched with increasing trepidation, the snake glided ever closer towards me.

Sounds of Sandra fumbling with door keys reached my ears. She managed to unlock the glass-panelled doors and together with our girls, descend the two steps from the house. The moment they stood on the grass-covered ground, an unexpected thing happened. The snake instantly reacted. Although it couldn't see Sandra or the children from where it lay, its head lifted slightly and turned to point in their direction. I guessed it must have sensed vibrations from their feet - as they made contact with the ground. Pausing for less than a second, the serpent quickened its pace. Gliding gracefully, it moved towards the edge of the kitchen stoep. Once there, it joined the longer grass, which grew as a fringe, from one end of the concrete slab to the other. I rushed to the kitchen window to gain a better view.

The snake was now weaving through the grass fringe towards the water tower - which stood at the corner of the house. Built with house bricks, the water tower was an oblong-shaped structure. Perched on its top was a hollow, concrete cylinder of around three feet in diameter. It held the household's water supply. Stacked against the base of the tower was a pile of concrete blocks, each of which measured a cubic foot.

Sandra arrived at the garage and took hold of the spade. Our two daughters stood by her side. Meantime, before the snake reached the far edge of the stoep, I flung open the kitchen door and rushed outside. Having navigated the last piece of open ground, the snake reached the water tower. Finding an opening in the top of the concrete blocks, it slid inside. So far as I could tell, that's where it remained. Hastily, I strode towards the concrete blocks, while Sandra and the children waited at a distance.

Responding to my request, Elanor took hold of the heavy spade. She struggled to drag it towards me. Panting lightly, she stood at arm's length while I gave her further instructions.

"Okay, this is what we do. The snake is in there somewhere. One by one, I'm going to lift the blocks off the stack. When we get to the snake, you hand me the spade. Okay?"

With her tiny face ablaze with excitement, Elanor nodded. Meanwhile, Sandra and Nicola nervously watched us. Feeling sure the enemy would not be near the top of the stack, I quickly lifted the first of five blocks. There was nothing there, and my arms swiftly swung the block to the ground. At that moment, I became aware it was a windless day, and no birds were to be seen. The sun itself seemed to hang motionless in the sky - as though time itself had been paused.

My heart beat faster as I cautiously lifted a second concrete block. Beneath it was another empty space. Heaving it to the ground, I turned to Elanor again. Considering the removal of two blocks must have brought me closer to the snake's hiding place, I posed a final question: "Are you ready?"

Grinning with excitement, she nodded.

Slowly, I took hold of the third block. With it held firmly in my grip, and in one rapid motion, I lifted it clear. But doing so, held it at an angle to shield my lower body. Looking down, I was shocked to see the snake! It was coiled in a hollow cavity in the top of the next block.

"Quick! Elanor," I cried, "Give me the spade!"

Throwing the block to the ground, I turned to face her but was unaware she had taken a step forward.

Inadvertently I stood on her foot! Elanor yelped! Our actions were not unlike a scene from a Laurel and Hardy movie - but this was no time for levity! Grasping the spade firmly, I turned again to face the enemy. To my surprise, the serpent had taken advantage of the distraction to make good its escape. Its body had uncoiled and was sliding down the back of the remaining blocks. The action was like that of a 'Slinky' toy moving down a flight of stairs. But with one murderous action, the spade's cutting edge fell squarely onto the escaping body and almost cleaved it in two halves.

Using the spade once more, I quickly dislodged another block and fully exposed the enemy. And with one mechanical motion, I used the spade to scoop up its injured body and pitched it into the middle of the exposed turf. Moving quickly, I stepped forward to administer the coup de grace. The spade fell like Madame Guillotine's blade. One blow almost severed the snake's head from its body. But a small portion of flesh kept the two parts connected. Both head and body were still moving! It wasn't a pretty sight.

"Ooh, kill it, Peter!!" cried Sandra in despair.

"I'm trying!!" I answered abruptly.

Taking a more careful aim, I made another thrust with the blade. This time, the head parted from the body. At that moment, the sounds of the day returned. It was as though an imaginary pause button had been released.

The snake's severed body lay motionless on the grass-covered ground. Foraging ants scurried over it. But that was not the case with the head as its underside rested on the ground.

Within seconds, an incredible spectacle unfolded before its audience. The mouth of the dismembered head began to open and then close with slow regularity. It was a surreal sight to observe. Curiously, the mouth appeared to be taking large gulps of air. For a full ten minutes, the motion continued.

Finally, beginning at the tip of the open mouth, the skin's surface formed into a visible 'ripple'. The 'ripple' travelled the full length of the head; like a miniature wave, rolling along the surface of the sea. The process took a few seconds for it to arrive at the severed end. At that moment, a flap of skin extended from each side of the head. Stretching outwards some two inches, they formed a kind of hood. And whilst keeping parallel with the ground, the complete head suddenly sprang upwards!

Like a tensioned spring having been released, it cleared the ground by two or three inches. Gravity pulled it instantly back to earth, where it lay for a second or two. And then, with one swift and final action, the head flipped over onto its upper side! And after that, there was no further movement!

A question which now presented itself was, "What to do with the lifeless reptile?" One suggestion was to put the remains in a bag and take them to my sangoma friends. But what if the snake was miraculously resurrected whilst I was driving my car? I had the notion that it might slide out of the bag and seek revenge! But another, and perhaps more rational thought, caused me to imagine friends of the snake, who might come looking for it.

Finally, I took the bag to the far end of the plot and buried it in the ground!

# 30
## 'BIG BALLS' GETS A SHOCK

Someone once said, "You don't own a cat - it owns you!" But speaking for our family, I prefer to say the time we spent at the plot was *shared* with six cats. All were treated well and, by the same token, were expected to keep any mice at bay. They appeared to have done their duty because I don't recall ever seeing a mouse!

Each cat was named from a choice of African tribes. The eldest one was named *Zulu*. She had matt-black fur, which - presumably due to her advanced age - had lost its youthful sheen. Her mood of the day was either grumpy or friendly, but undoubtedly, she was always unpredictable. Often, whilst being stroked, Zulu would slowly turn her head towards the caring hand. It was a gesture which suggested a show of appreciation. But on occasion, and usually without warning, she acted like a striking cobra. Her mouth would lightly bite the stroking hand, and her teeth graze the carer's skin!

The cats lived peacefully together until the day when a large, marauding tomcat strode into view. He appeared rough and tough as any cat could be. Whiskers grew from his gnarled face at precarious angles. His shabby, grey coat was peppered with various bald patches. The missing clumps of fur bore silent testimony to the many skirmishes he may have encountered.

Complimenting the coat's unkempt condition was a short, crooked tail. It poked - as best it could - towards the sky. But the casual observer could be distracted from all of this by the spectacle of the tom's large, protruding testicles! And after carefully considering their ungainly appearance, I decided to name him *Big Balls*.

At meal times, our pet cats would gather at their communal feeding bowl to eat the food. But quite often, and seemingly from nowhere, *Big Balls* would arrive and join them. He apparently knew when it was mealtime. His persona was such that his mere presence was enough to cause our cats to slink away. Usually after re-grouping, they would stand at a short distance, looking forlornly towards their surrendered food bowl. In the meantime, *Big Balls* was left to devour as much food as he wanted and at his own pace. His continuing visits might have been tolerated had it not been for one major transgression. It was when he was seen to have his way with a certain lady cat. From that moment, it was decided that Mister *Big Balls* would have to go!

My plan to rid us of this menace was put into action when I picked up a large sheet of corrugated, galvanised tin. Normally, it would be used for the roofing of storage sheds and the like. The sheet was placed on the flat grassy area in front of the kitchen's entrance door. As it lay on the ground, small blocks of wood were placed under each of its four corners. The wooden blocks would serve as insulators.

My next step was to remove a power socket from one end of an electrical extension cord. After rendering two of the exposed conductors safe, the third, or 'live' conductor, was attached to the tin sheet.

The remainder of the extension cord was run under the closed kitchen door. The three-pin plug, attached to the end of the cord, was pushed into a wall-mounted power socket.

At this juncture, I think the reader may realise the intention. Once the switch of the power socket was put into the 'on' position the galvanised tin sheet would become electrified!

Filled with a generous amount of food, the felines' feeding bowl was carefully placed in the centre of the tin sheet. Without any encouragement, the cats rapidly spaced themselves around the edge of the bowl and began to devour the savoury offering.

Meanwhile, I stood inside the kitchen with the door closed. And from my vantage point, next to the power socket, I could look through a window and secretly observe the cats. Incidentally, this was the window through which I had seen the visiting snake, mentioned in the previous chapter.

It didn't take long for *Big Balls* to make an appearance. As if by intuition - or maybe a super sense of smell - he seemingly knew that food was served. Rounding a corner of the nearby garage, the glare of the noon-day sun caused his eyes to squint. His face looked meaner than ever before. His four paws deftly made their way towards the pseudo dining table. Meanwhile, the regular diners were oblivious to the impending intrusion. The delicious food had completely captivated their attention. *Big Balls* arrived at the edge of the tin sheet.

Cautiously, he peeked from side to side, making quite sure he was safe to continue. Stealthily stepping onto the 'dining table', he moved gingerly towards the feeding-bowl. Somehow sensing his arrival one cat stopped eating and lifted her head.

Glancing sideways she came face to face with the monster! Instantly shocked, she quickly sidled away and, by so doing, left a gap in the ring of feeders.

Without encouragement, *Big Balls* moved into the breach and began to feed. One by one, the cats caught sight of him. And one by one, they withdrew from the bowl. At a short distance, they broodily gathered together. Each of them cast an accusing look, towards the offending intruder. There was, however, one exception, and that was Zulu. She was hesitant to leave. Perhaps confused due to her age, she simply sat motionless behind the unwanted visitor. Or maybe it was her inherent grumpiness which caused her to display defiance.

From the kitchen I watched the unfolding drama, with my finger poised in readiness to flick the power socket's switch. Zulu's reluctance to move caused me to delay. I found myself willing her to leave the tin sheet and let *el Matador* do his job. Incredible as it seemed, the dark, feline loafer began to respond. With slow and careful movements - not unlike a sloth - she stood up and stretched her legs. Pausing for a few moments, she turned her head and looked intently at *Big Balls*. It was as if she sought permission to leave - or maybe it was to utter a farewell curse!

At last, Zulu ambled to the edge of the tin sheet and climbed off. Excitedly, I waited until she reached the gathering of her friends. The coast was finally clear! With his head inside the bowl, *Big Balls* was oblivious to his surroundings. Taking a deep breath - I triumphantly flicked the socket's switch! When the electric power flowed, *Big Balls* instantly lifted clear of the tin sheet! With his four legs outstretched, stiff and straight, he resembled a Harrier jump-jet leaving the deck of a ship - albeit much faster!

Unable to defy gravity by a gap of several inches he immediately descended. But an instant before landing, the cat's furry legs were in motion. And like a hill climber struggling on a slippery slope, his legs were running, but he was going nowhere! In the space of a moment momentum had been gained and he darted away. The sudden burst of activity filled the gathering of cats with confusion. Scattering in different directions, they fled the scene! Leaving behind a trail of rising dust, *Big Balls* retreated around the corner of the garage and was never seen again!

As a foot-note - or should I say a *paw-note* - I wonder if the word 'Scatter' is derived from an action such as the above. When cats run away and in different directions - do they sCATter?

*'They fled the scene'*

# 31

## MEETING WITH SPIKE MILLIGAN

Spike Milligan was a British comedian and author of numerous books. He was a star of stage, radio, television, and the cinema screen. In September of 1983, he arrived in Johannesburg on what was described as his *First Farewell Tour of South Africa*. He starred in a variety show performed at Johannesburg's Linder Auditorium. The opportunity to see him live in action was not to be missed. Sandra declined the offer to tag along but agreed that I could take our two daughters. The theatre was full to capacity. Looking at the stage from the auditorium, we occupied front-row seats on the right-wing.

A couple of warm-up acts included a ventriloquist and a vocalist. The latter was a lad from Cape Town. His name was Rob Graham, although better known to everyone as *Crocodile Harris*. He had a number-one hit in South Africa with the recording *Give Me the Good News*. It also reached the number one slot in France and stayed there for ten weeks!

Spike Milligan's personal performance was packed with humour. Amongst other topics was a narration about jam rolls, which had to be eaten before midnight on the last day of the year! He also demonstrated his musical talent by playing a number or two on a trumpet.

Following that, he played an electric guitar, which was gifted to him by ex-Beatle George Harrison. Unfortunately, during his musical delivery, a brief electrical fault caused an interruption in the theatre's sound system. But appearing unfazed, Spike continued by ad-libbing. And after playing his guitar he began a comedy routine, which involved him wearing a series of false and over-sized noses. My young daughters laughed heartily. They spoke about Spike for months afterwards and remembered him as *'the man with the funny noses.'*

During the show, he produced a silver-plated water flask, which dangled from a thin chain. Swinging it like a pendulum, he called to the audience.

"This is an impression of John the Baptist!"

Surreptitiously, he removed the container's top, and whilst pointing the flask towards the audience, he shook it vigorously. Dollops of water sprang from its open neck and flew through the air. They fell like large raindrops onto the audience, who were seated directly beneath him. Taken by surprise, their smiling faces were given an unexpected wetting. Or, as Spike would prefer to say - they were *baptised*! Bringing this boisterous gesture to a conclusion, Spike was heard to utter the words:

"That'll teach you for sitting in the expensive seats!"

He ended his performance in the show by sitting centre stage and speaking about the notable times of his career. The story I enjoyed most was when he and his friend Peter Sellers had a brief encounter with the law. Sellers had bought a new Rolls Royce automobile, and although largely happy with its finish and its performance, there was a small niggling problem.

He called on his long-time friend, Spike Milligan, to offer some assistance.

"Spike, there's a squeak coming from the back end of my car, and it's most annoying. Would you help me to find it?"

"What do you want me to do?" asked Spike.

Holding a piece of chalk, Sellers explained his intended plan. He asked Spike to take the chalk and climb into the car's boot space. Sellers declared he would drive the car along the road. And when Spike heard the squeaky sound, he was to draw a chalk mark on the car's body work - as close to the sound as possible.

The request seemed plausible to Spike's adventurous spirit and he obligingly climbed into the boot. Peter Sellers started the car's engine and drove off down the road. But he soon discovered that when something is expected to happen, it usually doesn't. However, not to be outdone, Peter thought of a solution to the problem. He would drive the car up onto the pavement and then off again. "Surely?" he thought, "The jolting action would activate the squeak."

As Peter's plan unfolded, he was pleased to find that it did actually work! Although, Spike was not too happy about being bumped around inside the car's boot!

Going according to the plan, when the Rolls Royce mounted and then left the pavement, Spike was able to place chalk marks on the car's interior bodywork. However, during this procedure, a policeman happened to be walking in their direction. Spotting the vehicle from afar, he was puzzled by its erratic capers. At the opportune moment, he raised an arm - causing Peter to bring the Rolls Royce to a halt.

Striding over to the car, the policeman peered into the opened driver's door window.

"Good evening, sir," he said. "Is there something wrong with the car's steering?"

"No, officer. It's just that the car has a squeak. But I've got Spike Milligan in the boot, and he is looking for it."

The policeman was unsure whether to laugh or to frown.

"Yes sir, I understand," he said patronisingly. "But do you mind if I have a look inside the car's boot?"

Peter smiled as he obligingly stepped from the car. The two men stood in front of the car's boot. Watched closely by the policeman Peter opened the boot lid. Imagine the policeman's surprise when, like a Jack-in-the-box, up popped Spike Milligan. Smiling broadly and with his best Goon Show voice, he said, "Hallo!"

The show finished to rapturous applause and the audience began to disperse. With no curtain to close, the stage remained exposed. Spike Milligan walked from centre stage towards an exit door. His wife, who had joined him from off stage, was in close pursuit. Fortunately for me, they were heading in my direction.

During the show, I had schemed a way to get Spike's autograph. The present moment seemed like a golden opportunity. I begged my daughters to remain seated and to wait for me. Throwing a leg over a low barrier, I was quickly onto the stage and walking towards the withdrawing Milligan. I heard his wife call out from behind me.

"Bloody hell - let him get off the stage!"

Ignoring the outburst, I pressed forward.

"Excuse me, Mister Milligan!" I hollered, as I hurried to his side. "Could I please have your autograph?"

Spike stopped in his tracks and half turned towards me. I offered him a pen and my copy of the show's programme. He attempted to write but the pen failed to work properly. For a moment he stood motionless, as if in thought, and then voiced an idea.

"I've got a better pen in my dressing room" he said, and bade me to follow him.

The dressing room was spacious and its decor modern. Seated in a padded armchair Spike began to sign the programme. Some distance away his wife busied herself with items on a table. Standing next to Spike's chair, I made a comment.

"I'd like to thank you for all the joy you've given to the world down the years."

In all modesty, Spike replied, "Thank you." But immediately, downplaying the accolade, he casually stated, "It's just a job!"

Returning my programme, he looked at my shoes. Following his gaze, I noticed the heels were lightly coated with dried mud! They spoilt my otherwise smart appearance. At that moment I recalled it had rained that day. And leaving home in the semi-darkness, I had stepped into a puddle. Spike's attention left my shoes and his eyes peered directly into mine. They seemed to silently seek an explanation regarding the mud. His eyes had a remarkable colour. Like a cloudless summer's sky, they were pale blue with a greyish tint and appeared to have endless depth.

Fortunately, my embarrassing moment was brushed aside when I quickly voiced an inquiry.

"How are your children?"

"Oh, they're fine", he answered, taken by surprise.

As he spoke, his face broke into a smile, and he looked towards his wife. Still busy at the table, she reacted at the same moment by looking at him. My question appeared to have aroused their mutual interest. At that instant, he thought to introduce her.

"Oh, this is my wife," he said as he gestured in her direction. Stepping forward I politely shook her hand and she smiled in response. It was then I remembered my own children. Thanking my hosts, I quickly returned to the auditorium. Crocodile Harris breezed past me as he made his way from the stage. Gratefully, my daughters were safe and eagerly waiting to hear my tale of meeting *the man with the funny noses.*

After learning that Spike was due to attend a show in Durban, I had the notion to send him a letter. Addressing it to his Durban hotel, I offered him an invite to visit our home at Hillside. In addition, I included an 'Irish joke' which was popular at that time. The following is how it went.

"An Irishman named Paddy was at sea in a small fishing boat. A storm came up, producing an enormous swell. Thunder and lightning heralded a terrible wind. The fishing boat took on water and finally sank. When the storm eventually abated, Paddy found himself trying hard to stay afloat. He clung to a large piece of flotsam. Seemingly from nowhere, a helicopter arrived.

A man lowered a rescue cable and shouted to Paddy.

"Grab hold of the cable, and we'll pull you up!"

"No tanks, oi'll put my faith in the LORD!" said the Irishman.

Shortly after, a Royal Navy frigate appeared. Some sailors threw a rope to Paddy and shouted,

"Take hold of the rope, and we'll pull you aboard."

"No tanks, oi'll put my faith in the LORD!" said Paddy.

A few minutes passed before a submarine surfaced next to Paddy. From the conning tower, the Captain shouted.

"Swim towards us, and we'll take you aboard!"

"No tanks. I'm putting my faith in the LORD!" was the reply.

As the submarine submerged, it created a large swell, which caused the Irishman to drown. Paddy found himself in Heaven and standing in front of the LORD.

He turned to the LORD and said accusingly,

"I put my faith in you, and you didn't help me!"

The LORD looked at Paddy and said,

"I sent you a HELICOPTER, and a ROYAL NAVAL FRIGATE and then a SUBMARINE - What more did you want?"

Days after sending my letter, I received a reply. Spike Milligan thanked me for my correspondence and also for the 'Irish joke'. His letter ended with the words - 'Love, Light and Peace'. What more could anyone wish for?

# 32

# SEARCHING FOR A ZULU KING'S GRAVE

In September of 1873, a Zulu warrior named Cetshwayo, was crowned King of the Zulu nation. Almost six years later Zululand found itself at war with Great Britain. During the first half of 1879, a series of battles was fought between the British military forces and the warriors of Cetshwayo's impis (Regiments). Ultimately, the British army was victorious. Cetshwayo was captured and imprisoned at Cape Town. Following a brief spell of captivity, he and his entourage were transported by ship to England. The King of Zululand was presented to Queen Victoria. At the close of the regal meeting, Cetshwayo was instructed to return to Zululand and live in peace amongst his people.

During the interim, the British divided the Zulu nation into a number of separate areas. Each was to be governed by its own chosen leader. When Cetshwayo returned to his country, he found that he had lost the power he had previously enjoyed. Not content with the state of affairs, he mustered an impi of warriors and set out to conquer his biggest rival. Unfortunately for him, he underestimated the skill of his opposition and was defeated. During the battle, Cetshwayo was wounded but managed to escape with the help of some faithful followers.

He made a successful recovery and settled in an area which is present day Eshowe. Just two years later, in 1884, Cetshwayo died. Some say he was poisoned because he agitated to resume control of his broken nation. A few selected subjects transported the King's lifeless body to the hills of Nkandhla; in a remote part of Zululand. It was there he was interred within a secluded and pleasant glade. Afterwards, the dismantled pieces of the transport cart were used to surround and decorate the gravesite.

For decades thereafter, no white person is known to have visited the site. However, during the 1930s, author Carel Birkby made a tour of Zululand and attempted to find Cetshwayo's grave. In his book *Zulu Journey*, he writes the following:

"I came up from Eshowe to Nkandhla in search of Cetshwayo's grave, but I could not find it, for no native would tell me where it was. They looked stolidly at me and answered the cross-examination of Joshua Titus (His Zulu guide) with an unshakable, 'Don't know'". [6]

In September of 1961, author C.T. Binns wrote about the life of Cetshwayo in a book titled *The Last Zulu King*. He had also set himself the task of finding the grave. After travelling many miles along a 'bumpy and hilly route,' he parked his car and continued his journey on foot. A long and arduous walk over the 'mountainous country' took him to the top of a hill. From there he overlooked a wooded glade and saw where the grave was sited.

He stopped to gaze and weigh his options. But his ruminations were soon disturbed by a party of Zulus, who surrounded him. They were the guardians of Cetshwayo's grave and prevented him from entering the wooded glade.

He would first need to obtain the permission of a Zulu chief - who had been appointed by the Royal House of the Nation. A protracted conversation took place between the men and the author's interpreter. Eventually, he was able to convince the Zulu guardians that he wished to see the grave purely for historical interest.

Finally, C. T. Binns was escorted to the site, where he was able to see the grave and even managed to snap a photograph. When recording his adventure, he wrote the following:

"I was later informed that I was the first white man to visit that sacred spot for close to forty years. No wonder - the trip had taken nearly thirteen hours and had involved a rough motor tour of close to a hundred miles - and rounded off by a walk of eighteen miles over the rugged mountainous country - but it was all worth it." [7]

Not quite ten years later, a party of young men set out on their own quest to find the site of the Zulu King's grave. Maj. Justine Hulme, Midge Carter, Terry Wilson, S. B. Bourquin and Ken Gillings, began their journey from Durban. They travelled in a station wagon and made a temporary camp at the Eshowe caravan park. Having twice before, unsuccessfully attempted the journey, this time they were determined to reach their destination.

Early on a Saturday morning, they broke camp and proceeded, via the forest, towards Nkandhla. After driving reasonably well for about 65km, they turned onto a 'shocking road' and travelled a further 18km. Finally, leaving the car near an old storehouse, they decided to continue on foot. A young Zulu girl who worked at the store was said to live near the King's grave and would act as their guide.

Along the arduous journey, the five explorers became painfully aware of the weight of their backpacks. And what made matters worse was seeing the young Zulu girl carry a 50lb bag of mealies 'effortlessly' on her head! Many rivulets were crossed, which flowed amongst the hilly countryside. Furthermore, the heat of the day became oppressive, which caused the men to rest. For some minutes, they sat on a hilltop overlooking the Nkunzane River.

During this time, when perhaps they contemplated the sanity of their expedition, their Zulu guide suddenly pointed to a distant hillock. Behind it was the sought-after grave. After hiking for many more minutes, the men were confronted by the custodian of the King's grave. Since one of the men spoke fluent Zulu, a lively discussion took place. Naturally, some questions were raised as to why five white men would want to see the grave of the Zulu Nkosi. (King) Assured their intentions were good, there followed a customary sharing of uTshwala (Zulu beer) before the men were finally escorted to the gravesite.

Ken Gillings recorded the visit with the following words:

"Slowly, we entered the sacred grove of trees and silently followed the guardian to the grave, which is situated in the centre of the bush. We soon reached the sacred spot where we eagerly took photographs. All that can be seen of the grave is a collection of old pieces of metal - the rims, brake and other unidentified bits of the wagon, on which Cetshwayo's body was carried after his death on the 8th February 1884. Snake lilies grow in abundance, and the atmosphere is as serene as the site itself." [8]

The five men retraced their footsteps and, before nightfall, arrived at the Nkunzane River.

After making a campfire, they unrolled their sleeping bags and slept peacefully - contented they had finally achieved their goal. It wasn't until much later in their journey, they learned they had slept in an area infested with mambas!

Almost a hundred years after the death of Cetshwayo, the Kwa Zulu Natal authorities constructed a graded-soil road. It cut through the rugged hills in the Nkandhla region of Zululand. The road was designed to provide access to the wooded glade, where King Cetshwayo lay entombed. The remnants of the hand cart, which lay over the King's grave, were taken away to a museum located at Ulundi. In their place was laid a marble slab, engraved with an inscription in the languages of Zulu and English.

The following is a copy of the English text.

'Here lie the remains of King Cetshwayo, son of Mpande and his Queen Ngoumbazi (Daughter of Chief Mbondi Zungu.) He died at Eshowe on the 8$^{th}$ of February 1884 after a tempestuous reign of only five years. This stone was built through contributions from the Zulu nation and is erected in loving memory and gratitude for all he suffered in the defence of our land and heritage.

Unveiled by his great-great-grandson heir and successor, King Goodwill Zwelithini Ka Bhekuzulu Ka Solomon Ka Dinuzulu Ka Cetshwayo, the reigning monarch of the Zulu nation, on Saturday, 27$^{th}$ September 1980, 96 years after the King's demise.'

My passion for the history of the Zulu nation imbued me with a longing desire to find Cetshwayo's resting place. It was five years after the restoration ceremony when my desire was fulfilled.

With some gentle persuasion, the Farley family succumbed to my proposal to visit the gravesite.

Considering the tribulations experienced by previous explorers, I thought it prudent to make certain preparations. Resulting from a few annual visits to the Eshowe area, I had befriended a retired sugar-cane farmer. His name was Mr. Lees. Whilst enjoying his South African hospitality, we spent hours discussing the history of Natal and, in particular, Zululand.

Mister Lees was kind enough to guide our family to the local places of historical importance. Of particular interest was the site where Cetshwayo had lived, and later died. But when I disclosed my desire to visit the King's grave, Mister Lees expressed some concern. He soon convinced me that it was not an easy place to find. Furthermore, his dubious directions and descriptions of the difficult terrain caused the mission to seem precarious. In addition to this, he explained that along the route which we intended to take, the majority of Zulus could not speak English!

It was then I remembered the old adage, 'Necessity is the mother of invention'. An idea formulated in my mind. Since my portable cassette tape recorder was close to hand, and since Mister Lees spoke fluent Zulu, I asked myself a question. "What if he was to record his voice - whilst speaking the Zulu language - and ask for directions to Cetshwayo's gravesite on our behalf?"

I had the notion that on arrival to the general area of the gravesite, I might play the tape recording to a local Zulu. The hope was that it would produce a positive result. It was during the Easter weekend of 1985 when my plan was put into practice.

After stocking our faithful campervan with some necessary provisions, the Farley family began the trek. The following is an account of that exciting day.

"Easter Sunday - April 7$^{th}$ 1985.

Journey to Cetshwayo's Grave.

At about 0830hrs, we set out on our journey from the municipal campsite of Eshowe. There was intermittent rain along the route, although, for the most part, the sky was clear. After driving some distance along the Nkandhla road, the weather improved. And by the time we left the main asphalt road to proceed along one of gravel, the clear weather permitted some spectacular views. But from then onwards, the road surface progressively deteriorated. I told myself there was no cause for anxiety - well - perhaps a little. The camper-van followed the road down some almost vertical descents. They called for first-gear work and a liberal application of the foot brake. The road morphed into a track, where, at every turn, we saw rolling hills disappearing into the distance. Some were studded with kraals, and it was interesting to see how they were constructed.

Quantities of rocks were held together with compacted soil against the sloping side of a hill. On top of the projection, a level, semi-circular clearing was formed. A circle of upright tree branches, stripped of foliage, formed a cattle kraal. The traditional Zulu hut, dubbed the 'bee-hive', was largely superseded by a more permanent dwelling. Nevertheless, some scattered examples of the 'bee-hive' variety were evident. The permanent dwelling was a white-painted, circular mud-wall, with a single doorway. Its roof was an umbrella-shaped framework of thin tree branches covered with thatch.

We crossed a trio of streams, before arriving at a medium size, shallow river. Towering above it was a rocky ridge, while laid across the river was a wide concrete slab. It formed a flat road bridge, linking one side of the track to the other. The tyres of our campervan created small waves as they passed through the rushing water. At some distance below us was a riverbank. And since it may have been wash day, some Zulu ladies had gathered there. Gaily dressed in oddments of bright-coloured garments, they repeatedly dunked soiled clothing into the passing water.

Their action was followed by dashing the wet clothes against some nearby smooth boulders, while hoping to dispel any ingrained dirt. The washed garments were spread out to dry in the hot sunlight. Meanwhile, other ladies - who had gathered upstream - filled plastic containers with water. Placed on their shoulders - or, in some cases, their heads - they carried them home. Corpulent shapes - silhouetted against the sunlit sky - were seen to be moving in single file along the high rocky ridge.

Throughout our journey almost every vertical *descent* we encountered, presented in its turn, an almost vertical *ascent*. First-gear work was the order of the day. A number of times, I drove with heart in mouth - lest the camper-van slid backwards - or its engine should stall. The track ahead was gouged with a mix of wide and narrow furrows - all caused by earlier torrents of storm water. Above us we occasionally saw kraals, where curious dwellers looked down upon us. Whilst to our right and below us, the tops of huts were level with the camper-van's tyres. In this instance, the dwellers were looking up at us! At many stages of the journey, we saw random people observing our progress.

*"I drove with heart in mouth" (1985)*

*"We occasionally saw kraals" (1985)*

Almost everyone we saw, both young and old, waved a friendly arm. After driving a considerable distance, we reached a level area of ground. It lay beneath the brow of yet another hill.

Not far from the side of the track was a makeshift store. Above its entrance a large sign read, 'Inkayezi tea room.' Wondering if this might be a mirage, I contemplated seeking some refreshment. But whilst surveying the scene I noticed a *gogo* (an old Zulu lady) who was tilling a nearby piece of land. She happened to glance in my direction and I waved to her. Without further ado, she dropped her hoe and came hurrying towards us.

Turning to face Sandra, I announced the gogo's impending arrival.

"It looks as though it's time to put my master plan into action!" I proudly declared.

Sandra chuckled in anticipation of an unknown outcome. As the old lady approached I remembered a word of greeting in the Zulu language.

"Sakubona" (Hello, I see you)

"Yebo, Nkosi"- (Yes, sir) she replied.

Hastily, I brought my cassette player into view.

Pointing to the gadget I spoke another Zulu word, which I had managed to remember.

"Lalelani!" (Listen).

The wizened gogo curiously watched my finger press the gadget's 'play' button. Miraculously, a disembodied voice began speaking to *her* from *inside* the 'box'. The gogo's eyes widened.

She was stunned to hear the voice speaking in the Zulu language! I half expected her to run away but she stood her ground. Following a brief pre-amble, the electronic voice requested the listener to guide us to the grave of the Zulu King.

While listening to the recording, the gogo's head was level with the camper-van's steering wheel. From my seated position I studied her face. Its complexion was dark-brown and the skin texture appeared like shoe leather. Her fleshy ear-lobes sported small holes, each about the size of a one-cent coin. Her overall appearance was, undoubtedly, the result of regular exposure to the Zululand sunshine. Periodically, her head nodded in approbation of the message. Then suddenly, just as the recording was ending, her face brightened and expressed a knowing smile. She turned excitedly towards a grove of trees. Surprisingly, they stood a short distance behind us! A gnarled finger from her outstretched hand stabbed excitedly in their direction.

"Khona lapa!" (Over there!) She exclaimed, "Khona lapa!" she repeated.

Without the need for an interpreter, I instantly grasped what she meant. It was apparent we had unwittingly reached our destination!

As a show of gratitude, I handed the lady a pair of used but serviceable children's trousers. Her face became a study. Tired eyes lit-up and her wrinkled face erupted into a beaming smile. She turned to face a young woman who was standing in the veld, a short distance away. The young woman, who was possibly her daughter, had been watching our movements. Holding the trousers aloft, the gogo waved them triumphantly. Both women hurried towards each other across the recently furrowed land.

When I turned our vehicle around to face the Royal gravesite, I saw the two ladies admiring the gift. At that moment I had little doubt a Zulu child would soon be wearing it!

It was now mid-day. The sun was shining brightly and my family was hot and perspiring. The grove of trees, which graced a piece of level ground, was surrounded by a fence made of wire and wooden stakes. A simple gate prevented animals from entering, although it could be easily opened by visitors - such as us. A short path inside the grove led to another, albeit smaller, fenced enclosure. At its centre was the gravesite of King Cetshwayo.

Some nearby trees afforded plenty of shade, which, together with a natural breeze, created a cooling presence to the scene. Two individual trees grew close to the fenced enclosure. Standing like watchful guardians, their leafed branches cast shadows across a large marble slab which covered the Zulu King's gravesite. Edged with vertically-placed concrete pillars, the marble slab had an inscription in both Zulu and the English language. Each pillar stood two feet high, and each was connected to the next by a small-linked iron chain. Two of the pillars, placed at opposite corners of the slab, had toppled over. I suspect it was due to a weakness of the concrete base.

Having seen the gravesite, Sandra and our children ambled towards the campervan. At this moment their prime interest lay in consuming a cool drink. I lagged behind and spent a little more time making a few last photographs. Sunlight filtered through gaps in the overhead canopy - provided by the cluster of trees. The ambience was one of complete peacefulness and even the surrounding air was still.

*Nicola, Andrew and Elanor meeting new friends. (1985)*

*The author at the King's grave. (1985)*

There was a noticeable absence of mechanical sounds, such as motor vehicles or aeroplanes. Even natural sounds of children's voices or dogs barking were not to be heard. Only *one* sound had the affront to disturb the solitude and it was the clicking of my camera's shutter mechanism!

Slowly, I turned about and walked towards the campervan. At that moment, two small, yellow-coloured butterflies fluttered silently and playfully across my line of sight. Their bright yellow colour was enhanced by the Zululand sunshine and the backdrop of the sparse, green foliage.

With the camper-van's odometer registering 95618 km, we left the grave site at 1230hrs. One and one quarter hours later, we had travelled 23,5km, and our vehicle had reached a junction, which allowed us to join the Nkandhla road.

At 1515hrs, having travelled a further 11km, we arrived at the beginning of the asphalted section of the Nkandhla road. Finally, on our return to the Eshowe camping site, the time was 1545hrs, and the camper's odometer reading was 95682 km. All-in-all we had travelled a total of around 128 km that day.

During the evening, whilst sitting in the relative comfort of our tent, Sandra and I celebrated the success of our mission. Our children were given cool orange juice, while we had mugs of hot tea - it never tasted better! Pondering our adventure, I spared a thought for the Zulus, who had made the original journey, a hundred years before us. Where we had travelled, in the relative comfort of a campervan, they had done it on foot! And they had more than likely pushed and dragged the cart, which carried the lifeless body of their King!"

As a footnote to this story, it might interest the reader to know, thirty-three years after our Easter adventure, I made a return solo visit to the Royal gravesite. On that occasion, the old tracks of compacted soil, and the rough gravel roads, were now asphalted. Official tourist-type signposts pointed the way. Understandably, the combination of asphalted roads and official road signs made the journey far less stressful and much quicker.

Along the route, at previously isolated places, many small townships had sprouted. At one of them, a sizeable police station had been built. And on a high viewpoint, amongst the many hills, stands a transmitter mast. It caused me to wonder if television had now reached this part of Zululand. The concrete slab, which formed a 'flat road bridge' across the shallow river, was still there. But gone were the ladies, who had laughingly washed their clothes in the flowing water. Perhaps, with the passage of time, they had expired. And maybe their daughters, who represent a new generation, presently use electric washing machines to do the job for them!

The secluded wooded glade, which served as a resting place for the Zulu king, remained as before. But a short distance away stood a scatter of houses, where previously had been open veld. Inside the confines of the wooded glade was the Royal gravesite. It was mostly unchanged since my earlier visit. Except that now, it was surrounded by some additional chest-high steel railings and sported a padlocked gate. I suspect the extra security was perhaps due to an increased number of visitors.

Surprisingly though, within the wooded glade, the peaceful ambience still prevailed. However, on this occasion I noticed the absence of colourful butterflies to acknowledge my visit.

Instead of which, a pair of rummaging goats quietly emerged from the surrounding low-lying foliage!

Outside the wooded glade, I saw numerous Zulus. With a seeming sense of purpose, as they commuted on foot to untold destinations. And as I climbed into my car and was about to leave, a young couple walked passed me. They joyfully greeted me in perfect English. Concealing my surprise at their linguistic skill, I politely returned their greeting and drove away.

On my return journey to Eshowe, I fondly remembered my now redundant voice recorder. And my thoughts respectfully recalled my visit to the Royal gravesite. Taken all told, it seemed evident to me that in the space of a few years, some things had irrevocably changed in that part of Zululand!

# 33

## KARMA COURT

Arriving home from our visit to Eshowe, we were glad to see little had changed. But some dreadful news awaited us. Our neighbours' muntu announced that one of their young daughters was dead! A brick-built circular dam, which stood near their house, was mentioned. Always filled to the brim with water, it was used for irrigating their land. Seemingly, in an unguarded moment, the infant daughter had somehow climbed into the dam. What actually happened we don't know, but the fact was the child drowned!

The incident caused alarm bells to ring in my head. In the space of less than four years we had racked up a list of calamities. There had been the burning of the rondavel and the death of Jimmy-the-dog. Then our two daughters were bitten by 'Bull-nasty' - the neighbours' dog. Added to the list were the deaths of our two sheep and also the dispatching of a snake. And now there was this human tragedy.

Our neighbours' loss struck me as being one incident too many. At that moment, I made an unwavering decision.

"Sandra!" - I declared - "We have to get away from this place - or it is going to kill us!"

Her face grimaced. Perhaps inwardly, she questioned my decision, but outwardly, she simply didn't comment.

We put our property up for sale and made the move to a small town named *Florida*. Situated on the edge of the West Rand, its bustling community had become a melting pot for various immigrant nationalities. In terms of distance, it was midway between our plot and Johannesburg. Fortunately, there was no shortage of rented accommodation. A mix of old and relatively new properties was available. Many were low-rise buildings, and it was from them we chose a seasoned, two-storey apartment block. Displayed above its entrance doors were large ceramic letters. Coated with faded red paint, they formed the words - *Karma Court*.

Located in a quiet street, Karma Court was not far from an expanse of water known as *Florida Lake*. The lake was the focal point of a multi-functional area. At one end were tennis courts and a miniature railway, whilst at the opposite end were a crazy golf course and a yachting club. There was also a large cluster of freely growing bulrushes, which provided a breeding haven for wild birds. An asphalt pathway formed a perimeter around the lake and made a perfect route for walkers and joggers to exercise their legs. Of course, the lake was home to an abundance of fish and offered the opportunity for fishermen to practice their skills.

At Karma Court, our rented, two-bedroom apartment was on the upper storey. An attached balcony presented an open view beyond the street, which ran below us. It faced a tract of veld of around three hectares in overall size - which appeared to be the surviving portion of an old farmstead. Surrounded by an assortment of various-sized trees, a small farmhouse stood at its centre. From time to time, I watched the farmer and his Bantu employees at work.

It was predominantly a hands-on affair and focused on growing a limited range of vegetables. On one occasion I was amused to see the irrigation of crops in progress. Some parallel rows of carrots required watering. A length of small-bore hosepipe was strung across the veld. At the farmhouse, one end was connected to the water supply, whilst the farmer held the loose end.

What made this task amusing was the way in which the hosepipe was manoeuvred. Several Bantu - a mix of men and women - stood in a line and were spaced a metre or two apart. Each held their designated section of hose at shoulder level. Their task was to prevent it from snagging on the ground. A look of concentration on each face was worthy of a prize. And rather than holding a simple plastic hose, they appeared as if they were handling a portly python!

Meanwhile, the farmer stood at the head of the hosepipe and issued instructions to everyone. From my elevated viewpoint, I observed their earnest effort, which all seemed like a circus act. But I couldn't help thinking what a costly method was in play. However, at that moment, I had forgotten how the local labour was plentiful and relatively inexpensive.

The street at the front of Karma Court had a lay-by. When parked nose to tail, it could accommodate three cars. From our apartment's balcony it was possible to see any car which might be parked there. Meanwhile, at the end of the building was a drive-through car-port; with space for two vehicles. Because our Ford Escort was in good condition, we chose to park it there. We thought it would be protected from the sun. Unfortunately, it was some distance from our balcony and away from our line of sight.

Not long after moving to Florida a series of mishaps began - all of which involved our Ford Escort. One weekend morning I arrived early at the car-port, where an odd sight awaited me. Leaning next to a nearby wall was a glass windscreen. Surprised to see such a thing, I asked myself - "What's that doing there?" But when I looked at the rear of our car, the answer became clear. Someone had cut through the sealing-rubber and had removed the whole rear window! And that was not all. Two radio loudspeakers had been wrenched from the car's rear window-ledge. Also, the plastic dashboard, at the front of the car, had been maliciously hacked. The car's radio was stolen and all that remained was a gaping, jagged hole. It reminded me of a shark's open mouth!

In the fullness of time, the rear window was replaced and the other damage repaired. But would you believe that some days later, the car's windscreen wipers were stolen? Annoying as that was I was partially consoled by the thought that at least they were easily replaced. However, that was more than could be said for the next item to go missing. No sooner had the wipers been replaced when the plastic lens assembly for one of the rear-lights was taken!

A hunt to find a substitute began. My tours of vehicle scrap yards and visits to car-spares shops produced nothing. In the end, I ordered a new one from a Ford auto dealer. The subsequent waiting period for its arrival became a time for reflection. After considering the previous incidents, it seemed best for the future to park the car in the lay-by beneath our apartment's balcony. The idea was put into practice, and there was a temporary respite from torment.

But a few mornings later, I awoke and ambled to the balcony. From there, I looked into the street below. Fully expecting to see something untoward, it turned out I was wrong! Thankfully, the car was in its parking space and all appeared to be fine.

"But wait!" I told myself, "Something is not quite right. What is that dark-looking patch in front of the car?"

Beneath the front bumper bar and extending outward for two or three feet, the road surface appeared to be wet. Oddly enough, the sky was blue, the sun was shining, and there had been no rain the night before. There was no logical reason for the road surface to be wet. But then I thought, "Perhaps the car's radiator had sprung a leak - after all, it is a Ford Escort!" (I didn't have much confidence in the reliability of Ford automobiles at that time).

Hurrying downstairs, my thoughts wrestled with other possible reasons for the wetness. When I reached the car I soon discovered the cause for concern. Without a doubt, stemming from beneath the car was a patch of wet liquid. A touch from a finger, followed by a sniff from my nose, confirmed it was not water - it was in fact, petrol!

I cursed the possibility the petrol tank had sprung a leak. On my hands and knees I looked under the car. Astonishingly, a pipe, which connected the petrol tank to the carburettor, had been severed! Needless to say, the petrol had been drained, and the petrol tank was now empty! It was hard to accept that someone had the audacity to steal our car's petrol.

At that moment paranoia gripped me and I wondered what was coming next. From that night onwards I slept lightly.

To add to my mental torment, there was another distressing development. Following our recent move to the apartment, Sandra and I found it increasingly difficult to adjust to its confines. The situation felt particularly bad, after living in a house with five bedrooms, and with two and a half hectares of land, in which to stretch our legs!

As time passed, we became increasingly edgy and argued over minor disagreements. But in view of the recent happenings, we put aside our differences and agreed the car was to be regularly parked below our balcony. The master bedroom was adjacent to the balcony and sounds from the outside street could be easily heard. During the early hours of one particular morning, and whilst our family was sleeping, I awoke to the sound of a car engine. It was 'ticking over' in the street outside. Sliding out of bed, I quickly wrapped myself in a shirt. Reaching the bedroom window, I peered through a part-opened curtain. Parallel parked next to our Ford Escort was a large, open-top, grey saloon. Sitting in its front seats were two corpulent male-muntus. With heads turned towards our car, their facial expressions suggested devious thoughts were conjured in their minds.

For a better look, I slowly drew open the curtain. Its movement caught the visitors' attention. Reacting in unison, their rotund brown faces looked up and faced me. As calm as you like, both smiled. Their gesture appeared to say, "Hey there! We see you!" Then, like a crocodile leaving a riverbank and entering the water, the car slowly glided away. The reader may note we lived near the Bantu township of Soweto.

Over a million people were said to live in its small area. Criminals of all kinds lived and operated from there. At the time we lived in Florida, there was a joke 'doing the rounds'. Somehow, it seemed relevant to our present predicament. The following is how it was told.

"I have got some good news and some bad news for you. The bad news is that all the 'whites' are to be moved from their homes and to live in Soweto. The good news is that your possessions are already there!"

At breakfast time I told Sandra about my sighting of the two men and I stressed the importance of parking our car beneath the balcony. At least then, I might hear if anything untoward was happening. Arriving home some days later, Sandra found the parking bay was full. Seeing a convenient alternative, she diligently parked the car. Carrying a bag or two of shopping, she entered our apartment. With my paranoia now in full swing, I had previously checked the parking bay and knew it to be full. A further quick look revealed nothing had changed. As Sandra entered the kitchen, I turned from the window and anxiously called out:

"Where's the car dear?"

"It's across the street and parked under a tree!"

It was true. The car *was* parked across the street and under a tree. But the tree was some distance from the apartment block. And to view the car it required stepping onto the balcony, leaning out over the guardrail, and looking up the street!

When the evening meal was finished, our children went to their bedroom, and Sandra and I read our books.

Periodically, I looked out from the balcony to see if there was an available parking space. In due course, my persistence paid off.

"Hey, Sandra," I quickly hollered, "I can see an empty parking space. You're okay to move the car now".

Perhaps it was my assertion that *she* should move the car, which caused her to react the way she did. But following my announcement, she looked up from her book and snapped at me.

"Look! - If you want the car to be moved - YOU MOVE IT!"

With that said, she continued to read her book.

Naturally, I was cut down by the retort, but I chose not to argue. Of course, I could have done the manly thing and move the car myself but that is in hindsight. Instead of which, and yes, stubbornly, I replied, "All right - Leave it there."

The evening passed with few words spoken between us. The next morning, I arose early and rushed to the balcony. Looking up the street I was numbed by what I saw - or rather, by what I didn't see! It was all I could do to pour a mug of tea and nibble on a biscuit. Minutes later, Sandra entered the room. She appeared to be flummoxed. Perhaps the car's welfare had been on her mind, too. I wasn't to know. But excitedly, the first words she uttered were,

"The car has GONE!"

"Surprise, surprise" was my calm but sardonic response.

A search around the immediate area confirmed that our car *had* gone! At that moment how could I envisage that its theft would set the stage to completely change our lives? Our quest to buy a reliable and reasonably priced used car began in earnest.

Unfortunately, it proved to be fruitless. The reader may note, at that time the South African used car market was in its infancy. Available quality used cars were few and far between. But fortunately for us, we still owned the faithful Volkswagen campervan. And since my latest work-place was near to our apartment, Sandra and I were able to share its use. For a time, our transport arrangements were satisfactory, but not so our relationship. As spiteful words were frequently exchanged, it continued its journey on a downward spiral.

I could appreciate it hadn't been plain sailing for her living with me. She had shown patience and tolerance on many occasions. And in retrospect we had certainly taken some bold steps during our married life. The first of which was moving from a small English town to a large city in Southern Africa. After which, from initially living in a hotel room, we had aspired to live in a multi-roomed house with spacious land. But now, we were again confined to a small apartment. Maybe the moves from one house to another - and each time followed by a sense of impermanence - had become too much for her to bear.

Some days later, Sandra's action caused our paths to draw farther apart. And this time, the distance was to increase beyond redemption.

Late one bright afternoon, Sandra entered our apartment beaming with pride. She excitedly announced her latest purchase of an automobile. It was a used but late-model Volkswagen Golf. Her words were painful to hear. And to make matters worse, there had been no prior discussion. During our married life I had tried to avoid any form of debt. Suddenly, we now faced owing a loan company several thousands of Rand.

"What have you done?" I exclaimed. "We haven't got that kind of money to spend!"

Taking a deep breath, I remembered our Hillside plot was up for sale but as yet, there had been no offers. Any eventual sale money was intended to be used as a deposit on another house. When I explained this to Sandra, she reminded me of how *she* was now gainfully employed.

"The money that *I* earn shall pay for *my* car!" she exclaimed.

It was her words and actions which sealed our fate. Coincidently, as it would seem, some weeks later the lease on our Karma Court apartment expired. Sandra and I were no longer obligated to pay a joint rent. We, therefore, decided to separate and live in different homes. My choice was a nearby 'bachelor flat'. Its size was tantamount to little more than a large coffin!

I soon realised that gone were the benefits of married life - which included the daily sights and sounds of my children. Gone, too, were the caustic verbal exchanges between husband and wife. But Sandra's parting words still floated in my head.

"I'm still married to you" she said "But I'm not your wife anymore!"

Not many weeks later, our married status changed. Papers for our divorce were jointly signed. The reason was stated in bold letters - they read – 'Irretrievable breakdown of marriage'.

During the periods of solitude which followed, I contemplated what had gone wrong. A possible answer lay in the name of the apartment block we had previously occupied. The name, of course, was *Karma Court*. The original meaning of *Karma* literally meant 'ritual action'.

But according to the Upanishads - being the sacred texts of the Hindu tradition - *Karma* is generally known to mean the concept of rewards and punishments. These are attached to various acts. It dictates that human beings gain merit [punya] or demerit [papa] from every action they perform. But good deeds and bad deeds do not simply cancel each other out. One has to experience the fruits of all actions. [9]

As I lay on my bed the words, *one has to experience the fruits of all actions*, caused me to think more deeply. My fixed gaze focused on the bedroom's blank ceiling. I recalled the time when our family first arrived at the Hillside plot. With little effort, I visualised the Bantu couple I had ushered from the corner of our land. Their cold, staring eyes and expressionless faces appeared before me.

Could it be they who had put a curse on me and, by association, my family too? Or was it maybe a malicious spirit? One perhaps connected with the empty gravesites which were situated to the rear of our plot? I believe such things could happen.

But after all was said and done, in the end, it became obvious to me it was time to move on. I needed to open my life's book and find the next blank page on which to start a new chapter.

# THE END

# REFERENCES

[1] National Geographic magazine - June 1977.

[2] *Panoramic South Africa* - C. Struik Publishers Pty., Ltd., Cape Town, 1979.

[3] Venterspost Gold Mining Company Limited, Study 307, JvD/pag., 22 May 1978.

[4] *Journal of the S.A. Institute of Mining and Metallurgy, p.127, April 1989 - Spotlight on Randfontein Estates Gold Mining Company Witwatersrand 1889-1989.*

[5] In the year 2021, the city of Port Elizabeth was renamed 'Gqeberha' from the Xhosa language.

[6] Birkby, Carel, *Zulu Journey* – p.77.

[7] Binns, C. T., *The Last Zulu King*, (Longmans, Green & Co Ltd., London, 1963, p.229.)

[8] Gillings, Ken, *Durban members' visit to Cetshwayo's grave and Mome Gorge*, (South African History Society-Military History Journal Vol. 2 1-6 June 1971 to December 1973)

[9] *Eastern Religions* - Coogan Michael D., Duncan Baird Publishers Ltd., - 2005 - London.

## THE FOLLOWING TITLES ARE WRITTEN BY THIS AUTHOR

## THE RED TABS – SOUTH AFRICANS AT WAR IN EAST AFRICA AND THE WESTERN DESERT 1940-1942

During World War II over 126,000 South African combatants wore a strip of red material on their tunic's epaulettes. Known as the 'Red Tabs,' the strip denoted each soldier was a volunteer. South African troops pushed the Italian forces out of East Africa and later faced Hitler's Afrika Korps in the Western Desert. At a small area of the desert called Acroma Keep, the South Africans fought against overwhelming odds. Amidst the action, a truce was held – just long enough to gather their dead and attend to their wounded. Many of the battles in which they fought are described in this book. Anecdotes from veteran soldiers and numerous previously unpublished photographs, contribute to making the book an interesting read.

## MYSTERIOUS TALES FROM TURTON TOWER

Turton Tower has stood near the Lancashire village of Chapeltown for over six hundred years. During that time, it has spawned numerous reports of paranormal happenings. Ghostly figures of men, women and even dogs have been sighted. The Tower Museum plays host to an ancient cradle which is said to 'rock' unaided at midnight. There are also two human skulls which have a long history of poltergeist activity. The author has painstakingly collected the many and varied 'Mysterious Tales from Turton Tower' and put them together in this book.

## LAUGH 'N' SCRATCH

Early in 1963 at a north of England town, the *Beatles* pop group is due to play at the local dance hall. Stuart is a young projectionist in the town's only cinema. His eccentric colleagues have dark secrets to share. A clairvoyant cleaner predicts his future with uncanny accuracy. And when Stuart meets Suzie, a teenage usherette, his coming of age begins. The teenagers fulfil a prophecy when they come face to face with The Beatles.

## A PENSIONER VISITS PERU

Did you know there are pyramids in Peru or that mummified corpses can talk? This book reveals how a pensioner found answers to those questions during his visit to Peru. After standing on the Nazca Lines, a light aircraft flew him over the mysterious geoglyphs that stretch for miles in the desert. When visiting Cusco, he paraded with the locals during the traditional religious festival of Corpus Christi. At Machu Picchu, he climbed amongst the famous Inca ruins.

www.ingramcontent.com/pod-product-compliance
Lightning Source LLC
Chambersburg PA
CBHW052010070526
44584CB00016B/1691